U·X·L

ASIAN AMERICAN

BIOGRAPHY 2ND EDITION

U·X·L
ASIAN AMERICAN
BIOGRAPHY 2ND EDITION

Volume I
A-L

**Edited by Helen Zia
and Susan B. Gall**

Detroit • New York • San Diego • San Francisco • Cleveland • New Haven, Conn. • Waterville, Maine • London • Munich

THOMSON
GALE

U•X•L ASIAN AMERICAN BIOGRAPHY, 2ND EDITION
Helen Zia and Susan B. Gall, Editors

Project Editor
Diane Sawinski

Permissions
Margaret Chamberlain

Imaging and Multimedia
Lezlie Light, Randy Bassett

Product Design
Cindy Baldwin

Manufacturing
Rita Wimberley

Composition
Evi Seoud

ISBN 0-7876-7601-2 (set)
ISBN 0-7876-7602-0 (v.1)
ISBN 0-7876-7603-9 (v.2)

Library of Congress Control Number: 2003110046

Printed in the United States of America
10 9 8 7 6 5 4 3 2 1

CONTENTS

Volume 1: A–L

CONTENTS

READER'S GUIDE

U•X•L Asian American Biography, 2nd Edition, profiles more than 150 Americans who trace their ancestry to Asia and the Pacific Islands. Included are prominent men and women of Asian Indian, Cambodian, Chinese, Filipino, Native Hawaiian, Hmong, Japanese, Pacific Island, Pakistani, Taiwanese, and Vietnamese descent. Profilees are notable for their achievements in fields ranging from civil rights to sports, politics to academia, entertainment to science, religion to the military. Early leaders in Asian American as well as contemporary figures are among those included. A black-and-white photograph accompanies most entries, and a list of sources for further reading or research is provided at the end of each entry. The volumes conclude with an index listing all individuals by field of endeavor and a subject index.

Related Reference Sources:

U•X•L Asian American Almanac, 2nd Edition, explores the history and culture of the major ethnic groups comprising Asian America. The *Almanac* is organized into 17 subject chapters, including immigration patterns, women and family, religion, employment, civil rights and activism, education, literature and theater, and sports. The volume contains more than 90 black-and-white photographs and maps, a glossary, and a cumulative subject index.

U•X•L Asian American Chronology, 2nd Edition, explores significant social, political, economic, cultural, and professional milestones in Asian American history. Arranged by year and then by month and day where applicable, the chronology spans from prehistory to modern times.

Entries range from a few lines to one page in length and describe topics such as immigration, discriminatory legislation, the world wars, the formation of activist organizations, and the contributions Asian Americans have made to all aspects of American society.

The *Chronology* contains more than 100 illustrations and maps as well as charts and boxes that highlight important information. The extensively cross-referenced volume concludes with a list of sources for further reading or research and a cumulative subject index.

U•X•L Asian American Voices, 2nd Edition, presents 20 full or excerpted speeches, orations, testimony, and other notable spoken works of Asian Americans. Each entry is accompanied by an introduction and a glossary explaining terms and events to which the speech refers. The volume is illustrated with 100 black-and-white photographs and drawings and features a cumulative subject index.

Comments and Suggestions

We welcome your comments on *U•X•L Asian American Biography,* 2nd Edition, as well as your suggestions for persons to be featured in future editions. Please write: Editors, *U•X•L Asian American Biography,* U•X•L, 27500 Drake Road, Farmington Hills, MI 48331-3535; call toll-free: 800-877-4253; fax: 248-699-8097; or send e-mail via http://www.gale.com.

Advisors

Special thanks are due to Helen Zia, Frank Wu, Kristine Minami, and Karen Narasaki, each of whom provided valuable information and insights.

PHOTO CREDITS

The photographs and illustrations appearing in *U•X•L Asian American Biography,* 2nd Edition, were received from the following sources:

On the covers: Margaret Cho: **Courtesy of Margaret Cho;** Amy Tan: **Courtesy of G. P. Putnam's Sons;** Lance Ito: **AP/Wide World Photos.**

AP/Wide World Photos: pp. 31, 83, 95, 118, 158, 160, 173, 183, 199, 203, 267, 284, 301, 317, 328, 344, 356, 361, 363, 388, 408, 413, 421, 444; **Corbis Corporation:** pp. 128, 175, 180, 212, 275, 335, 441; **The Kobal Collection:** pp. 294, 394; **Courtesy of NASA:** pp. 49, 63, 314, 399, 416; **Courtesy of Daniel K. Akaka:** page 2; **Photo by Frank Ockenfels 3, ©Sony Music, courtesy of Columbia Records:** page 4; **Courtesy of Benihana:** page 7; **Courtesy of George R. Ariyoshi:** page 10; **Photo by Liane Enkelis Photography, courtesy of Kavelle Bajaj:** page 16; **Courtesy of Atlanta Ballet:** page 18, 19; **Courtesy of Lynda Barry:** page 22; **Filipino American National Historical Society Collection, used by permission:** page 25; **Photo by Ackerman Photography, courtesy of Phyllis J. Campbell:** page 29; **Courtesy of Subrahmanyan Chandrasekhar:** page 33; **Photo by Russ Adams Productions, courtesy of Michael Chang:** page 37; **Photo by Christian Steiner, courtesy of ICM Artists:** page 41; **Courtesy of Elaine Chao:** page 43; **Courtesy of Stephen Chao:** page 47; **Photo by Roland Neveu, courtesy of Warner Bros. Productions Limited:** page 53; **Courtesy of William Shao Chang Chen:** page 56; **Photo by ILM, courtesy of Doug Chiang:** page 59; **Courtesy of Margaret Cho:** page 65; **Courtesy of Vernon Chong:** page 68; **Courtesy of Harmony Books:** page 70; **Photo by Tony Esparza, courtesy of CBS Inc.:** page 73; **Courtesy of New England Patriots:** page 77; **Liaison Agency:** page 79; **International Swimming Hall of Fame:** page 82; **Harry Langdon Photography, courtesy of March Fong Eu:** page 84; **Courtesy of Hiram Fong:** page 87; **Photo by Dianne Fong-Torres, courtesy of Hyperion:** page 89; **Courtesy of John L. Fugh:** page 93; **Courtesy of Lillian Gonzalez-Pardo:** page 99; **Photo by Hideo Yoshida, courtesy of Philip Kan Gotanda:** page 102; **Courtesy of James Hattori:** page 104; **Courtesy of David Ho:** page 106; **Courtesy of David Henry Hwang:** page 109; **Courtesy of Daniel K. Inouye:** page 112; **Courtesy of Paul Isaki:** page 116; **Courtesy of H.W. Pak:** page 122; **Photo by Mr. Jerry Bauer:** page 126; **©Capital Cities/ABC, Inc., used with permission:** page 132; **Courtesy of Elaine H. Kim:** page 135; **Courtesy of Jay Kim:** page 139; **Courtesy of San Francisco Giants:** page 141; **U.S. Army Center of Military History:** p. 147; **Courtesy of Maxine Hong Kingston:** p. 151; **Courtesy of Harold Hongju Koh:** page 154; **Courtesy of Paul Kuroda:** page 167; **Courtesy of U.S. Figure Skating:** page 170; **Photo by Robert Zuckerman, courtesy of *A. Magazine:*** page 178; **Photo by Marty Umans:** page 187; **Courtesy of Roosevelt University Library:** page 191; **International Swimming Hall of Fame:** page 193; **Photo by Ascherman, courtesy of The Cleveland Orchestra:** page 206; **Courtesy of *National Geographic Traveler:*** page 209; **Courtesy of the Office of Governor Gary Locke:** page 215; **Photo by Robert McEwan, courtesy Lone Dragon Produc-**

tions, Inc.: page 218; **Photo by Bachrach, courtesy of Ivy Books:** page 221; **Courtesy of Greg Louganis:** page 225; **Photo by J. Henry Fair, courtesy of ICM Artists, Ltd.:** page 230; **Courtesy of Mako:** page 233; **Courtesy of Tom Matano:** page 236; **Courtesy of Robert T. Matsui:** page 239; **Courtesy of Nobu McCarthy:** page 244; **Courtesy of Sonny Mehta:** page 246; **Courtesy of Zubin Mehta:** page 248; **Photo by Satoru Ishikawa, courtesy of The Midori Foundation:** page 252; **Courtesy of Dale Minami:** page 254; **Courtesy of Norman Mineta:** page 258; **Courtesy of Gap, Inc.:** page 261; **Courtesy of Patsy Mink:** page 264; **Courtesy of Mee Moua:** page 270; **Courtesy of William Mow:** page 273; **Photograph © Jerry Bauer, courtesy of Knopf:** page 278; **Photo by Christian Steiner, courtesy of Columbia Artists Management Inc.:** page 281; **Photo by Michael Geissinger, courtesy of Irene Natividad:** page 288; **Courtesy of Josie Natori:** page 291; **Courtesy of Dallas Cowboys:** page 297; **Courtesy of Gyo Obata:** page 304; **Photo by Frank Wolfe, LBJ Library Collection:** page 311; **Photo by Christian Steiner, courtesy of Seiji Ozawa:** page 320; **Courtesy of the Los Angeles Dodgers:** page 323; **Clarion Books:** page 325; **Courtesy of Arati Prabhakar:** page 332; **Courtesy of Beulah Quo:** page 339; **Courtesy of AST Research:** page 341; **Courtesy of Patricia Saiki:** page 350; **Courtesy of Richard Sakakida:** page 353; **Courtesy of Allen Say:** page 358; **Courtesy of The White House:** page 368; **Photo by John Eddy, courtesy of Cathy Song:** page 372; **Photo by Kevin Leong, courtesy of Anna Sui:** page 377; **Photo by Carol Takaki, courtesy of Ronald Takaki:** page 381; **Courtesy of Paramount Pictures:** page 384; **Photo by John Blaustein, courtesy of Chang-Lin Tien:** page 391; **Photo by Deborah Storms, courtesy of the estate of Yoshiko Uchida:** page 403; **Courtesy of Huynh Cong Ut:** page 405; **Courtesy of John D. Waihee:** page 411; **Courtesy of Vera Wang:** page 419; **Courtesy of Michiko Nishiura Weglyn:** page 424; **Courtesy of the Academy of Motion Picture Arts and Sciences:** page 427; **Courtesy of Touchstone Picture & Television:** page 430; **Courtesy of Flossie Wong-Staal:** page 434; **PGA Tour, Inc.:** page 437; **Photograph by Taro Yamasaki, courtesy of the photographer:** page 447; **Courtesy of Bruce Yamashita:** page 450; **Courtesy of Martin Yan:** page 454; **Gamma Liaison Network:** page 459; **Photo by K. Yep, courtesy of Laurence Yep:** page 462; **Courtesy of Shirley Young:** page 465; **Photo by Danny Feld, courtesy of Teddy Zee:** page 468.

Daniel K. Akaka

Politician, educator
Born September 11, 1924, Honolulu, Hawaii

"I use my Hawaiian abilities and the spirit of Aloha [to] bring people together."

In 1990, following the death of Hawaii's longtime senator Spark Matsunaga, Daniel K. Akaka was appointed to fill Matsunaga's seat in the U.S. Senate. He was sworn in on May 16, 1990, and then won a special election called for November of that year. He is the first Native Hawaiian to serve in the U.S. Senate and is currently the only Chinese American in the upper house of Congress. Prior to his appointment and election to the Senate, Akaka served as Hawaii's 2nd Congressional District's representative in the House for fourteen years. Akaka also taught in both rural and urban public schools and in a military school; he served as a principal as well. Akaka was married in 1948 and has four children, fourteen grandchildren, and one great-grandchild.

In the Senate, Akaka keeps a low profile. "I am not a born politician," Akaka said in an interview with *Asian American Biography (AAB)*. "People tell me I have to be feisty to get my way in Congress. But that's not my style. I use my Hawaiian abilities and the spirit of Aloha that brings people together."

Humble beginnings

Akaka was born into a devoutly religious family of eight children. The family lived in a cramped, two-bedroom house. Akaka's father had only a third-grade education and worked in a machine shop that made molded steel vats used to boil sugarcane. "My big goal as a boy," the legislator said, "was to work at Pearl Harbor [the massive American naval base]. But somehow I never made it there." Instead, Akaka began pursuing an education at the insistence of his parents, who recognized the importance of schooling in achieving one's dreams. He enrolled in the Kamehameha School for Boys, a private school from which he graduated in 1942. He began looking for work to earn money for college and became a welder with the Hawaiian Electric Company before joining the U.S. Army Corps of Engineers as a welder mechanic. Immediately after World War II, Akaka was stationed with the Corps in the Pacific.

After his discharge from the army, Akaka enrolled in the University of Hawaii to fulfill his dream of becoming a teacher. He earned his bachelor's degree in education in 1953, a certificate to teach secondary school in 1954, and a master's degree in education in 1966. Meanwhile, Akaka worked as a teacher, beginning in 1953.

Public service

Akaka told *AAB* that he learned about the importance of community service from his parents. "My parents believed in feeding and helping others. My mother would yell to our visitors, 'Hele mai e ai,' which means 'Come in and eat.'" In 1963 Akaka, by then an elementary school principal, was selected as a delegate to the National Convention of the Department of Elementary School Principals. Akaka attended the event

Daniel K. Akaka

determined to spread good will and the "Aloha spirit" on Hawaii's behalf. He arrived at the convention with a truckload of flower leis [wreaths] and macadamia nuts, two well-known symbols of Hawaii. But his hospitality didn't end there, as he told *AAB*. "They needed some impromptu entertainment so I ended up singing 'Blue Hawaii' before 6,000 delegates," Akaka recalled. Before the convention was over he was approached to run for the national board of directors.

In 1969 Akaka was named chief program planner for Hawaii's department of educa-tion. Six years later, Democratic gubernato-rial candidate **George Ariyoshi** persuaded Akaka to run as lieutenant governor. Akaka lost the Democratic primary, but Ariyoshi was elected governor and appointed Akaka as his special assistant for human resources.

National politics

In 1976 Akaka decided to run for Con-gress in Hawaii's 2nd Congressional Dis-trict. He won the primary and went on to take 80 percent of the vote in the general election—about average for Democrats in Hawaii. He was elected by similar margins in each of his next seven elections. In 1990 he was appointed to fill the Senate seat left vacant by the death of Spark Matsunaga, Hawaii's longtime senator.

In both his House and Senate positions, Akaka has voted as a liberal Democrat. In 1984 the House Democratic leadership was one vote shy on a crucial vote to block Pres-ident Ronald Reagan's request for funding for the production of the MX missile, a con-troversial nuclear weapons system. Akaka's last-minute vote was critical in defeating the initiative.

In the Senate, Akaka spoke out vigor-ously against the confirmation of Justice Clarence Thomas to the Supreme Court. Thomas, a George Bush, Sr. appointee, was viewed by many as lacking in judicial expe-rience and too ideologically conservative to sit on the bench. On another front, Akaka successfully fought an effort by Democratic Senator Bill Bradley of New Jersey to cut federal sugar subsidies by two cents per pound, a move that would have been very unpopular with Hawaii's huge sugar indus-try. His motion to table Bradley's amendment to the 1990 farm bill passed by a margin of 54–44. In 1993 Akaka worked to pass a joint congressional resolution (through both houses) that acknowledged U.S. wrongdoing in the 1893 overthrow of the government of the Kingdom of Hawaii; the measure also offered an apology to all Native Hawaiians on behalf of the United States. Akaka also served as the chairman of the Hawaii Congressional Task Force.

Akaka has been especially concerned about the environment of his native state. Hawaii relies heavily on tourism for its economic survival, but the tremendous number of people who visit the islands every year has a negative impact on the state's environment. Also, about 70 percent of all endangered species protected by federal law live in Hawaii. The senator from Hawaii has worked on the creation of strict safeguards against the introduction of destructive alien species into Hawaii's delicate environment. He established the Spark M. Matsunaga Renewable Energy and Ocean Technology Center at Keahole Point and pushed for a prohibition on consideration of U.S. territories in the Pacific as nuclear waste disposal sites. Akaka is also concerned about Hawaii's forests, and has authored the Hawaiian Tropical Forest Recovery Program.

Akaka has become a role model for many Native Hawaiians; he frequently speaks to young people, urging them to get involved in community service. Speaking before the National Asian Pacific American Bar Association in Honolulu in 1994, Akaka urged Native Hawaiians to consider running for public office. "You are our strength," he said. "You are our hope. Your skills and commitment provide the tools we need to change what is wrong today and build what

is right for tomorrow. You do indeed hold the keys to power ... the power to help. All I ask is that you never let anger and fear and hurt displace the pureness of your hearts as the force that drives your search for it or your use of it. Mahalo! (Thank you). Aloha!"

Sources:

Akaka, Daniel, professional resume and press releases supplied by Bob Ogawa, press officer, 1994.

Akaka, Daniel, telephone interview with Melanie J. Mavrides, June 23, 1994.

Congressional Quarterly's Politics in America: 1994, the 103rd Congress, Washington, D.C.: Congressional Quarterly, Inc., 1994.

"Senator Daniel Akaka," *United States Senate,* http://www.akaka.senate.gov/about.html (accessed March 2003).

Toshiko Akiyoshi

Musician, composer
Born December 18, 1929, Manchuria, China

Akiyoshi is "... the only woman in history to have composed and arranged an entire library of music."—The Book of Women's Firsts

Toshiko Akiyoshi is a highly regarded jazz pianist, composer, and arranger. (An arranger is someone who decides how the various parts of a composition will be performed, determining the overall feel of a recording or performance.) As the head of the Toshiko Akiyoshi Jazz Orchestra, a 17-piece band, she has received 12 Grammy Award nominations. In 1978 she became the first woman in jazz history to head a group named by the greatly respected magazine *Down Beat* as best big jazz band, a title won by her ensemble for four consecutive years. In 1992, celebrating Akiyoshi's 35th year in the United States, she and her band recorded *Toshiko Akiyoshi Live at Carnegie Hall,* their first album for Columbia Records.

Akiyoshi's music is traditional American big band music that was widespread in the 1930s and 1940s and consisted of large ensembles playing popular tunes, frequently in the upbeat jazz style known as "swing." Akiyoshi, however, regularly adds an international flair sometimes described as "world music." Influenced by her Asian ethnicity—she was born to Japanese parents in occupied Manchuria, China—her compositions also contain shades of Caribbean calypso and African music.

Born in China

Akiyoshi was the last of four daughters born to a Japanese family living in Japanese-occupied Manchuria, now a province of the People's Republic of China. Her father had originally wanted her to become a doctor, and she briefly considered it. "My father always wanted me to go to medical school.... I suppose he was disappointed he never had a son, and for some reason he thought I would be the one to accomplish something," she said in a 1992 press release.

After Japan's defeat in World War II, the Akiyoshi family settled in the resort town of Beppu, Japan, which, like most of American-occupied postwar Japan, was home to a massive American troop presence. She'd had some training in classical piano, and one day

Toshiko Akiyoshi

she happened by a dance hall established for use by American servicemen and noticed a "Help Wanted" sign for a pianist. Her family was initially opposed to her taking such a job but eventually gave in. At first, the music she played in the dance hall was not true jazz; then she met a young man who played her a recording of Teddy Wilson's "Sweet Lorraine" and other classics. In her press release, Akiyoshi recalled her reaction to hearing the music, remarking, "I thought, 'Wow! Jazz can be so beautiful, and so musical.'"

By the late 1940s, Akiyoshi had grown restless with small-town life and had moved to Tokyo. By 1952, she had her own group and was becoming a key participant in the westernization of Japan. Western music (generally thought of as American and European) was very popular. American jazz greats were touring Japan, and often they would stop and play with local musicians, including Akiyoshi. In 1953 she was noticed by Canadian pianist Oscar Peterson during jazz promoter Norman Granz's "Jazz at the Philharmonic" tour of Japan. Peterson told Granz that Akiyoshi was the greatest female jazz pianist he had ever heard. His interest led to Akiyoshi's first recording, which featured Peterson's own rhythm section (bass and percussion).

Move to America

As a jazz musician, it was almost inevitable that Akiyoshi would come to the United States, the birthplace of jazz. In 1956 she earned a full scholarship to the prestigious Berklee School of Music in Boston, becoming the first Japanese musician to study there. (Berklee awarded her an honorary doctorate in 1998.) She graduated in 1959, and began playing around the United States, encountering racial and gender prejudice for the first time: many people just couldn't imagine an Asian woman playing jazz. It is something she herself has commented on, stating, "I come from a different musical culture ... and it's always considered a handicap."

After years of performing as a solo artist and with small groups, Akiyoshi left the East Coast for California with her husband, Lew Tabackin, a saxophonist. In Los Angeles they formed what Akiyoshi refers to as a "rehearsal band," which would eventually become the Toshiko Akiyoshi Jazz Orchestra. Their first recording, *Kogun,* was very successful and is one of the bestselling big band albums in history. In 1976 Japan's *Swing Journal* chose Akiyoshi's album *Insights* as the best jazz album of the year, and in 1977 she was voted the number-one big band leader by *Swing Journal*'s readers. During this period she also received two Grammy nominations.

Musical output

Akiyoshi's orchestra has recorded dozens of albums in its long career, including *Tales of a Courtesan, Wishing Peace, Farewell to Mingus,* and *European Memoirs.* Akiyoshi records original compositions almost exclusively, prompting *The Book of Women's Firsts* to describe her as "the only woman in history to have composed and arranged an entire library of music." Her compositions often address social themes and reflect her Asian background as well. For example, the title cut from her *Tales of a Courtesan* describes the emotions of an Asian courtesan—a woman in royal societies kept by a powerful man as a lover and companion—caught between a superficial life of luxury and the reality of her virtual slavery. Akiyoshi's compositions are considered standard textbook study among jazz students at music schools across the United States.

In 1982 Akiyoshi's remarkable career was the subject of a documentary called *Jazz Is My Native Language.* In it she discusses the many changes her orchestra has weathered over the years. Akiyoshi herself often plays with trios and quartets, and she is also a teacher. In 1991 she and her band signed a record deal with Columbia/Sony. Their first album for the new label was a live recording at New York City's Carnegie Hall. Her latest recording, *Monopoly Game,* was released in 2002. Akiyoshi hopes that the exposure a major record label brings will help increase the band's visibility and bring it financial success equal to its critical success. As Akiyoshi told *Down Beat,* "The recording goes just about any place in the United States. Even in a small town of 5,000, they can buy the CD if they want."

Sources:

Akiyoshi, Toshiko, press release, 1992.

Seidel, Mitchell, "The Perils of Toshiko," *Down Beat,* vol. 60, no. 2, February 1993, pp. 30-32.

Stephen, Lynnea Y., "Toshiko Akiyoshi: Jazzing It Up at Carnegie Hall," *Ms.,* May–June 1993, p. 82.

Rocky Aoki

Entrepreneur
Born October 9, 1939, Tokyo, Japan

"He spent a lot of time going around and seeing other restaurants to see what made them so successful. He never talked about the restaurant failing. He believed in his idea even when it looked like it would fail for sure. His energy was completely focused."—Aoki's wife, Chizuru Aoki.

Hiroaki "Rocky" Aoki is the founder of Benihana Restaurants, a chain of very popular Japanese-style eateries now located in the United States, Canada, Mexico, England, South Korea, Japan, Australia, and Thailand. Aoki began this chain with a single restaurant in Midtown Manhattan. Like most small businesses, including restaurants in Manhattan—which have an extremely high failure rate—Aoki's first restaurant had a slow start, but through a combination of good luck and hard work, he was able to make a success of it. Aoki is also well known as a world-class sportsman, participating in long-distance road rallies, speedboat racing, and ballooning. Moreover, he is a noted philanthropist and fundraiser for international art exchanges and environmental causes.

The original Benihana

Aoki's parents, Yonosuke and Katsu Aoki, were the owners of an upscale Tokyo coffee and tea shop called Ellington, named after the legendary American jazz musician and composer Duke Ellington. It was a popular night spot in prewar Tokyo and the Aokis enjoyed a prosperous lifestyle. After the beginning of World War II, when Rocky was three years old, the family's fortunes changed. America became the enemy and its culture was no longer viewed as glamorous by the Japanese people. When the U.S. Air Force began bombing Tokyo, the Aokis fled to Rocky's mother's home in the rural province of Gumma. After the war, the family returned to the nearly destroyed city of Tokyo and started a restaurant called Benihana, a Japanese word that can be translated as either "flower" or "saffron" (a prized ingredient in exotic dishes).

Aoki was educated at Keio, an exclusive private high school, after which he attended Keio University. He was a gifted student and very popular among his peers. He was also an athlete accomplished in a variety of sports, including track and field, karate, and, most successfully, wrestling. He became captain of the Keio University wrestling team and by the age of 19 was one of Japan's top wrestlers. In 1959 he toured the United States as an alternate on Japan's Olympic team, emerging undefeated in his weight class. During his trip, he became fascinated by the United States; when he returned to Japan he vowed he would try to win a scholarship to study in America.

Move to America

Aoki applied as a transfer student to several American universities and was offered scholarships to a few. He took up residence in New York City while deciding which school to attend. (While in New York he roomed with an old family friend from Japan, **Seiji Ozawa,** who today is conductor and music director of the Boston Symphony Orchestra.) Aoki ultimately enrolled in Massachusetts's Springfield College, but after moving to campus he changed his mind, transferring to C.W. Post College on Long Island, New York. While there, however, Aoki got into trouble for fighting, a problem that had dogged him since his middle-school days in Tokyo; he was eventually thrown out of school. He then gave up on a four-year degree and collegiate wrestling and enrolled in New York City Community College (NYCCC), where he earned an associate's degree in management in 1963.

Aoki had for some time wanted to open a restaurant in America. It was a business he knew well from his parents, and he felt he could be successful. Since his arrival in the

Rocky Aoki

United States, he had been putting aside money and had saved $10,000 by 1963, the year he graduated from college. That year he was offered some prime restaurant space in Midtown Manhattan by the owner of a struggling Chinese restaurant. Aoki enlisted the aid of his parents, who helped him secure a loan, and in May 1964 the first American Benihana restaurant opened.

There were many ethnic restaurants in New York, especially in Midtown, and a restaurant needed more than just good food to succeed. Aoki recognized this and decided to set his restaurant apart by the way the food was prepared. His new restaurant featured steak, chicken, and seafood— fairly standard fare—but Aoki had his chefs prepare the food on a *teppanyaki* (steel-topped) grill right at the patron's table. His restaurants featured tables built around these grills so that guests could watch as the chefs prepared their food, always with a dramatic flair.

Pursuing his dream

That first restaurant took some time to become successful. Soon, however, word got around that there was a new, unique little restaurant in town. Then Benihana got a glowing review from the food critic for the *New York Herald Tribune.* Aoki's wife, Chizuru, whom he married in 1964, recounted the early days at the first Benihana to Jack McCallum in his biography of Aoki, *Making It in America: The Life and Times of Rocky Aoki, Benihana's Pioneer.* She said that she recalls Aoki "running around like a chicken with his head cut off. He spent a lot of time going around and seeing other restaurants to see what made them so successful. He never talked about the restaurant failing. He believed in his idea even when it looked like it would fail for sure. His energy was completely focused."

This intensity paid off. On May 15, 1966, the second Benihana opened on Manhattan's East Side. The restaurants became huge successes among the fashionable set in New York. At both his restaurants, Aoki counted celebrities as regular customers. In 1968 the first Benihana opened in Chicago, and in May 1969, Aoki expanded to the West Coast when he opened Benihana San Francisco.

The Aoki flamboyance

In the early years of the restaurant, Aoki lived frugally and worked long hours to make sure everything was perfect. By the early 1970s, however, as the restaurant succeeded and became a chain, Aoki started to live much more lavishly. He began investing in splashy businesses that netted him notoriety but very little money. He backed a Broadway play starring comedian Joan Rivers that flopped, and he promoted a boxing match in Japan for his longtime friend, Muhammad Ali. While these ventures attracted attention and gossip column name recognition, he lost money on all of them.

Aoki spent his extensive leisure hours on a variety of pursuits. He became a world-class backgammon player in 1974. He started collecting antique cars, mostly sports cars and racing cars. Aoki is the first to admit that he wasted a lot of money and behaved impulsively. He told McCallum, "When I first started making money, my personal life got poorer.... I bought a nice house, yes, but that was it. I didn't put any furniture in it.... I started buying clothes, Rolls Royces, Cadillacs....I wanted to put [the money] where it would show." Aoki continued his flamboyant lifestyle throughout the 1970s and 1980s. He became a champion powerboat racer, he piloted a helium gas balloon across the Pacific, and in 1987 he won the first Milan-Moscow Road Rally, driving the 1,300 miles from Italy to Moscow's Red Square in a 1959 Rolls Royce Silver Wraith.

In the 1990s Aoki began to settle down, devoting his time and money to more socially responsible endeavors. He was recognized by the United Nations Environmental Program Directorate for his sponsorship of the *New York Times* environmental supplement "Imagine." He also established a Green Arts Program promoting international understanding through the arts.

In the 1990s, Aoki expanded the Benihana restaurant chain, opening several Haru Sushi restaurants. However, in 1999, Aoki stepped down as chairman of Benihana after pleading guilty to insider-trading charges and had to pay a large fine. (Insider trading is simply the use of internal company information in making stock-purchasing decisions.)

Sources:

McCallum, Jack, *Making It in America: The Life and Times of Rocky Aoki, Benihana's Pioneer,* New York: Dodd, Mead & Company, 1985.

George Ariyoshi

Politician, attorney
Born March 12, 1926, Honolulu, Hawaii

Ariyoshi recognized that something had to be done to slow the economic development of the Hawaiian Islands before their natural beauty was destroyed.... He was one of the first nationally significant politicians to promote environmentally friendly technologies.

In 1974 George Ariyoshi became the first American of Japanese descent to be elected governor of a state. The state was Hawaii, where traditionally there has been a large Japanese American population. Ariyoshi served three terms as the island state's governor, leaving office in 1986. One of his consistent concerns as governor, and throughout his political career, was the stimulation of economic development in Hawaii. While he was in office, Hawaii experienced rapid economic growth, especially in the area of tourism. However, with the growth in tourism came threats to the natural beauty of the islands. Ariyoshi attempted to ensure that economic expansion did not come at the expense of the environment and that the benefits of a bustling economy in Hawaii would be shared by as many people as possible.

The son of immigrants

Ariyoshi was born in 1926 to Japanese immigrants to the Hawaiian Islands, which were not yet part of the United States. His father, Ryozo Ariyoshi, had been a sumo wrestler in Japan and had worked as a stevedore (cargo handler) and, later, was the owner of a dry cleaning shop. His mother, Mitsue (Yoshikawa) Ariyoshi was from Kumamoto, Japan. The elder Ariyoshis emphasized the importance of education, and they were very supportive of their son's youthful desire to become a lawyer, despite the unpleasant reality that there were few opportunities for Japanese immigrants in the territory of Hawaii at that time.

Winning his first elected office, Ariyoshi served as class president during his senior year in high school. He graduated from McKinley High School in 1944, during World War II, and he enlisted in the army and served as an interpreter for the U.S. Military Intelligence Service in U.S.-occupied Japan after the war's conclusion.

George Ariyoshi

Following his military service, Ariyoshi enrolled in the University of Hawaii, where he stayed only briefly before transferring to Michigan State University. There he studied political science and history and earned a bachelor's degree in 1949. He then continued his studies by earning a law degree from the University of Michigan Law School in 1952. With his long-held dream of becoming a lawyer realized, Ariyoshi returned to his native Hawaii in 1953 and set up private practice as a criminal lawyer.

Entering politics

It was not until 1952 that Japanese immigrants or their descendants living in the territory of Hawaii could become citizens of the United States. Once granted this status, the large Japanese community in Hawaii began to emerge as a serious political force in Hawaiian politics. The Japanese immigrant and Japanese American populations were especially drawn into Democratic politics. This was partially in recognition of the work Democrats had done in defense of their civil liberties during the unconstitutional imprisonment of Japanese Americans during World War II. (Asian Americans were viewed with suspicion during the war, and 120,000 Japanese Americans from the West Coast were held in desolate "internment" camps, the result of a racist American policy that was supposedly enacted to prevent Japanese Americans from helping the Japanese in the event of a Japanese invasion of the United States.)

In 1954, Ariyoshi was approached by the chair of the Hawaiian Democratic party, John A. Burns, who urged him to run for a seat in the territorial house of representatives, the legislative body of the territory. Ariyoshi won that race, and when his term ended in 1958, he ran for a seat in Hawaii's other legislative house, the territorial senate, which he won as well. In 1959, Hawaii was admitted as the fiftieth state of the United States of America, and Ariyoshi continued to serve as state senator. He then began rising to successively more powerful posts within the Democratic party. In 1964, he was named chair of the powerful Ways and Means Committee; in 1965, he became the senate majority leader; and in 1969, majority floor leader. All the while, Ariyoshi maintained his law practice and in 1968 was named vice president of the Hawaii Bar Association and then president the following year. Ariyoshi was becoming a popular and well-connected figure in both Hawaiian politics and the state's legal community.

Meanwhile, Burns had become governor of the state, and in 1970, he invited Ariyoshi to run as his lieutenant governor. They won the election with 55 percent of the vote. The Burns/Ariyoshi administration saw considerable economic growth, notably in tourism, and was very popular with the people of the state. It also sought to expand Hawaii's role in international affairs. Burns and Ariyoshi recognized early on the importance of Hawaii's position as the state with the closest geographical and cultural ties to the growing economic force of Japan, a remarkably farsighted view considering the huge importance of Asia to the international economy today.

In 1973, Governor Burns became ill with cancer and in October of that year, he turned over the day-to-day operations of the state to his lieutenant governor. Less than a year later, Ariyoshi announced that he would seek the Democratic nomination for governor in the October 1974 primary. At this point Ariyoshi began to modify some of his views on development. He began to push for greater investment in areas beyond tourism, such as agriculture, to keep the state's economy from growing too dependent on any one industry. He won that year's election and spent his first term tackling problems such as the effects of the global recession (the slowing down of economic activities worldwide) on Hawaii, years of unchecked development, and a state population explosion resulting from an influx of immigrants from Asia and mainland America.

A new vision of growth

It is hard for any politician to try to limit economic development. The business sector, which pumps huge amounts of money into political campaigns to see its interests protected, has little patience for policies that slow growth. Yet Ariyoshi recognized that something had to be done to slow the economic development of the Hawaiian Islands before their natural beauty was destroyed. In 1977, he established what he called the Growth Management Task Force—a panel of 40 experts from various fields—to initiate legislative proposals that would stimulate economic growth without such drawbacks as environmental damage and immigration expansion. He also made a bid for multinational corporations—giant firms that operate throughout the world and dominate international trade—to use Hawaii as a base of operations when doing business with the countries of the Pacific Rim. In addition, Ariyoshi took steps to ease the congestion of Oahu, Hawaii's main island, and worked to reduce the state's dependence on imports.

Ariyoshi was one of the first national politicians to promote environmentally friendly technologies, such as ocean thermal energy conversion and the development of aquaculture, the planting and harvesting of sea plants. He also supported a controversial measure, the Hawaiian Land Reform Act of 1967, that granted the state the right to redistribute land owned by large private estates to the tenants who lived on it.

In 1978, Ariyoshi ran for reelection, facing stiff competition in the Democratic primary from the mayor of Honolulu, Frank Fasi, who bitterly opposed many of the governor's more controversial policies. It was a tough campaign, but Ariyoshi defeated Fasi in the primary by the slimmest of margins and then won the general election in another close vote. It is widely thought that Ariyoshi's economic policies—called "preferred growth"—which had attracted strong business sector opposition but gained wide public acclaim, won him both elections.

In 1982, Ariyoshi began his campaign for a third term in office. Two major labor disputes in his troubled second term weakened the governor's support among organized labor. In the midst of the 1982 campaign, Ariyoshi also faced controversy when the federal government opened an investigation into charges of brutality at the Oahu Community Correctional Center. In addition to these troubles, Ariyoshi was again challenged in the Democratic primary by Frank Fasi, who was fast becoming his archrival. Ariyoshi was elected again and served his third term with distinction, working on the same popular reforms that he had initiated during his first two terms.

Awards

The Hawaiian constitution limits governors to three terms, so Ariyoshi stepped down in 1986. In recognition of his long and distinguished career in Hawaiian politics, Ariyoshi has received many awards, including honorary law degrees from the University of the Philippines at Quezon City and the University of Guam at Agana. He served as chair of the Western Governors' Conference in 1977 and 1978, and was president of the Pacific Basin Development Council in 1980 and 1981. In his entire political career, from 1954 to 1986, Ariyoshi never lost an election. He remains busy, as a businessman and a politician, serving as president of Prince Resorts Hawaii, co-chair of Asia Pacific Consulting Group, on the governor of Hawaii's East-West Center board, and as a member of the Presidential Advisory Committee on Trade Policy and Negotiation.

Ariyoshi married Jean Miya Hayashi in February 1955, and the two now live in Honolulu. They have three children and two grandchildren.

Sources:

Current Biography Yearbook, New York: H. W. Wilson, 1985.

The office of George R. Ariyoshi, Watanabe, Ing & Kawashima, Attorneys at Law, Honolulu, Hawaii.

Jose Aruego

Author, illustrator
Born August 9, 1932, Manila, the Philippines

"[My stories] must take off from something funny. If they are serious, I cannot get my juices working. Kids like to be happy and my books give them the opportunity."

J ose Aruego is an award-winning children's book illustrator and writer, cartoonist, and graphic artist. He has illustrated more than 60 books, including several of his own. But Aruego almost didn't become an illustrator; he comes from a family of successful lawyers in the Philippines and was raised to follow in his father's footsteps and become an attorney. His father was a very prominent legal scholar who helped draft the Philippines' constitution and published several books.

As a child Aruego showed an interest in drawing and art. In school he noticed that his ability attracted attention and admiration, and he practiced his skills throughout his childhood. He also collected comic books, the artwork of which he greatly admired. In their 1992 children's book, *Famous Asian Americans,* Janet Nomura Morey and Wendy Dunn quoted Aruego as saying, "If I am good at drawing, people notice me."

A short career in law

After graduating from high school, Aruego enrolled in the University of the Philippines, where he earned a bachelor of arts degree in 1953; he then enrolled in the university's law school, earning a law degree in 1955. Although discontented with his studies and not at all eager to enter the field of law, he felt bound to it by the expectations of his family. Barely passing the bar exam, which enables lawyers to practice, he began what would turn out to be a very short career in law. Aruego was a practicing attorney for all of three months. He tried one case, which he lost, and decided to stand up to family pressure by changing careers.

Aruego's father eventually came around and decided to support his son's chosen vocation. He financed a move to New York City, where Aruego studied graphic arts and advertising at the Parsons School of Design, one of the most prestigious design schools in the United States. Aruego spent the summer between his sophomore and junior years traveling and studying in Europe, where he learned the technique of line drawing (in which subjects are represented using solid lines). He also became interested in promoting cultural understanding among nations and worked as a member of an international friendship program.

In 1959, Aruego graduated from Parsons with a degree in graphic arts and advertising. His first several jobs were with design firms and advertising agencies. He also took on freelance drawing and design work. One freelance job of which Aruego is especially proud was an assignment to paint a mural at New York's International House, a dormitory for international and nontraditional students at Columbia University, Teacher's College, and Union Theological Seminary. While working on this important project in 1961, Aruego met and married another artist, colorist Ariane Dewey.

Cartoons and illustrations

In addition to this work, Aruego had for some time been submitting cartoons to magazines for publication. Soon they were accepted, and his work began appearing in such popular magazines as *The New Yorker, The Saturday Evening Post,* and *Look.* He continued working at various agencies until 1968, by which time he was making enough money from his cartoons to support himself.

In 1968, Aruego's son Juan was born. The new father quickly submitted a children's book he had written and illustrated to publishers in New York. Called *The King and His Friends,* it was published in 1969 by the second publisher to see it. The book was fairly successful and helped Aruego land a job as the illustrator of a book by Robert Kraus, with whom the artist would work often in coming years.

Published in 1970, *Whose Mouse Are You?* was honored as a notable book by the American Library Association. That year proved an extremely productive one for Aruego; altogether, he had five books published—two he had written and three he had illustrated for other writers. One book that he authored, *Juan and the Asuang: A Tale of Philippine Ghosts and Spirits,* was named an outstanding picture book of the year by *The New York Times.*

In 1976, Aruego was chosen as the Outstanding Filipino Abroad in the Arts, an award granted by the Philippine government. He described going home to receive the award to Dunn and Morey, recalling, "It was nice being recognized in my new profession. Lots of lawyer classmates and professors were proud of me that I made it as an illustrator. I changed professions and changed to what is successful." He believes that though he did not succeed as a lawyer, going to law school nonetheless taught him discipline and helped him to mature.

Aruego's later work—some of which he illustrated with his wife—includes *We Hide, You Seek* (1988), *Birthday Rhymes, Special Times* (1993), *Rockabye Crocodile: A Folktale from the Philippines* (1993), *Alligators and Others All Year Long: A Book of Months* (1994), and *Weird Friends: Unlikely Allies in the Animal Kingdom* (2002).

The nature of his work

Since he began his career in the late 1960s, Aruego has illustrated or written over 60 books and has won several awards for his work. By the mid-1990s, he had given up drawing cartoons—the work that first inspired him to pursue art and that first supported him as an independent artist—and had devoted himself exclusively to writing and illustration. He offers the following advice to those wishing to pursue a career in the arts: "Art has many facets—books, magazines—one should go where their talent lies. Some are good artists but cannot tell stories..... You must be ready to compromise.... You cannot always do what you want. In the beginning you have to adjust your style to earn money. Do what you want on the side. The most beautiful thing is doing what you want when that earns money."

Aruego often incorporates Philippine folk tales into his writing and uses tropical jungle motifs in his illustrations. His books are generally comical and center on endearing, eccentric animal characters. He told Dunn and Morey, "I have written mostly animal stories. The ideas have humor. They must take off from something funny. If they are serious, I cannot get my juices working. Kids like to be happy and my books give them the opportunity."

Sources:

Morey, Janet Nomura, and Wendy Dunn, *Famous Asian Americans,* New York: Cobblehill Books, 1992.

Simon and Schuster, publicity and press releases, http://www.simonsays.com (accessed April 15, 2003).

Kavelle R. Bajaj

Entrepreneur
Born June 15, 1950, India

"Success can be measured only by one's self. We set a goal and try to reach it. Reaching it is the only success."

Kavelle R. Bajaj is the founder and president of I-Net, a computer services firm that specializes in computer-based networking. (A computer network is a group of computers connected to each other and thus capable of communicating with each other, allowing their operators greater efficiency.) The company is one of the computer industry's great success stories, as is Bajaj's story itself. She started the company in 1985 with $5,000 from her husband. At the time, she knew nothing about computers or operating a company, but she had ambition and drive and, as she told *Asian American Biography (AAB)*, "I knew I could never work for anyone. It's not in my character."

During its start-up phase, always a difficult time for companies, I-Net benefited from being a registered minority-owned business. As such it was eligible for government contracts, a certain percentage of which were then required by law to be given to minority-owned businesses and businesses owned by women. I-Net soon earned a reputation for fine service and professionalism, and its subsequent growth has been based exclusively on merit.

A traditional upbringing

Bajaj's mother was a traditional Indian homemaker, and her father was an entrepreneur who had started his own construction company. His work took him to remote districts of India. Bajaj and her two siblings traveled with him, an experience that gave them an opportunity to see the immense diversity of India, which, like the United States, is made up of very different cultures.

Bajaj was taught from an early age that a woman's role is as caretaker of the family, but she did not accept this limitation easily. "I was a free spirit," she told *AAB*, "independent, headstrong, and stubborn as a child. I did whatever I set my mind to. I gave my parents quite a few gray hairs." In an interview with the *Chicago Tribune*, Bajaj described her upbringing, relating, "I was born into a family that had very traditional values for the majority, except they did believe in getting their daughters an education. Granted the education they wanted was everything that would prepare you to be an ideal housewife and a desired partner in life." Given that philosophy, it is not surprising that when Bajaj went to college—at the University of New Delhi—she earned a degree in home economics.

An arranged marriage

In 1973 Bajaj married Ken Bajaj, a computer engineer. The marriage was arranged, as is the custom in India, and Bajaj had only met her future husband on a few occasions prior to the wedding. In 1974 the couple immigrated to the United States, settling first in Michigan, where Bajaj's husband

Kavelle R. Bajaj

was offered a teaching position. From there, they moved to Maryland, where Ken Bajaj had accepted a position in private industry. For the next several years Bajaj fulfilled the traditional role of mother and homemaker, raising her children and caring for the family home.

In the mid-1980s, though, Bajaj began thinking about pursuing greater intellectual stimulation. For a long time she could not decide whether she should enter the professional world or go back to school, feeling the obstacles before her in either direction were too great to overcome. Here her hus-

band proved inspirational, telling her that if she didn't act soon to get into the business world, she would have nothing to occupy her time when their children grew up and moved out.

Bajaj had been interested in computers for some time and felt that with the growth the industry was expected to experience, she would have no problem finding a niche for herself. She told the *Chicago Tribune,* "At that point, you had software people and network people and maintenance people and systems analyst people. What I felt was missing was accountability. There was so much finger pointing when the system didn't work that I felt—and this is what I told my potential customer—'let I-Net be accountable for your requirements. Let us be your analysts and bring you the solutions you need.'"

The beginnings of success

I-Net's first office was in the basement of the Bajajs' suburban home. The company's first contracts were government set-asides, but in time Bajaj began competing against the giants in her field, including IBM, AT&T, and EDS. Bajaj attributes I-Net's early success to her decision to specialize in constructing computer networks that fit her clients' specific needs. Her success is also attributable to the timing of her entry into the market; the computer revolution was exploding, and many companies had needs that only a few were equipped to meet.

In its initial years, I-Net grew at a phenomenal rate of 80 to 90 percent. In 1988 Bajaj's husband joined the company as executive vice president. The decision to include her husband was a difficult one for

Bajaj, who did not want to disrupt the harmony of the family. Still, she was having trouble finding someone who could bring computer expertise and business savvy to her growing company.

Defining success

In 1996, I-Net was sold to Wang Laboratories. Despite her immense financial rewards, Bajaj does not believe that this is the final definition of a job well done. "Success can be measured only by one's self," she said in an interview with *AAB*. "We set a goal and try to reach it. Reaching it is the only success." She does not believe in external barriers. "Obstacles are self-imposed," she has said. "We can't blame outside sources for our failures." As an Indian woman working in unfamiliar surroundings, Bajaj's hurdles have been personal as well as professional; she measures her success by her ability to rise above considerable cultural barriers as well as by the dollar value of her company.

Bajaj is working to help others in situations similar to hers—women and minority small-business owners. She works with a local mentoring program in which she helps budding entrepreneurs on a one-to-one basis. She is also involved in organizing a national resource center for Asian Indian women that would provide information at the governmental, industrial, and political levels. Ultimately, Bajaj hopes such a resource will help provide training for Asian Indian women in many occupational fields.

Bajaj has been recognized for her contributions, and for her achievements as an immigrant. In 1996, she was awarded the Women of Distinction Award from the American Association of University Women. In 1997, she received the American Immigration Law Foundation Washington Immigrant Achievement Award.

Sources:

Bajaj, Kavelle R., personal profile produced by Bajaj, June 1994.

Bajaj, Kavelle R., telephone interview with Shamita Das Dasgupta, June 20, 1994.

"A Network Hit," *Working Woman,* May 1994, p. 49.

Maniya Barredo

Dancer
Born November 19, 1951, Manila, the Philippines

"When I was seven I knew I wanted to be a dancer. I sang and took up the piano and acted, but the minute I went into ballet I knew this was what I wanted. It was my best way of reaching people and made me very happy. It still does."

Maniya Barredo is a prima ballerina and dance coach with the Atlanta Ballet. She is a highly regarded figure internationally and has danced with some of the most important ballet companies in the world, including New York's Joffrey Ballet, Montreal's Les Grands Ballets Canadiens, and the Paris Opera Theater. She is widely known for her classical repertoire, which includes the lead roles in *Giselle, Sleeping Beauty, Romeo and Juliet, Swan Lake,* and *The Nutcracker.* Barredo has also starred in the dance film *Ali Babba and the Forty Thieves*, an international production. In 1983, in addition to dancing as prima balle-

Maniya Barredo

she was four years old; she later took ballet lessons from her aunt, one of Manila's best-known ballet teachers. In an interview with *Asian American Biography (AAB),* Barredo said, "When I was seven I knew I wanted to be a dancer. I sang and took up the piano and acted, but the minute I went into ballet I knew this was what I wanted. It was my best way of reaching people and made me very happy. It still does."

Barredo's rise to fame was quick and seemingly charmed. By the time she was nine years old she had her own children's television show and was contributing money from her earnings toward her siblings' educations. When she was 14, she joined the Hariraya Dance Company in Manila and became the star of the troupe. While she was with the Hariraya, there was a teacher in residence from the Bolshoi Ballet in Moscow, one of the most important ballet companies in the world. This teacher recognized Barredo's talent and selected her to train for a new ballet he was then mounting for the Bolshoi.

rina, Barredo was named dance coach of the increasingly prestigious Atlanta Ballet.

Early ambition

Barredo's family had mixed feelings about her desire to be a dancer. Her father, a businessman, saw no future in dancing and pushed his daughter to pursue a more practical, academic career. Her mother was more sympathetic, herself a frustrated dancer who'd shown early promise but had spent her most productive dance years raising her nine children. Barredo began dancing when

A scholarship in New York

In 1970, Barredo received a scholarship to study ballet at the American Ballet Center, the official school of the Joffrey Ballet, for which she had been recruited by the founder of the company, Robert Joffrey. She trained from nine in the morning until seven in the evening for two years. Her teachers included some of the top names in American ballet. Barredo also performed during this period, touring with the company's student group, Joffrey II, and then later joining Joffrey I.

After her second year of training, auditions were announced for the National Ballet

The Atlanta Ballet–Maniya Barredo as Juliet, Nicolas Pacana as Romeo

of Washington, and Joffrey sent six of his students to try out—Barredo was not among them. She went to the auditions anyway, on her own, and competed against 60 of the finest dancers in the country. Here Barredo faced a long-standing problem: as a Filipina she did not look the part of the traditional European ballerina. Aside from her Asian coloring and features, she was short—only five feet tall—and weighed a mere 83 pounds. Remarkably, Barredo so impressed the judges that she was offered a contract with the company. This was a dream come true, but Barredo consulted Joffrey and others as to her course; they advised her to continue her training. Again, her physical appearance played a part in the decision. She described her dilemma to *Sunburst* magazine, revealing, "I had a special problem being ... short and dark, I couldn't possibly get into any company as a member of the corps. I would stick out like a sore thumb. I had to come in immediately as a soloist or not at all." She decided to continue her education in hope of being hired as a soloist.

A career as a soloist

In May 1972, Barredo gave a solo dance concert at Carnegie Hall, the first such performance by a Filipina in the United States. In 1973, she joined Montreal's Les Grands Ballets Canadiens, one of three major ballet companies in Canada, becoming its youngest principal dancer. While with Les Grands Ballets, Barredo spent a month's residency at the Paris Opera Theater Ballet. She also met and married Mannie Rowe, another principal dancer. In 1976, Barredo represented Canada at the International Dance Festival in Cuba. She then left Les Grands Ballets to join the

Atlanta Ballet, a small company with a modest budget. She had fallen in love with Atlanta and was also eager to escape the harsh Canadian winters.

Barredo's move from a traditional company with an established history and legacy to a relatively new company in a city lacking a strong cultural tradition was much discussed in the ballet world; some wondered if she would ever be heard from again. But the Atlanta Ballet grew in size and funding over the years.

In 1979, Barredo was invited to join the "Stars of the World" ballet tour, where she was the only dancer not with a New York or European company. However, some still viewed Barredo's move to Atlanta as a professional mistake. She addressed the issue in an interview with the *Atlanta Constitution*: "An artist is not rated by where she works. It doesn't make me any less of a dancer to dance here. I believe in the Atlanta Ballet.... Having been with Joffrey, I have seen the pitfalls of a big New York company. Here I have room to grow without the pressures of all the politics. I have found my little corner of the hemisphere."

A chorus of acclaim

During her career as a dancer, Barredo won wide praise. Back in her days with Les Grands Ballets, she was described by the *Toronto Financial Post* as "the star of the show ... a slim, slight, but voluptuous dancer who has the audience in the palm of her hand from the moment she steps on to the stage until, with a switch of her elegant back, she leaps into the wings after her curtain call." The Philippine magazine *Focus* reviewed her work with the Atlanta Ballet, reporting,

"Only a wisp of a girl, she could mesmerize an audience completely into ecstasy.... When performing onstage, she seemed to breeze through her repertoire as she danced her roles, executing with artistry and maturity the technically demanding steps."

In January 1994, Barredo danced her farewell performance in Manila, performing *Giselle* at the Cultural Center of the Philippines. When she finished she received a 15-minute standing ovation. Barredo retired from dancing in 1995. Since then she has kept busy working with arts organizations. She has been an artistic consultant to Ballethnic and artistic director of the Atlanta School of Ballet and Metropolitan Ballet Theatre. She served as cultural attaché for the Philippines in 2001, where she was presented with the National Artist Award from the Cultural Center of the Philippines.

Barredo lives in suburban Atlanta with her second husband, L. Patterson Thompson, and their five dogs. Looking back on her life in an interview for *AAB*, she recalled, "When I left the Philippines, everyone told me I'd never make it: my friends, my teacher, my family. I said, 'Well, we'll see.' I believed in who I was and that with hard work, I could do just about anything."

Sources:

Atlanta Ballet, press releases and biographical materials, 1994.

Barredo, Maniya, telephone interview with Ferdinand M. de Leon, May 5, 1994.

Smith, Helen C., "Maniya Barredo Celebrates 10 Years in Atlanta," *Atlanta Journal and Constitution,* November 2, 1986, p. 1J.

Viana, Francis, "Honey Barredo," *Sunburst,* pp. 46-47.

Lynda Barry

Cartoonist, playwright
Born 1956, Seattle, Washington

"I have a strong commitment to bringing certain things to light... what people go through. I'm very fierce about it."

Lynda Barry is one of the most popular alternative comic strip artists in America. Her strip, *Ernie Pook's Comeek,* appears in over 60 alternative newspapers around the country, as well as in Canada, Russia, and Hungary. In 1991 she adapted her 1988 novel, *The Good Times Are Killing Me,* for the stage. It appeared off-Broadway in New York before touring nationally. Barry is also a commentator for National Public Radio and a former columnist for *Mother Jones* magazine.

The benefits of art

Barry was raised in a working-class neighborhood that was predominantly black and Asian. Her Filipino mother worked as a hospital janitor and her Irish-Norwegian father was a meatcutter at a supermarket. When she was in the second grade, Barry discovered her budding artistic talents when one day she drew an orange grove to illustrate the letter "O"; the popular girls in school liked her drawing and for a few days she enjoyed a sort of celebrity she had never known before. Until then, Barry had been interested in insects and thought of becom-

Lynda Barry

become a problem, left home, leaving her mother to support her and her two brothers. In *Elle* magazine, Barry described how a teacher used to send her off with a pad and pencil when she was particularly distressed, saying it had a calming effect on her.

Barry discussed the difficulties of her childhood in *Mirabella:* "People say to me, 'But look at all it's given you!' And I think that's such a ... transparent hope. Like the idea the people who had a good childhood and money and good things are actually less than people who had to suffer. In the end, it's like saying my childhood was good. And I refuse to say that. I came out of it—others didn't. There's no way to turn around a difficult childhood." This deeply held feeling—that childhood is often not the peaceful and fun-filled playground we have come to expect—marks much of Barry's work. Her comic strip addresses such subjects as alcoholism, divorce, incest, and suicide. "I have a strong commitment to bringing certain things to light ... what people go through. I'm very fierce about it."

Her first comic

Barry studied fine arts at Evergreen State College in Washington state, where she became friends with other cartoonists, including Matt Groening, who would go on to create the animated television show *The Simpsons.* As a student of art she was influenced by the French painter Henri de Toulouse-Lautrec and by writer Raymond Carver, both of whom chose simple settings and working-class characters to portray universal themes and ideas. Barry did not consider a career in cartooning until one day, after breaking up with her boyfriend, she

ing a veterinarian. But with the attention her drawing brought her, the young girl reconsidered her calling. She told *Mirabella* magazine, "It turned out to be a good thing, but I chose it so I could be better liked. I can remember all the brain action behind it." This is a typical Barry story, one that captures the social maneuvering of childhood; it is just the sort of thing that might appear in one of her strips.

Once she discovered art, Barry often turned to drawing to cope with the increasing turbulence of her home life. When she was 14, her father, whose drinking had found herself doodling a strip in which men looked like cactuses—cactuses that smoked and tried to lure women. A friend at the University of Washington liked her drawings and published them in his school's paper.

Barry's first big professional break came when the *Chicago Reader,* an alternative weekly (an alternative to the large daily newspapers, often featuring extensive coverage of the arts and a liberal point of view), began running her strip. It soon caught the attention of other weeklies, including the biggest in the country, New York's *Village Voice*, which led to national syndication. This strip eventually became *Ernie Pook's Comeek* and can now be read all over the country.

Ernie Pook's Comeek

Barry's strip is named for a pet turtle her brother kept as a child. It is a four-panel, black-and-white serial strip drawn in a scratchy, childlike style. It follows the adventures of Arna, Arnold, Freddi, Maybonne, and Marlys, a group of children growing up in the 1960s. The characters face all sorts of honest, raw traumas of the kind that seem ordinary, but their stories capture the anguish of adolescent stress. *Elle* called Barry "the reigning queen of adolescent pop psychology [who] has a monopoly on growing pains," and went on to say, "[The] characters suffer from king-sized inferiority complexes ... and pin names like 'the hairy eyeball' on teachers who torture them with tired platitudes." The strip is hugely popular and has attracted a dedicated following, earning Barry a cultlike status.

Over the years, Barry has collected her works into books. In 1994 she released her eighth, *It's So Magic*. While the early books chronicled innocent rites of passage like bad haircuts and a shared first smoke, her most recent collections have tackled more serious subjects. Her 1992 book, *My Perfect Life,* for instance, takes on issues like race, sex, alcoholism, and religion.

Novelist and playwright

In 1988 Barry published her first novel, *The Good Times Are Killing Me,* which later won the Washington State Governor's Writer's Award. The novel tells the story of two 12-year-old girls growing up in the mid-1960s—Edna, who is white, and Bonna, her black friend who lives next door. Barry developed the novel into a play that premiered Off-Broadway in 1991 and then toured the country and Canada, earning rave reviews. *Now,* a weekly in Toronto, described Barry's style in the play: "She's not interested in bloodlessly using the tales of kids to soothe adults. She's drawn to the vividness of childhood life lived full of possibilities and peril.... The children of Barry's raw world don't live in idyllic isolation, but have real problems. Bouncing off adults, they detail the grown-up world that dominates them with the searing and unrestrained perception that only a child can have."

In 1990 Barry became a commentator for National Public Radio's *Morning Edition* program. Prior to that she wrote a strip about relations between men and women for *Esquire* magazine, and for several years she wrote a column for the magazine *Mother Jones*. She has also released a recording, in which she reads her short stories, called *The Lynda Barry Experience.* Barry has had her paintings featured in several exhibits around the country and has completed her first television show, *Grandma's Way Out Party,* which aired on station KCTS in Minneapolis, Minnesota.

Barry, however, loves cartooning most of all. "It's my favorite thing," she has said. "A comic strip doesn't take that long to do, and I only do one a week. I do it right before it's due. I sit down until I hear the first line and then I just write it and draw it right there on the paper. It's like the live performance of a writer. It's the closest you can get to being live." More recent books by Barry include *Cruddy* (2000), *One Hundred Demons* (2002), and *The Greatest of Marlys* (2000).

Sources:

Barry, Lynda, "Biography," May 1994.

Hollett, Michael, "Lynda Barry: Fearless Cartoonist's Razor-Sharp Recollections Explode on Stage," *Now,* April 8-14, 1993.

Mifflin, Margot, "A Not So Perfect Life: The Anxious Humor of Lynda Barry," *Elle,* April 1992.

Oppenheimer, Judy, "Lynda Barry Outstrips Them All," *Mirabella,* April 1991.

Carlos Bulosan

Writer, poet
Born November 2, 1911, Binalonan, the Philippines
Died September 11, 1956, Seattle, Washington

"Writing is a pleasure and a passion to me."

Carlos Bulosan was a great writer, poet, and labor organizer who produced most of his important work in the 1930s and 1940s. He wrote poetry, fiction, and nonfiction and was associated with the radical politics of the day. His most famous work, *America Is in the Heart,* was very successful when it was published shortly after World War II, but then the book—and its writer—were largely overlooked until the volume was rereleased in the early 1970s. Bulosan is now looked upon as one of the pioneer Asian American writers and as a brave voice of the oppressed.

An ocean crossing

Bulosan grew up in a peasant family in a rural area of the Philippines. As a child he would go to the market with his mother and sell vegetables and fish sauce. He also worked as a laborer in the mango fields. His family was impoverished and struggled for years with greedy landowners over ownership of the family land. During this period, the Philippines were a colony of the United States, and there were many stories about how easy it was to make money in America—how luxurious a life one could lead even working as a bellhop or bartender. Many Filipinos were leaving their country to work in the sugar fields of Hawaii and on the West Coast. After high school, Bulosan joined the growing numbers of young men who were making the long ocean voyage to what they hoped would be a better life. He paid $75 for passage to Seattle, Washington. During the long voyage an epidemic of meningitis broke out and several of the Filipino passengers, who were confined to the steerage section, became ill or died.

Bulosan arrived in the United States in July 1930, less than a year after the 1929 stock market crash that devastated the Amer-

Carlos Bulosan

ican economy and marked the beginning of the bleak period in American history known as the Great Depression. The unemployment rate was enormous and competition for the lower-end types of jobs Filipino immigrants usually held became fierce. White Americans began to look at the Filipinos, whom they had encouraged to emigrate during better times, as a threat to their ability to support their families. Bulosan was unable to find work in Seattle and so went north to work in the fish canneries of Alaska. The work was incredibly difficult and the hours long. After one season of hard labor, Bulosan's total earnings were just $13.

Lessons about America

After this experience, Bulosan began working his way south to California, where two of his older brothers had settled. Along the way he worked as a field hand or crop picker with other Filipino immigrants. The horrible conditions and low pay made Bulosan see that all was not as it was supposed to be in the United States. When he got to California, there was further proof of this: the Filipino community had been singled out by politicians and the media as the cause of serious social problems. Racist laws made it illegal for Filipino men to marry white women, and cars driven by Filipino men were randomly stopped and searched by police. These injustices outraged Bulosan, who then sought political movements prepared to fight for reform. He would later write, "I came to know ... that in many ways it was a crime to be a Filipino in California. I came to know that the public streets were not free to my people."

Soon after his arrival in California, Bulosan became involved in an effort to organize independent unions as a way for Filipinos to fight the arbitrary firings and wage cuts they routinely suffered. This organizing effort led to the establishment of a new international union known as the UCAPAWA, the United Cannery and Packing House Workers of America. The union represented workers in Seattle's fish canneries and in the packing houses of Salinas, California.

The writer emerges

Bulosan was sickly and had difficulty holding jobs. He worked for a while in restaurants as a dishwasher. Finally, he moved to Los Angeles to stay with his brother Aurelio, who was able to support him. Bulosan began spending his free time in the public libraries, reading everything he could find. He was especially interested in philosophy and sociology, particularly in the way these disciplines interacted with the labor movement. He was becoming an avid follower of Communist theorist Karl Marx and would often tell friends of the rising power of the working classes and what they would achieve in the coming revolution.

Bulosan also spent his time in the libraries practicing his writing. In 1932, he published his first poem in an anthology of the work of California poets. In 1934, he began publishing *The New Tide,* a bimonthly radical literary magazine that brought him into contact with some of the great writers of the era, including the poet William Carlos Williams and the novelists William Saroyan and Richard Wright. He also befriended Harriet Monroe, the editor of *Poetry,* an important literary journal that published some of the most successful poets of the time. Monroe became a champion of Bulosan's work and played a significant role in his future success. In addition, Bulosan wrote political articles that were published in the *Philippine Commonwealth Times* and at least two other Stockton-Salinas newspapers that focused on the problems of Filipino workers. There was much interest in radical politics in the United States at this time. The labor movement began to emerge as an important force, and there were thousands of small working-class magazines and newspapers all over the country.

In 1936, Bulosan was stricken with tuberculosis and had three operations for a lesion in his right lung. He also had problems with his knee and his kidneys and spent the better part of 1936 through 1938 in the hospital. Again, he used his idle time productively, reading and writing voraciously. "Writing is a pleasure and a passion to me," he wrote at the time. "I seem to be bubbling with multitudinous ideas, but my body is weak and tired. I locked myself in the room, unplugged the phone, pulled down the shades and shut out the whole damned world. I knew enough of it to carry me for a lifetime of writing."

The beginnings of success

When the United States was drawn into World War II, the Philippines was its ally against the Japanese in the Pacific theater. Around this time, Bulosan began to achieve wider success. In 1942, he published two books of poetry: *Letter from America* and *Chorus for America.* Later that year, he was included in *Who's Who in America.* In 1943, he published *The Voice of Bataan,* a collection of poems dedicated to the men who died in that crucial battle of the Pacific war—all of them Filipino, American, and Japanese. That same year, the *Saturday Evening Post* published four articles on what they called "the four freedoms": freedom of speech, freedom to worship, freedom from want, and freedom from fear. Bulosan was chosen to write the article on freedom from want, a topic he knew well after living in deprivation for years. The author took the opportunity to express some of his most deeply held political beliefs in a magazine with a huge circulation. He wrote a biting essay about the oppression of the working class, the police-state intimidation techniques routinely used against unions, and the racism running wild in America. He ended his essay with a not-so-subtle warning: "If you want to know what we are—we are Marching!"

In 1944, Bulosan published his first collection of short stories, *The Laughter of My Father.* The book was translated into several languages and established Bulosan as an important writer. Then, in 1946, he published his most enduring work, the autobiographical *America Is in the Heart.* The book is a merciless critique of a racist society immersed in the Great Depression. The *Saturday Review of Literature* responded, "People interested in driving from America the scourge of intolerance should read Mr. Bulosan's autobiography. They should read it that they may draw from it the anger it will arouse in them ... the determination to bring an end to the vicious nonsense of racism."

Political backlash

But by the early 1950s, Bulosan, like many of his generation of radicals, had fallen from favor. His published works and his involvement in union activities raised suspicions during this time of fierce anti-communism, when Senator Joseph McCarthy was overseeing a national witch-hunt for communist sympathizers. Bulosan claimed to have been blacklisted—put on a list of allegedly "disloyal" people whom companies were pressured not to hire. Bulosan once again fell into poverty and his health began to deteriorate anew. He spent his final years in Seattle, hospitalized periodically. On September 11, 1956, he died of tuberculosis and malnutrition.

For nearly 20 years after his death, Bulosan and his works were largely forgotten. However, a generation of young Asian Americans rediscovered him when *America Is in the Heart* was reprinted by the University of Washington Press in 1973. It has since become a fixture in Asian American Studies programs at universities across the nation.

Sources:

Bulosan, Carlos, *America Is in the Heart,* 1943; reprinted with an introduction by Carey McWilliams, Seattle: University of Washington Press, 1973.

Evangelista, Susan, *Carlos Bulosan and His Poetry: A Biography and Anthology,* Seattle: University of Washington Press, 1985.

Phyllis Campbell

Banker
Born July 25, 1951, Spokane, Washington

"In my life I have always tried to stand out in positive, not negative ways. I'm proud of the attributes I can bring to business, civic roles, and other life experiences. Living each day to the fullest and taking advantage of each page as it is turned is my goal."

Phyllis Jean Takisaki Campbell has become very successful in a field generally reserved for white males: upper management banking. Through 20 years of hard work she has risen through the ranks in one of the West Coast's premier financial institutions, the U.S. Bank of Washington, headquartered in Spokane. She was hired as a trainee fresh out of college and then served in a variety of positions. As president and chief executive officer, Campbell was responsible for the leadership and management of all U.S. Bank of Washington retail and business banking in the state, including three area banks representing over 160 branches.

A close family

Campbell was born the oldest of five children to Marion and Raymond J. Takisaki. Her father owned and operated a dry-cleaning business in Spokane. Campbell's grandfather had emigrated from Japan and was the owner of a grocery store. He instilled in his children a sense of community service and emphasized the virtue of hard work. In an interview with *Asian American Biography (AAB),* Campbell recalled, "My grandfather always said that this country had afforded him great opportunities, and he taught us that we had a responsibility to give back to people what had been given to us." Even her family's experiences during World War II did nothing to shatter her grandfather's view of the United States. "During the war," she related, "my grandfather and my uncle and aunt were forced to liquidate the business and were interned in North Dakota [in an internment camp where Japanese Americans were detained, supposedly as a national security risk], but even after that my grandfather never spoke ill of the government." In his mind, the government's later apology and restitution payments to Japanese Americans who were interned were taken as proof of the nation's resolve never to let a similar experience happen again.

When Campbell was a child, her family was poor, and the children helped out in the dry-cleaning business. This communal effort had a big impact on Campbell, who learned about the importance of family and perseverance. Her mother worked outside the home throughout Campbell's childhood, a rarity at the time. "My mother worked and maintained a career throughout her whole life," Campbell told *AAB,* "even raising five children. She was a role model for me as a strong woman, a person in her own right. My sister and brothers and I took care of each other and occasionally, a lady in the neighborhood would come in to help. Back in those days neighborhoods were safe places. My brothers and sisters and I are still very close today."

An early interest in business

As she grew up and worked in the family business, Campbell became interested in the management aspects of business. She also learned to enjoy working with people. Ultimately, however, her sights were set beyond staying in the family business. "I wanted something larger with corporate finance and corporate structure," she explained.

Campbell was educated in the Spokane public school system and after graduating from high school, she enrolled in Washington State University. Working part time to finance her education and to support herself at college, she received a bachelor's degree in business administration and then went on to earn a master's degree in the executive marketing program. She has also earned degrees from the University of Washington's Pacific Coast banking school and Stanford University's marketing management program. In recognition of the success she has achieved in banking, she was awarded honorary doctorates from Whitworth College and Gonzaga University.

Her banking career

Campbell was hired as a management trainee by the Old National Bank of Spokane after finishing her graduate degree. Her first job was as a branch manager. She soon worked her way up the ladder, however, and within a few years had become senior vice president of all the Spokane branches of the bank. In 1987 Old National Bank was acquired by U.S. Bank of Washington. The new owners not only kept Campbell on, they promoted her to senior vice president and area manager for eastern Washington. In 1989 she became executive vice president and manager of the distribution group for U.S. Bank, and in 1992 she was named head of the Seattle-King County area. From 1993-2001 Campbell served as president of U.S. Bank of Washington. In 2002, she was elected to the board of directors of Alaska Air, as well as serving on the boards of SAFECO, Puget Sound Energy, and the Pacific Science Center. Throughout her career, Campbell has shown herself to be an excellent manager and a keen businessperson, especially during the occasionally difficult transitional period of banking deregulation that began in the early 1980s.

As seemingly effortless as her rise to the top of her profession was, Campbell ran into some large obstacles, most notably being diagnosed with cancer at the age of 32. "Having cancer at such a young age was a lot to assimilate," she admitted. "I underwent radiation therapy and won the battle, but it forced me to reassess my life and

Phyllis Campbell

rethink where I was going. Now I try to live each day to the fullest and I want to be a role model in giving back to others, just like my grandfather was for me."

Community service

In 1992 Campbell received the Puget Sound Matrix Table's Woman of Achievement Award in recognition of her professional achievements and community service. One of her favorites charities is Success by Six, a program that emphasizes the need to help young children get ready to learn. "Our children are our future," she told *AAB*, "and their education is the key. But *we* will determine the world our children will live in. For this reason, I am working to give something back to young people." Campbell is also vice chair of the Greater Seattle Chamber of Commerce, vice president of the Board of Regents at Washington State University, and chair of the Association of Washington Business. In addition, she is a member of the board of the Washington Roundtable and Puget Power and Light.

In 1996 Campbell received the Human Relations Award from the American Jewish Committee. In 1999 she received the Champion of Youth Award from the Seattle chapter of B'nai B'rith. The International Women's Forum honored her in 2000 with the Women Who Make a Difference Award.

Campbell lives with her husband, a civil engineer. She views her Japanese American heritage as "two sides of the coin." As a result of her background and the trials her family experienced during World War II, she is proud of her heritage, but she views it and the qualities that are a product of it as a responsibility. "In my life I have always tried to stand out in positive, not negative ways. I'm proud of the attributes I can bring to business, civic roles, and other life experiences. Living each day to the fullest and taking advantage of each page as it is turned is my goal."

Sources:

Campbell, Phyllis, telephone interview with Nancy Moore, June 27, 1994.

U.S. Bank of Washington, executive profile, Seattle, Washington, June 1994.

Tia Carrere

Actress, singer
Born January 2, 1967, Honolulu, Hawaii

"My upbringing in Hawaii has taught me that family is the most important thing."

In 1992, Tia Carrere rose to national prominence, landing major roles in two Hollywood movies. In the huge box-office success, *Wayne's World,* she played a character described in *Cosmopolitan* as a "heavy-metal kung-fu sex kitten" who was the girlfriend of the main character, played by Mike Meyers, formerly of *Saturday Night Live.* In *Rising Sun,* a thriller based on the bestselling novel by Michael Crichton, she played a computer specialist and the love interest of the film's star, Sean Connery.

In addition to her acting, Carrere has also released an album of dance music. Music has always been a passion of Carrere's, and she contributed two cuts to the *Wayne's World* soundtrack, which went platinum, selling one million copies. But her solo album showcased a different musical side. She described her style for *Cosmopolitan* as "a little bit dancey.... Completely different from what I did in *Wayne's World.*" In 1993 Tia recorded *Dream,* an album released by Reprise Records that became a platinum hit in the Philippines.

A couple of lucky breaks

Carrere was born Althea Rae Duhinio Janairo in 1967 in Hawaii to Alex Janairo, a general contractor, and Audrey Kim, a data processor. As a child she was given the nickname Tia. Her family is of Filipino, Chinese, and Spanish origin. Carrere has two sisters, Alasaundra and AudraLee. She was educated in private schools and graduated at 17 from an all-girls' Catholic high school. When she decided to pursue a career in acting, she changed her name to Carrere, which she thought sounded more interesting and exotic than Janairo.

Shortly after graduation Carrere was approached by the parents of the producer of a low-budget beach movie called *Aloha Summer;* they felt she would be perfect for their son's film. The role mainly required that Carrere look good in a bikini, which she accomplished easily. The film quickly faded, but Carrere's star had begun to shine.

From this beginning Carrere moved to television. Her first big role was on the television soap opera *General Hospital.* Carrere played Jade, a nursing student who became a favorite with the show's fans. The popularity of her character, along with the exaggerated promises of her then-boyfriend-manager, led Carrere to sue the soap to get out of her contract so that she could pursue another, more lucrative deal. When that deal did not materialize, Carrere recognized the foolishness of her actions and ended her personal and professional relationship with her manager. Luckily for the young actress, the producers of *General Hospital* re-signed her for six more months. Carrere reflected on this experience in *Cosmopolitan,* saying, "He wanted to represent me and be a big shot. I was stupid. I let it happen."

After her stint on *General Hospital,* Carrere moved to Los Angeles to pursue a career in films. She landed small roles in pictures like *Harley Davidson and the Marl-*

Tia Carrere

boro Man and *Showdown in Little Tokyo.* One day, while she was having a meeting with Mo Ostin, then chair of Warner Bros. Records, Ostin got a call from Paramount Pictures, which was looking for an Asian woman to play Cassandra, the heavy-metal rock musician who would be Mike Meyers's love interest in the upcoming movie *Wayne's World.* He said he knew just the actress.

After making *Wayne's World,* Carrere secured a role in *Rising Sun,* a film that caused some controversy in the Asian American community for its stereotypical portrayal of the Japanese. Her next roles were in *Quick,* an action/adventure movie in which she portrayed a police officer on the trail of drug smugglers, and in *Wayne's World II* (1993), in which she reprised her role as Cassandra.

In 2002 Carrere provided the voice for Mami in the animated Disney film *Lilo and Stitch.* In 2001, Carrere starred as a history professor in the television series, *Relic Hunter.* Carrere's other films include *True Lies* (1994), *Jury Duty* (1995), *The Immortals* (1995), *High School High* (1996), *Kull the Conqueror* (1997), *Scarred City* (1998), and *Night of the Headless Horseman* (1999).

From 1992 until their divorce in 1999, Carrere was married to Elie Samaha, a Lebanese entrepreneur and real estate tycoon. Carrere became a partner with Samaha in several of his real estate dealings and on several film projects with Phoenician Films, the company founded by the couple.

Sources:

Green, Tom, "Tia Carrere," *Cosmopolitan,* August 1993, p. 102.

Levitt, Shelley, "Tying the Not!," *People,* December 7, 1992.

Subrahmanyan Chandrasekhar

Astrophysicist
Born October 19, 1910, Lahore, India
Died August 21, 1995, Chicago, Illinois

"Chandrasekhar probably thought longer and deeper about our universe than anyone since Einstein." —Martin Rees, Great Britain's Astronomer Royal.

A strophysicist Subrahmanyan Chandrasekhar shared the Nobel Prize for physics in 1983 with William A. Fowler. Chandrasekhar's award-winning theory, completed some thirty years earlier, concerned the structure of white dwarfs, which are medium-sized stars that have used up all of their fuel and collapsed into dense, white-hot balls about the size of the Earth. His work eventually led to the discovery of black holes. He was one of the first scientists to combine the study of astronomy with the study of physics and thus became a pioneer in the new field of astrophysics.

A young physics student

Chandrasekhar (also called Chandra) was born in Lahore, India (now Pakistan). His father was a distinguished musicologist (someone who studies music as a branch of knowledge rather than studying to compose or perform music), and his uncle was the physicist Sir Chandrasekhar V. Raman, who was awarded the Nobel Prize in 1930. Subrahmanyan was very excited by his uncle's

Subrahmanyan Chandrasekhar

work and decided at a young age to study physics himself. Chandra was home-schooled until the age of twelve, and later attended a Hindu high school. He published his first paper—an analysis of the thermo-dynamics (the physics of the mechanical action of heat) of the interior of stars—at the age of eighteen in the *Indian Journal of Physics.*

After graduation from high school, Chandrasekhar studied theoretical physics at the Presidency College in Madras, where he was especially interested in the field of astrophysics and the pioneering work then

being done by two British scientists, Sir Arthur Stanley Eddington and Ralph Howard Fowler. Chandrasekhar earned his bachelor's degree in 1930 and received a scholarship from the government of India to continue his studies at Cambridge University in England.

The Chandrasekhar Limit

At Cambridge, he concentrated his studies on the behavior of stars that have run out of fuel, or "died." Chandrasekhar believed he had detected an error in the standard scientific literature about the way in which stars larger than the sun died. Contrary to the theory of that time, he believed that the tremendous gravitational force of large stars would prevent their stabilizing at the white dwarf stage. Instead, the electrons in the star's gasses would keep moving faster, approaching a state known as "relativistic degeneracy." In this state, molecular matter is moving near the speed of light. Under these conditions, the young astrophysicist thought, stars would not collapse into white dwarfs but simply continue to collapse.

What we now call a "black hole" is thought to be the aftermath of the collapse of a massive star as Chandrasekhar described the event. Any star will collapse once its nuclear fuel is spent. Without the radiation from nuclear fusion pushing outward from the star's core to balance its immense gravity, a star will begin to fall into itself. A star the size of the sun will end up as a white dwarf star, the size of Earth. But Chandrasekhar showed that as a larger star collapses, the mass becomes so concentrated that the force of gravity ends up being overpowering. As the star becomes more and more dense, gravity increases until not even light has enough velocity—or speed—to escape the collapsed star's surface. Anything crossing that surface—including light—is forever trapped within its invisible confines. The only way a black hole can be detected is by seeing its effect on visible objects like adjoining stars, dust, or gas.

Going against the tide

In 1932, Chandrasekhar published his first paper on the death of stars. The next year he received his Ph.D. from Cambridge, where he was offered a fellowship to continue his studies. By this time he had developed a complete theory explaining the details of his new hypothesis, and the Royal Astronomical Society invited him to present his findings at their annual meeting.

When Chandrasekhar presented his theory, however, it was not well received. The scientific establishment was reluctant to adopt a new theory that contradicted the work of a prominent member, which Chandrasekhar's certainly did. It questioned the theories of Sir Arthur Stanley Eddington, perhaps the most respected English physicist of his time. After Chandrasekhar delivered his presentation, Eddington stood up and ridiculed the young scientist's ideas, saying that, if taken to their logical conclusion, they would suggest the existence of tiny balls of energy so dense and with such a tremendous gravitational field that not even light would be able to escape. And in fact, time appears to have proven this idea to be correct; Chandrasekhar's theories prevail. Today the point that separates stars that will collapse into white dwarfs and those that

will collapse into black holes is called the Chandrasekhar Limit. Black holes are not only believed to exist, they are thought to make up 90 percent of the universe.

In *A Passion to Know* by John Tierney, Chandrasekhar discussed how differently his life could have been had Eddington not ridiculed his now-proven hypotheses. "It's very difficult to speculate. Eddington would have made the whole area a very spectacular one to investigate, and many of the properties of black holes might have been discovered twenty or thirty years ahead of time. I can easily imagine that theoretical astronomy would have been very different.... My position in science would have been radically altered as of that moment. Eddington's praise could make one famous in astronomy."

Immigrating to the United States

Following his dispute over theory with England's greatest astronomer, Chandrasekhar felt he had few academic options left in England. In 1937, he and his wife Lalitha, whom he had married the year before, left for America. The two would become American citizens in 1953. In Chicago, he took a position as a research associate at the University of Chicago. In this position he continued his work on the death of stars and in 1939 published *An Introduction to the Study of Stellar Structures*. Largely ignored at the time of its publication, the book was recognized as a classic work only twenty years later.

In the next several years Chandrasekhar began studying various other aspects of astrophysics while being promoted to associate professor in 1942 and to professor in 1944. In 1947, just ten years after settling in Chicago, he was appointed distinguished service professor of theoretical astrophysics. Throughout his career Chandrasekhar has easily been able to change areas of expertise. In 1942, he published his second book, *Principles of Stellar Dynamics,* which described the behavior and evolution of star clusters. Toward the middle of the 1940s, Chandrasekhar began studying yet another field, the radiative transfer of energy in the interior of stars. He followed these studies with many others in the rapidly developing field of astrophysics.

In the 1970s, Chandrasekhar returned to the first field he had studied, the creation of black holes. Finally, the scientific community had come to validate his work. He has written several books, many of which are considered classics. Among them are: *Radiative Transfer* (1960), *Hydrodynamic and Hydromagnetic Stability* (1961), *Ellipsoidal Figures of Equilibrium* (1969), and *The Mathematical Theory of Black Holes* (1983).

Recipient of many honors

Chandrasekhar has received many honors during his career, including the 1983 Nobel Prize. The announcement from the Swedish Academy stated: "Chandrasekhar's possibly best-known achievement, accomplished when he was in his 20s, is the study of the structure of white dwarfs. Although many of these investigations are of older dates, they have, through the great process of astronomy and space research, in recent years gained renewed interest."

Chandrasekhar also received twenty honorary degrees, held membership in twenty-one learned societies, and was the recipient of the Gold Medal of the Royal Astronomical Society of London, the Rumford Medal of the American Academy of Arts and Sciences, the Royal Medal of the Royal Society of London, the National Medal of Science, and the Henry Draper Medal of the National Academy of Sciences.

In mid-1994, Chandrasekhar retired from the University of Chicago and began working on translating Isaac Newton's classic work *The Principia* into the language of modern mathematics. He died the next year. In 1999, NASA launched an X-Ray observatory which they named "Chandra" in honor of the man who inspired a whole new field of research study.

Sources:

Chandra X-Ray Observatory Center, http://www.chandra.harvard.edu (accessed March 2003).

Nobel Prize e-Museum, http://www.nobel.se (accessed March 2003).

Tierney, John, "Subrahmanyan Chandrasekhar: Quest for Order." In *A Passion to Know,* edited by Allen L. Hammond, New York: Charles Scribner's Sons, 1984.

Michael Chang

Professional tennis player
Born February 22, 1972, Hoboken, New Jersey

"Tennis is a high profile sport...I realize I have a wonderful opportunity to touch people's lives, particularly kids growing up."

In June 1989, at the age of 17, Michael Chang became the youngest male tennis player in the world to win a Grand Slam tennis tournament and the first American man in 34 years to win the French Open. Chang's win followed a series of shocking upset victories against the best players in the game. In the semifinals he defeated the world's top-ranked player, Ivan Lendl. Then, in the championships, he defeated the heavily favored Stefan Edberg. Chang had come into that year's open ranked nineteenth in the world. By 1992, he was ranked fourth, and as of early 1994, this remarkable young player was ranked seventh. Although he hasn't won a major title since his 1989 triumph, Chang is a consistent and powerful force on the international tour and generally wins one or two singles titles a year. His winnings have amounted to $19 million since he turned pro at age 16.

Early interest in tennis

Michael Chang was born February 22, 1972, into a family that thrived on tennis. His parents, Joe and Betty Chang, were research chemists who had immigrated from Taiwan to the United States and met on a blind date in New York City. Chang and his older brother, Carl, were born in Hoboken, New Jersey. As a toddler, Chang remembers watching his father play tennis in local tournaments in St. Paul, Minnesota, where the family had moved when he was two. At age six, he picked up a racket for the first time. He and Carl got more than a little encouragement from their father; Joe Chang would spend hours coaching the two boys, setting up matches between them and suggesting pointers to improve their game. From this experience, Chang picked up a keen sense of competition. At age eight, he played his father. When his father won, Chang was so disappointed that he broke his racket. Recognizing his competitive streak, his parents started encouraging him to enter matches.

As Chang's interest in tennis grew, his family moved to San Diego, California, partly so he could practice outdoors year round. Shortly after this move, Chang began winning junior tournament titles. In 1984, at age 12, he won the Junior Hard Court singles title of the United States Tennis Association (USTA). He also won a doubles title in the same tournament with Marco Zuniga. One year later, he won the Fiesta Bowl 16s. The following year, 1986, his rise to the top of the juniors rankings continued.

Chang joined the U.S. Sunshine Cup team and the World Youth Cup team, and he became the European Indoor 14s champion and a runner-up in the USTA's Boys 16s. In 1987, he won the USTA's junior championship, which gave him the chance to play in the U.S. Open, one of tennis's four Grand Slam events. Though expectations for him were not high in the U.S. Open, he won his first-round match.

Michael Chang

Turning pro

Up to this point, Chang had played tennis purely for the joy of competition. He thrived on pressure, and he had developed a gritty determination to win, whatever the price. But he did not see tennis as a profession. His parents always stressed the importance of education and limited his playing to four days a week—if he got his homework done. Chang understood that school was important, but by age 16, he faced a dilemma: he'd gone as far as he could on the junior circuit and needed to seek greater challenges to improve his tennis skills. The next step would be to turn professional, but this would also mean dropping out of high school. He decided to choose tennis and managed to pass a final exam to receive a high school diploma. He turned pro in February 1988.

Suddenly, the pressure to excel intensified. Media attention began to focus on him; the pro circuit began to watch his progress. He met the challenge, displaying poise under pressure. *Sports Illustrated* wrote that Chang's skill was "based on anticipation, reflexes, speed—nobody has been quicker to the ball since Bjorn Borg [the Swedish champion who dominated the sport in the 1970s]—and defensive instincts that make an opponent feel as if he is slugging away at Chang's garage door." He also remained coolly unemotional on the court, thinking through his technique. He reached the quarterfinals of two major tournaments in 1988.

The French Open

In the 1989 French Open, Chang first shook the tennis world with his semifinal victory over Ivan Lendl, then the world's top-ranked player. Lendl, as expected, had won the first two sets and seemed ready to head for the final round. But Chang took the following two, setting the stage for a decisive final set. In that encounter, Chang's legs cramped up so badly that he could barely move. But he ran for water and bananas during breaks and managed to keep himself in the game. He broke Lendl's serve three times, and Lendl broke Chang's serve twice. Then, with the set at 4-3, Chang lobbed an underhand serve—sending the ball into a high arc—which distracted Lendl and caused the more seasoned player to lose his composure. Chang then tried to break Lendl's concentration by moving near the service box. As Lendl's serve failed to reach its goal, Chang fell to his knees in tears of joy. He later admitted to *Sports Illustrated* that he had been trying to break Lendl's concentration. "I would do anything to stay out there. It was that mental thing."

Despite the upset victory, Chang's maneuvers did not win praise from tennis fans or the press; many called his efforts to distract Lendl poor sportsmanship, and some sportswriters went so far as to wonder whether Chang's leg cramps were for real. Chang also became the victim of blatant racism. A French journalist made reference to Chang's "vicious Oriental mind," while another newspaper ran a headline referring to Chang as "the Chink." A third called the Chinese American player "our little slant eyes."

Nevertheless, Chang remained cool on the court. His mother, who had left her job as a chemist to travel with him, fed him fortifying Chinese noodles in their hotel room, and Chang continued to concentrate on his game. Early on, he'd learned that the road to success contained no short cuts. He kept this philosophy in the back of his mind as he prepared for the French Open finals against Stefan Edberg. Edberg was heavily favored, but Chang walked away with the victory in five sets.

Setback

Though 1989 was the high point of Chang's athletic life, it also produced a stunning low: late in the year, after competing at Wimbledon and the U.S. Open, he fractured his hip during practice, an injury that put him out of circulation until mid-1990. Though he knew when he turned pro that injury was a risk he'd have to accept, he acknowledges that the broken hip discouraged him a great deal. But it also gave him time to put tennis in perspective. In 2003 Chang, who was once ranked number two in the world, announced his plans to retire. During his professional career, he won 34 major tennis tournaments, including the 1989 French Open.

Through the late 1990s and into the twenty-first century, Chang continued to hammer away relentlessly at his technique. He was also learning to relax. Growing up in Minnesota, he developed a passion for fishing, which he pursues when he needs a sense of peace. He calls the sport more complicated than tennis in some ways, because it requires more preparation. Though he held a total of fourteen singles titles as of early 1994, Chang claims one of his most cherished accomplishments was hooking an eight-pound carp after a tournament in Cincinnati.

Off the court, Chang does all that he can to be a good role model for youth. In 1992, he helped establish the Tennis Stars of the Future program in Hong Kong to reach out to underprivileged children. In 1999, Chang and his close-knit family established the Chang Family Foundation. The Foundation's goal is to provide support for sports and community programs that serve as a Christian outreach to youth. This has already been accomplished by youth tennis camps and scholarship programs. In 2002, the foundation started the Christian Sports League, a program to support sports programs in churches and other organizations.

Sources:

Deitsch, Richard, "Q and A with Michael Chang," *Sports Illustrated,* April 7, 2003.

Dell, Pamela, *Michael Chang,* Chicago: Children's Press, 1992.

IBM/ATP Tour Media Information System, "Michael Chang," player biography, 1994.

Kirkpatrick, Curry, "Giant Killers," *Sports Illustrated,* vol. 70, no. 26, June 1989, p. 34.

"Michael Chang," Official Web site, http://www.mchang.com (accessed March 2003).

Sarah Chang

Violinist
Born 1981, Philadelphia, Pennsylvania

"I think performing is a part of me, and I really love what I'm doing."

S arah Chang's career as a classical violinist has spanned just a few years, but she has performed all over the world with some of the most important orchestras. Chang burst onto the classical music scene at the age of eight when the internationally renowned conductor **Zubin Mehta** invited her to perform as a surprise guest soloist with the New York Philharmonic at Avery Fisher Hall in New York City. Her performance of nineteenth-century Italian violinist Niccolò Paganini's *Violin Concerto No. 1* earned her a standing ovation and wide media coverage and praise.

In the 1990s, Chang performed at the Presidential Gala Concert in South Korea and the Concert for the Planet Earth at the Rio de Janeiro Earth Summit, as well as with the London Symphony Orchestra. The international fame and intense public curiosity about child prodigies had a great impact on Chang, but she has maintained a life much like that of any other young woman.

Chang's early inspiration

Chang is the daughter of Korean immigrants with a tradition of classical music. Her father, Dr. Min Soo Chang, is a violinist, and her mother, Myoung, is a pianist and composer. She began taking lessons from her father at the age of four. Her hands were too small to play a full-size violin, so her father bought her a 1/16-size replica for her to use until her hands grew. Chang's performing career began at age five, when she started playing with local orchestras. The next year, she began to study with Dorothy DeLay, an acclaimed teacher from the Juilliard School of Music in New York, perhaps the most renowned music school in America.

Chang excelled at the violin, impressing everyone who heard her play. One such person was Zubin Mehta, then conductor of the New York Philharmonic, who was looking for someone to replace a solo violinist who had canceled an upcoming performance. He was so overwhelmed by Chang's playing that he invited the eight-year-old to stand in for the soloist. Chang's performance drew rave reviews from the press and national attention from concert managers and directors.

The child prodigy tours the country

Chang began playing with various orchestras around the United States and Canada in 1991, at the age of nine. After her New York performance, her next stop was her hometown of Philadelphia, where she was invited to perform with the Philadelphia Orchestra by its conductor, Ricardo Muti. She then went on to performances with the California, Chicago, Montreal, and Pittsburgh symphonies. About her Pittsburgh performance, a *Washington Post* critic wrote, "Nine-year-old Sarah Chang mixed supple phrasing and mind-boggling technique in virtually tossing off Paganini's fiendish *First Concerto*. Chang plays with controlled abandon, never distorting her gorgeous tone or the music's structure and leaving plenty of room for her maturing lyric sense to shine."

The *San Jose Mercury News* also had flattering things to say about Chang after her performance with the California Symphony, calling her "formidable" and "dazzling." The paper went on to say that Chang played "with an adult's poise, a virtuoso's touch." The *Chicago Tribune* called her performance in Lalo's *Symphony Espagnole* a demonstration of her "astonishing technical dexterity."

In 1992, Chang's concert and recording career continued to accelerate. Her performance at the Concert for Planet Earth was broadcast all over the world, airing on public television's *Great Performances* in the United States. It was later released on disc by Sony Classical records. In May 1992, Chang became the youngest musician ever to win the prestigious Avery Fisher Career Grant. Four months later, she performed Tchaikovsky's *Violin Concerto* with the Los Angeles Philharmonic at the Hollywood Bowl. The *Los Angeles Times* deemed her performance an example of a "prowess and vision rare at any age."

In October 1992, Chang made her European debut when she performed Tchaikovsky's *Violin Concerto* with the London Symphony Orchestra. Her appearance was widely acclaimed, including a glowing review in the London *Times*. That same year, Chang released her first album. Entitled *Debut,* it includes recordings of the works of composers Prokofiev, Gershwin, Sarasate, and others. The record quickly became a bestseller on *Billboard*'s classical music sales chart.

Chang's busy schedule continued in 1993. She performed with the New York Philharmonic, Philadelphia Orchestra, Montreal Symphony, Toronto Symphony, New World Symphony of Miami, Orchestre National de France, Leipzig Gewandhaus Orchestra, Monte Carlo Philharmonic, and Japan's NHK Symphony. She also released as her second album a recording of her performance with the London Symphony

Sarah Chang

Orchestra. That year she was named Young Artist of the Year by *Gramophone* magazine and was described by the *New York Times* as the "definitive violin prodigy of her generation, a child with the requisite dazzling technique but also considerable expressiveness."

In 1997 Chang made her Carnegie Hall debut and also released *Simply Sarah*, a collection of short works for violin and piano recorded by EMI Classics. In 1999, the same year she graduated from high school, she was awarded the prestigious Avery Fisher Prize.

Chang continued her ambitious recording schedule, with one or two new releases every year. In 2001 she recorded an album of popular shorter works for violin and orchestra, with Placido Domingo conducting the Berlin Philharmonic. Her recording that same year of chamber music was released in 2002.

Life in the spotlight

Sarah Chang spent a great deal of her childhood in a way few can imagine. While still a young girl, she achieved an international stature very few adults have known. She practiced violin four hours a day and attended a full Saturday program at Juilliard that includes classes in theory, ensemble, and chamber music. Despite all of that, Chang managed, with her parents' help, to do some more traditional activities for a teenager. Her parents have insisted that she not perform live more than twice a month, and she attended regular classes at Germantown Friends School, a private high school, where her favorite subjects were social studies and French.

Many people drew parallels between Chang and **Midori,** another young performer often referred to as a prodigy, because both were Asian and both studied under the same teacher at Juilliard—Dorothy DeLay. DeLay, however, did not agree with such comparisons. She told *Town & Country,* "I have compared her playing with records of other prodigies and I don't think anything quite like her has ever happened before. But one never knows what's going to happen in the next ten years. She might

decide she wants to become a professional golfer, or who knows."

Music continues to be a passion for the young woman. Chang herself has said that she loves the life she is leading. She told *People,* "I think performing is a part of me, and I really love what I'm doing."

Although she graduated from the pre-college program at Juilliard in 1999, Chang postponed the decision about college, electing to concentrate on her music career. She continues an ambitious concert schedule that takes her to such places as Los Angeles and New York—as well as Zurich, Switzerland; Vienna, Austria; and Beijing, China.

Sources:

EMI Classics, http://www.emiclassics.com (accessed March 2003).

Frohman, Jesse, "String Fever," *Town & Country,* April 1994, p. 85.

"Philadelphia, There She Goes: Violin Prodigy Sarah Chang Has the World on Her Strings," *People,* January 11, 1993, p. 88.

Elaine Chao

United States Secretary of Labor
Born March 26, 1953, Taipei, Taiwan

"Getting people back to work is what this department does. Giving people hope in their future is our job."

I n 2001 Elaine Chao was confirmed by the Senate as the 24th U.S. Secretary of Labor. Nominated to this position by President George W. Bush, she is the first Asian American woman to be appointed to a presidential cabinet position. Prior to this appointment, Chao was the president of the United Way, a charitable organization. She also had held several top posts in the Republican administrations of presidents Ronald Reagan and George Bush. Her first governmental appointments were in transportation and shipping; in 1991, she assumed her highest profile in government when she was named director of the Peace Corps (a group of trained volunteers sent to places throughout the world, especially to assist underdeveloped nations).

Born in Taiwan

Chao's father, Dr. James S. C. Chao, left the island of Taiwan in the early 1960s to start a new life for his family. A few years later, Chao, her mother (the former Ruth M. L. Chu), and her sisters went to the United States to join him. The family moved to New York, where the elder Chao had settled to pursue an education. "It was a wonderful trip," Chao told the *Los Angeles Times*. "My first port of call was Los Angeles. That's where I laid my first foot on America." Her father, who was then studying at St. John's University, would later go on to found a well-known ship brokerage and agency business, Foremost Maritime. Chao was educated at Mount Holyoke College, where she received her bachelor's degree in 1975. She earned a master's degree in business administration from Harvard in 1979.

Chao's first jobs were in banking. She worked from 1979 to 1983 as an international banker at Citicorp in New York. She

Elaine Chao

was selected as a White House fellow in 1983 and 1984, then joined BankAmerica Capital Markets Group in San Francisco as vice president of syndications. (A syndicate is a group of persons or concerns that combine to carry out a particular transaction.) After moving to California, Chao became involved in politics, campaigning for prominent Republicans like Ronald Reagan and California governor Pete Wilson. In 1988, she served as national chairman of Asian Americans for the George Bush/Dan Quayle campaign and delivered a speech at that year's Republican convention.

From private to public service

In 1984, President Ronald Reagan appointed Chao to her first government post when he named her the deputy administrator of the Maritime Administration, a federal agency that regulates shipping. After two years in this position, she was named chairman of the Federal Maritime Commission and then was appointed deputy secretary of the Department of Transportation. As Chao worked her way through the bureaucracy of Washington, she gained a reputation as a confident, hardworking manager and also as an independent thinker, who often took political stances outside the mainstream. For instance, she shuns the terms "chairperson" and "chairwoman," which would be appropriate to a woman holding such a position, preferring instead to be called simply "chairman." She also opposed the 1991 Civil Rights Act because she believed it promoted quotas, which she feels inhibit minority achievements.

The Peace Corps

Chao was named director of the Peace Corps in 1991 by President George Bush. The Peace Corps at this time was going through drastic changes. Whereas prior to this period the corps had served primarily in developing countries, providing services like agriculture reform and road building, its new focus was providing assistance to the countries of the former Eastern Bloc in their conversion from a Communist economy to a capitalist one (a transition marked by private or corporate, instead of government, ownership of goods, and by distribution of goods based on competition). With her experience as an interna-

tional banker, Chao was a perfect candidate to propel the corps in this new direction.

Very shortly after her swearing in, Chao traveled to Bulgaria to represent President Bush at the opening of that country's first American university. Prior to that, she had met with representatives of Latvia, Estonia, and Lithuania, the former Soviet republics on the Baltic Sea that had been the first to secede from the former Soviet Union. Other countries seeking banking and financial training from the Peace Corps included Hungary, Poland, the Czech Republic, Slovakia, Romania, and Albania. There were plans to offer substantial help for the former republics of the Soviet Union.

As director of the Peace Corps, Chao oversaw a budget of $117 million. One of her priorities was to streamline the volunteer application process. She told *American Shipper,* "It takes 9 to 18 months to process an application. That's too long. We lose a lot of people because they can't afford to wait around." Chao also believed that her personal background would help her as director. "I understand very well the kind of work the Peace Corps does," she said. "I understand instinctively what local nationals feel about Americans. I still remember growing up in Taiwan how valuable tissue paper was and how rich Americans seemed because they would use it up and throw it away so easily."

The United Way

Chao's tenure as director of the Peace Corps was short-lived. When George Bush was defeated by Bill Clinton in the 1992 presidential elections, she resigned her post. Later that year, she was named president of the United Way, a well-established charitable agency in turmoil. Former United Way president William Aramony had been pulling in a salary of $390,000 a year. He had spent agency money on first-class airplane tickets and had hired a friend with questionable bank dealings as the agency's chief financial officer. When these facts became public, local United Way agencies began withholding dues in protest, and Aramony resigned under fire. United Way donations plummeted by $140 million between 1991 and 1992.

Chao's job was to reform the agency and help it regain its credibility. Selected from a list of 600 candidates, she was singled out for her integrity, honesty, and management skills. She did not actively seek out the position, but when she was offered the job, she was happy to accept. "United Way of America is a challenge that I could not decline," she told the *Washington Post.*

In her first months with the agency, Chao visited as many of the organization's local affiliates as she could, trying to assure them of her intentions and gain an understanding of what was required of her. She felt strongly that making the national organization more sensitive to local needs would be a key to turning the United Way around. "This is a redress that is badly needed and is long in coming," she said in an interview with the *Christian Science Monitor.*

To restore public confidence in the agency, Chao started at a salary of $195,000, half that of her controversial predecessor. She imposed new travel and expense controls and restructured programs to put more emphasis on training, field regulation, and service. Like most restructurings, the changes at United Way were painful. Nearly one-third of the agency's staff was let go,

and its budget was cut by one-third. But Chao achieved results. By late 1993, most affiliates that had withheld dues had resumed payments. And, though a difficult economy caused a slowdown in charitable contributions, Chao said her prognosis for the future was "cautious optimism." Chao appeared in commercials for the agency as a way to boost public confidence in United Way programs, usually in association with NFL Charities, a longtime United Way partner.

Labor Secretary

When President George W. Bush took office in 2001, he nominated Chao for the position of Secretary of the Department of Labor. The nomination was accepted by the U.S. Senate and Chao became the first Asian American woman to receive an appointment to the president's cabinet. The Department of Labor works to promote and encourage the welfare of all workers, job seekers, and retirees in the United States.

In fulfilling these goals, Chao has supported legislation to help provide health insurance to uninsured workers, and announced plans for a workplace safety initiative. She has helped open ten resource centers across the country for injured energy workers and is working to increase the number of qualified Asian Pacific Americans in positions within the federal government.

Secretary Elaine Chao is married to U.S. Senator Mitch McConnell of Kentucky.

Sources:

Baum, Geraldine, "An Insider Moves Up," *Los Angeles Times,* January 19, 1993.

Canna, Elizabeth, "Free Market Peace Corps," *American Shipper,* March 1992.

MacLachlan, Suzanne L., "United Way Hit by Weak Economy, Old Scandal and Competition," *Christian Science Monitor,* May 18, 1993.

Melillo, Wendy, "United Way Names New President," *Washington Post,* August 27, 1992.

United States Department of Labor, http://www.dol.gov (accessed March 2003).

United Way, biographical materials, 1994.

Stephen Chao

Television producer
Born 1956, Ann Arbor, Michigan

"I don't have a story where I creep into the theater and dream about the nickelodeons. But I remember seeing Road Warrior *six times. It was, to me, totally original.... I had no idea this could be done on film."*

S tephen Chao is considered to be an extremely innovative and creative television programmer. He has worked with companies such as U.S.A. cable and Fox Television, where he created such innovative, controversial shows as *America's Most Wanted, Cops,* and *Studs.*

Chao has combined an excellent, traditional education with creativity and sometimes outrageous behavior to become one of the television industry's most prominent, promising executives.

Conventional childhood

Stephen Chao was born in Ann Arbor, Michigan, in 1956 to a middle-class family. His maternal grandfather had been a prominent political figure in China in the 1940s and 1950s, serving for a time as economic minister to the United States. When Chao was eight years old, his parents divorced, and he moved with his mother and two older brothers to New Hampshire. He was an excellent student and earned a scholarship to Exeter Academy, one of the finest private boarding schools in the country. From there he went on to Harvard, where he studied the classics. He graduated with honors in 1977, and earned his MBA from Harvard Business school in 1984.

Beginning a career

After graduation Chao took a job as a reporter for the *National Enquirer,* perhaps the best known of the supermarket tabloids that feature sensational headlines and stories. It was not the type of job usually pursued by Harvard graduates. Chao, however, enjoyed being unconventional and genuinely considered the *Enquirer* to be a serious and important part of society. At the paper he covered many celebrity stories and funerals. He stayed with the paper for two years and then returned to Harvard for a master's degree in business administration.

After graduation, Chao became interested in the movie business. In a *New York* magazine article in 1993, he said, "I don't have a story where I creep into the theater and dream about the nickelodeons. But I remember seeing *Road Warrior* six times. It was, to me, totally original—visually, emotionally, countrily [sic], everything! I had no idea this could be done on film."

Chao tried unsuccessfully to get a job at a major studio in Hollywood. He ended up working in New York for film producer Dino De Laurentis as a fundraiser—work he hated. He saw a chance to make it in Hollywood when he read that international newspaper executive Rupert Murdoch was trying to buy a Hollywood studio. He eventually landed a job with the Murdoch News Service in a business area—not exactly what he was looking for, but a foot in the door. After two years he got what he wanted: a creative job at Murdoch's newly established Fox Television network.

Fox Television

At Fox, Chao worked directly for Barry Diller, president of the network. His job was to develop innovative shows with low production costs. As the first broadcast network to challenge the domination of the big three—ABC, CBS, and NBC—Fox faced intimidating competition. Chao's first efforts often were not very successful. These shows included *The Ron Reagan Show,* a late-night talk show that featured as host the son of the former president; *Dr. Science,* which *New York* magazine described as "a cross between *Pee-Wee's Playhouse* and *Watch Wizard* "; and *King of the Mountain,* a game show in which contestants attempted to climb a hill while being rained upon by papier-mâché boulders.

Chao finally launched a successful show with *America's Most Wanted.* The program features dramatic recreations of violent crimes and then asks viewers to help find the criminals. At the time of its creation it

Stephen Chao

was a new concept and had a rough time gaining acceptance with the network. The fact that it was very inexpensive to produce helped make it successful.

His next show for the network was *Cops,* in which a cameraman follows police officers on duty in some of the more violent neighborhoods of various cities around the country. The show has been criticized for its brutal realism and seeming lack of interest in the consequences of violence. In discussing these criticisms, Chao said in *New York* magazine, "That was the beauty [of *Cops*]—to me there isn't a lesson. We're just showing something that *is*. It's not coded with music and narration and writing and directing. It's just edited, in a really simple way. It's pure, and you derive your own lesson."

Chao's final successful show for Fox was *Studs,* a late-night game show of sorts in which attractive young men and women discussed dating. The program was incredibly successful, making $20 million a year. Murdoch, however, decided to cancel the show because he didn't like some of its topics and language.

Life after Fox

Chao was fired from Fox Television for outrageous behavior at a conference of television executives and other powerful men and women, including the then-U.S. secretary of defense (later vice president) Dick Cheney. He then spent a year traveling with his family and considering the future. He worked briefly for Fox's movie division as a developer of ideas for films, a position that did not work out.

In 1993 Chao founded his own company, Stephen Chao Incorporated (SCI) and was able to create and produce programs for major network channels as well as networks such as Nickelodeon. SCI launched the 24-hour animation channel called Locomotion as well as a Playboy television channel in Latin America.

In 1998 Chao joined U.S.A. Networks as president of programming and marketing. In 2000 Chao was promoted to president of U.S.A. Cable, a division of U.S.A. Networks which includes the Sci-Fi Channel, the U.S.A. Movie Channel, and the Home Shopping Network.

In 2001 Chao left the company after administrative reorganization.

Sources:

Smith, Chris, "Chao, Baby," *New York*, October 18, 1993, pp. 68–75.

Yang, Jeff, "Power Brokers," *A. Magazine*, vol. 2, no. 3, December 15, 1993, pp. 25–34.

Kalpana Chawla

Astronaut
Born July 1, 1961, Karnal, India
Died February 1, 2003, aboard Space Shuttle
Columbia, U.S.A.

"Pioneers don't have role models."

When the space shuttle *Columbia* disintegrated over the southern United States during its descent back to earth on February 1, 2003, Americans mourned for the seven crew members who died an immediate, fiery death in flight. Among the members of that crew was 41-year-old Kalpana Chawla, an employee with National Aeronautics and Space Administration (NASA) since 1988 and an astronaut since December 1994.

Chawla, who was born in India and completed her education in the United States, logged a total of 34 days, 14 hours, and 54 minutes in space during her life. She was a crew member not only of the ill-fated sixteen-day flight of the STS-107 *Columbia* mission, but also of the STS-87 *Columbia* mission in late 1997.

Although Kalpana Chawla's life ended suddenly and tragically, many feel she lived a life that most can only dream about.

In heralding Chawla's participation on the *Columbia* missions, Caryl Rivers noted that Chawla's position as a NASA astronaut marked another step forward for women and minorities in the United States. Rivers, a Boston University professor of journalism, stated that because of Chawla and the other shuttle crew members, young girls today will continue to dream.

"What is not so important is that they died," Rivers observed about the shuttle crew. "What is important is that they went."

Roots in survival

Chawla was born July 1, 1961, the youngest of four children. Her father, Banarsi Lal Chawla, founded a successful tire-manufacturing company. Her mother, Sanjogta Kharbanda Chawla, is the well-educated daughter of a physician. Kalpana Chawla grew up in comfort, in a home that fostered achievement. However, her family's success was rooted in a struggle for simple survival. In 1947, when the South Asian subcontinent was partitioned (divided into separate countries), her father had been a refugee.

The largest country on the South Asian subcontinent is India. India became a British colony in the late 1800s. Until 1947, there was a British colonial government in India. As the British prepared to end their rule of India in 1947, the colonial administrators tried to quell (put a stop to) growing unrest between the two religious groups in India:

Kalpana Chawla

Hindus and Muslims. The British decided that, to keep the two groups from fighting with each other, India should be divided into three sections: a Hindu-dominated section that would be called India, and two Muslim-dominated sections. At that time, the two new Muslim countries were called West Pakistan and East Pakistan. (West Pakistan later became known as Pakistan, and East Pakistan became Bangladesh.)

Independence Day for the three newly created countries was set for August 15, 1947. As the day neared, 14-year-old Banarsi Lal Chawla and his family found themselves in the position that nearly fourteen million other inhabitants of the subcontinent faced. They were living in Lahore, India, which was to become a part of the Muslim nation, West Pakistan. As non-Muslims, they decided that they had no choice but to flee.

The family survived bullets, mob violence, hunger, and thirst as they traveled east to India. They settled in the small town of Karnal, approximately 70 miles (110 kilometers) north of New Delhi. They did what they could to survive. With his father in ill health, Banarsi Lal Chawla supported the family by selling chutney and auto parts. Eventually, he began manufacturing metal boxes for storage.

The hardship from those days still pains him. But, with the birth of his children—daughters Sunita and Deepa, son Sanjay, and finally Kalpana in 1961—the pain gradually began to heal. Banarsi Lal Chawla ventured into tire manufacturing and developed one of northern India's most prosperous industrial plants.

Daring to dream

As his youngest daughter, Kalpana, perished in flight, Banarsi Lal Chawla grieved. But he also made note of what his daughter achieved. For him, the death was a tragedy. But the mission itself was a milestone. Shortly before *Columbia* left Earth, he declared, "Good things happen in families where good people are born."

Kalpana Chawla must have inherited her father's steadfastly optimistic streak. For, as her brother Sanjay recalled, she sensed from the outset that even if boys had more opportunities than girls, she was not going to let herself be labeled as "just another girl."

She was not just another girl in Indian society. She was a hard worker and an exceptional student. Yet, she didn't dare dream of becoming an astronaut. Her dream was much more practical: becoming an aerospace engineer.

She graduated from the Tagore School in her hometown in 1976, and completed a bachelor of science degree in aeronautical engineering from the Punjab Engineering College in India in 1982. She earned the highest grades in engineering at her college and was offered a teaching position there. But she already had set her sights on a different path. Without her father's knowledge, she had already applied to graduate schools in the United States. Her father, who was busy running his tire business, had paid little attention to his youngest daughter's academic achievements and dreams. If anything, Sanjay Chawla recalled, their father expected him and Kalpana to begin working with the family business.

Kalpana was accepted by the University of Texas for a master's degree in aeronautical engineering. Her father was traveling overseas on business, however, and could not be reached to make a decision in time for her to request a visa (permission to stay in the United States) and other documentation required to study in the United States. As a result, she ended up accepting the teaching job at Punjab Engineering College, putting her dreams on hold.

Her father—once he became aware of what had occurred—was determined that his daughter would not have to accept this disappointment. He raced to the college where Kalpana was teaching in Punjab, and urged her to follow through with her dream. As a businessman, Banarsi Lal Chawla knew ways to get things done quickly. Using the influence and connections that come with the building of a successful business, he managed to get Kalpana everything she needed to study in Texas: a passport, visa, and airline ticket. He then began calling friends and business associates in the United States, to make sure that his daughter could enroll even though the semester had already started.

Kalpana Chawla completed a master of science degree in aeronautical engineering in 1984, and earned a doctorate four years later. By then, at age 27, she had a job offer from NASA in hand. For the first time, it entered her mind that she could apply to be an astronaut.

She started working at NASA's Ames Research Center, focusing on a specialized area known as computational fluid dynamics. (This field uses mathematics to help scientists predict how fluids—gases or liquids—flow. Aerospace engineers and weather forecasters, to name just two types of scientists, use it.) Kalpana's research projects involved solving complex problems related to this special topic.

In 1993, while she was waiting for a decision on her application to become an astronaut, she accepted a position as vice president and research scientist at Overset Methods Inc. in Los Altos, California. She remained with the firm until NASA sent her the news in December 1994 that she had been accepted as a candidate for astronaut.

"Going into space?" Chawla remarked in a 1995 interview with *India-West*. "I never dared dream of it. I think it's the coolest thing that could happen to me."

Embarking in space

Chawla was chosen by NASA in December 1996 to join the STS-87 *Columbia* shuttle mission, from November 19 to December 5, 1997. As the shuttle prepared to take off, students from her high school in Karnal, India, paraded through the streets of the town in her honor.

"Kalpana Chawla will go to meet our Moon uncle on a rocket," one kindergarten student enthusiastically declared.

Chawla served on that mission as a prime robotic arm operator, and during that flight, traveled 6.5 million miles in 252 orbits of the earth. However, the mission itself was marred by the failure of one of its most important tasks: the capture of a Spartan satellite. Chawla released the satellite from a robot arm properly but was unable to catch it again when it failed to execute an expected maneuver. As a result, the crew was forced to perform a spacewalk to retrieve the satellite.

Media reports initially placed the blame for the error on Chawla. However, after an investigation, NASA determined that a series of errors involving both the ground control and the flight crew contributed to the mishap. Chawla noted that she and the other scientists learned some lessons from the experience, so that a similar mistake would not occur in the future. Most important, she added, the shuttle was ready to fly again.

Poetics of flight

Much has been made of Chawla's position as the first female of Asian ancestry to travel in space. She overcame challenges because she was a woman and an immigrant from India to win her spot on the astronaut team. She was often poetic in expressing her feelings about flying in space.

"You feel like Alice in Wonderland," she told a reporter with the Indian-American magazine, *India Currents,* in 1998, shortly after returning from her first journey into space.

"The combination that you are weightless and looking out, lends a story-book feeling. The colors of sunrise and sunset are awesome ... you see a whole range of colors ... very dark ... violets and blues ... they change very fast."

Being above Earth, circling the globe in a mere hour-and-a-half gives one a sense, Chawla added, of "how small this planet really is."

Sources:

"Biographical Data," National Aeronautics and Space Administration, Lyndon B. Johnson Space Center, Houston, Texas.

Fears, Darryl, and Rama Lakshmi, "'Golden Girl' Gave Youth in India a Chance to Dream." *Washington Post,* February 2, 2003, p. A31.

Lavilla, Stacy, "Shuttle Astronaut: The First Asian American Woman in Space," *AsianWeek,* January 28, 1998, vol. 19, no. 22, p. 9.

Prasad, Leena, "Pioneers Don't Have Role Models: From Karnal to Outer Space with Kalpana Chawla," *India Currents,* May 31, 1998, vol. 12; no. 2, p. 30.

Watson, Paul, "The Columbia Disaster; Astronaut Encouraged Others to Reach for the Stars." *Los Angeles Times,* February 3, 2003, p. A-9.

Joan Chen

Actress
Born April 26, 1961, Shanghai, China

"We need an ideal.... our lives should be subject to an ideal."

J oan Chen is an acclaimed actress who has appeared in several films and popular television shows both in the United States and in her native China. She is perhaps best known in the States for her role as the Empress Wan Jung in Bernardo Bertolucci's critically hailed film *The Last Emperor.* She is also recognized for her portrayal of Josie Packard on the short-lived but widely watched television series *Twin Peaks.*

In China, Chen is a highly respected actress, known for the sweet, demure characters she plays. She began her film career at the age of 14, winning China's version of an Academy Award—called a Golden Rooster—at the age of 18. She was declared China's best-loved actress and often referred to as the nation's Elizabeth Taylor. Chen acted in three more Chinese productions before heading to the United States in 1981.

Doctors' daughter

Chen was born Chen Chong and is the second of two children born to Chinese physicians. She described her mother in *USA Weekend* as a "renowned scientist, a medical doctor." The family was persecuted during the Cultural Revolution of the late 1960s and early 1970s, when communist leader Mao

Zedong led a fanatical purge of Chinese society, trying to weed out all capitalist and Western (mostly European and American) intellectual influence. Her parents, like many educated middle-class people, were forcibly sent to farms and factories to be "reeducated" in Communist Party doctrine. Chen and her brother were sent to live with her grandparents. She remembers this time as being full of fun and was totally unaware of the sinister nature of her parents' absence.

When she was just 14, Chen was seen in school by a local studio scout looking for people to appear in a film. She was chosen for a tiny role as a guerrilla (unconventional warfare) fighter and got to speak all of two lines. Still, she was fascinated by the industry and knew she wanted to pursue a career as an actress. After the film was released she applied to a two-year course of study in acting and was accepted. Her parents, who by this time had returned to their normal lives, were not entirely supportive of this decision and insisted that she not abandon her regular studies completely.

As part of her training as an actress, Chen traveled throughout China, meeting workers and seeing how people lived so that she could more accurately portray the working class. At the boarding school she attended she at first had a difficult time adjusting. She told *Interview* magazine, "I wasn't a very graceful teenager, and I became quite fat. My teachers told me if I continued to gain weight I would have no future, no career.... At the same time I was also very worried about being stupid, because I hadn't finished high school. I wouldn't talk to people because I was afraid of saying the wrong thing. I suppose a lot of teenagers go through weird things like that."

Joan Chen

Before she had completed the course, Chen was chosen to star in a film about a deaf mute that became a huge success in China. After a few more parts, Chen became a celebrity. She told the *New York Daily News* that she was recognized wherever she went: "It's the same as in this country, but China has a lot more people." After finishing her acting training she took an entrance exam to attend a university that trained people for the diplomatic corps. She continued to doubt her intellectual abilities and was terrified of flunking out and disappointing her parents, who longed for her to become a doctor. Instead, she became one of only five percent of the applicants to pass the exam. By this time her parents had moved to the United States, and they urged her to join them.

American success

Chen first attended college at the State University of New York at New Paltz, where she pursued premedical studies. Her mother was convinced that her fame in China was meaningless in America and that she would never be able to work in Hollywood. After a year, though, Chen transferred to California State University, where she took up film studies. Two years into film school, Chen started searching for acting jobs and ran into the obstacles most young actors confront. She told the *New York Daily News,* "I had to start all over again. Agents didn't want me. I had no photos, no film. They all said the same thing: 'Leave your photos and call me back.' I finally prepared a resume and found an agent who would take me."

Chen's first roles were stereotypical Asian woman on network television shows like *Miami Vice.* Her big break came in a strange encounter on a Hollywood studio lot where she was walking to an audition. She told the story to the *New York Daily News,* reporting, "A gruff voice called out from a limousine: 'Did you know that Lana Turner was discovered in a drug store?'" Chen had no idea who Lana Turner was or what the man was talking about, but he introduced himself as Dino De Laurentis, a major film producer, and told her on the spot that she would star in a movie he was casting. (Lana Turner was a Hollywood star and sex symbol in the 1940s and 1950s.) The movie was

Tai-Pan, based on the James Clavell novel about nineteenth-century China's contact with the colonial powers of Europe. *Tai-Pan* was shot in China, offering Chen her first opportunity to see her home in several years. Instead of a welcome homecoming for one of the country's most beloved stars, however, there was heated controversy over her playing the part of a concubine to a European colonialist. The part was considered a disgrace, and Chen was seen as a sellout for accepting it.

When she returned to the United States, Chen married Jimmy Lau and settled in Los Angeles. Her marriage lasted only a short time, however, and she was soon back on location in China, filming *The Last Emperor.* The movie was hugely popular all over the world and won an Academy Award for best picture in the United States. Chen told *Interview* that the movie was "shown in China and was controversial because the chronology was inaccurate. But the Chinese audience admired the beautiful way [the director] filmed it." In 1988, Chen remarried, to Peter Hui, a cardiologist, and moved to San Francisco.

In 1989, Chen was hired to play Josie Packard on the strange but much-watched television show *Twin Peaks.* The role extended her popularity to many Americans who had not seen the epic *The Last Emperor.* Her next big film role came in 1993, when she was chosen to play a Vietnamese peasant woman in Oliver Stone's *Heaven and Earth.* In the film, Chen's character ages from her early twenties to seventy years old. While preparing for the film in Thailand, Chen suffered infections and burns on her legs from extensive work in rice paddies. She talked about the role in

USA Weekend, explaining, "This was another experience.... I have three children [in the film] who are older than me, and I had to play this old woman... as ugly as you can make me to be." *Heaven and Earth* fared poorly at the box office, but Chen earned positive reviews for her demanding performance and was credited with taking on a risky role sharply in contrast with the glamorous parts that had made her reputation.

Chen believes she has enough fame and power to break through the kinds of stereotypes that limit Asian actors in America. She told the *New York Daily News,* "I want to play a real woman with complexity, with style." In 1994, she was pursuing work on a film about Burmese pro-democracy activist Aung San Suu Kyi, the Nobel Peace Prize winner who was held in Myanmar under house arrest for several years until her release in summer 1995. Chen admires her idealism and determination and told *USA Weekend,* "We need an ideal... our lives should be subject to an ideal."

That movie has not yet been produced. Meanwhile, Chen has starred in *The Joy Luck Club* (1994), *Golden Gate* (1994), *Judge Dredd* (1995), *In a Class of his Own* (1999), and *What's Cooking?* (2000). Chen has also been able to turn her hand to directing and producing.

In 1998, Chen teamed with novelist Yan Geiling to adapt the novel "Tian Yu" to film. The result was the film *Xiu Xiu: The Sent Down Girl.* The film was shot on a location near the border of China and Tibet, an area which has restricted access through the Chinese government. Unfortunately, Chen did not have the required permission to be there. She was banned from working in that country and ordered to pay a large fine. But Chen was not to be deterred. She directed the 1999 film *Autumn in New York* and has plans for two more Chinese films, *Fu Song* and *Unwanted.*

Sources:

Bruden, Martin, "China's Liz Taylor and the Foreign Devil," *New York Post,* September 1, 1986.

Carter, Gayle Jo, Monika Guttman, and Richard Vega, "Joan Chen Moves 'Heaven and Earth,'" *USA Weekend,* December 24, 1993, p. 8.

Hollywood.com, http://www.hollywood.com (accessed March 2003).

Lurie, Rod, "On Deadly Ground," *Los Angeles Magazine,* February 1994, p. 110.

Morgan, Susan, "Joan Chen," *Interview,* August 1990, pp. 80-83.

Thomas, Bob, "Beauty and the East," *New York Daily News,* September 4, 1986, p. 71.

William Shao Chang Chen

Engineer, retired military officer
Born November 11, 1939, Shanghai, China

"Go into and be a part of the mainstream of America. [Asian Americans] should tend to avoid being stereotyped, but be all you can be to be a part of the mainstream."

William Shao Chang Chen served more than 30 years in the U.S. Army. He steadily rose through the ranks to become the first Chinese American major general in the armed forces. His highest post was as commanding general of the U.S. Missile Command, where he was charged with management of all the army's missile systems, from development through procurement and support.

A family of refugees

Chen's father was a Chinese American who was orphaned at the age of ten. He nonetheless managed to put himself through school and trained to become a pilot. During the Great Depression of the 1930s, in which the U.S. economy experienced an extreme decline and unemployment reached a staggering high, he left the United States to work as a commercial pilot with an airline that Pan Am, the huge American carrier, was developing in China. While living there he met and married a Chinese woman with whom he would have two children.

At the time of William Shao Chang Chen's birth in 1939, China was at war with Japan. Japan occupied large parts of the country and was committing massive slaughter of civilians and other human rights abuses. When the United States declared war on Japan after the surprise Japanese attack on Pearl Harbor, Hawaii, the Chens fled China for the United States. They first moved to Canton, Ohio, where they had relatives. The elder Chen joined the American war effort and served in the air corps in the China-Burma-India theater of operation, fighting the Japanese as they sought to create a giant, pan-Asian empire.

The family stayed only briefly in Canton before moving to New York City and then on to Washington, D.C., where Chen spent most of his childhood. He was educated in the public school system except for his last two years of high school, which he spent at Storm King School, a private boarding

William Shao Chang Chen

school in Cornwall-on-Hudson, New York. He graduated in 1956 at the age of 16 and enrolled in the University of Michigan in Ann Arbor, where he studied engineering and math. In 1960 he earned his bachelor's degree; he stayed on at Michigan for an additional year to earn a master's degree in astronautical engineering.

The Reserve Officer Training Corps

While in college, Chen had enrolled in the Reserve Officer Training Corps (ROTC).

This was at the beginning of the Cold War between the global superpowers—a period of tension between the United States and the Soviet Union that defined the post-World War II era. Chen reasoned he would eventually have to serve in the military in some capacity, and with an ROTC background he would be able to serve as an officer. These were all entirely practical decisions—he had never considered a career in the military.

In 1961, after earning his master's degree, Chen was offered a regular army commission as a first lieutenant. He took the commission for what was supposed to be a three-year commitment. His first assignment was at Fort Meade, Maryland, where he worked in an army air defense unit during the Cuban Missile Crisis, which was brought about when American reconnaissance airplanes detected Soviet missile deployments in Cuba, 90 miles from the coast of Florida. The missiles were thought to be equipped with nuclear warheads, and Washington issued a stiff warning to Moscow to remove them. The military was put on high alert throughout this tense period, which is generally regarded by historians as the closest the two superpowers ever came to entering into nuclear warfare. Working at an air defense installation, Chen was right in the middle of this, and in an interview with *Asian American Biography (AAB)* he said it was a very exciting time. He recalls being put on heightened alert, monitoring all incoming flights from the coast, running drills, and manning the defense systems on 12-hour shifts. At this time Chen decided he might stay in the army beyond his commission.

Managing weapons systems

In 1963, Chen was appointed research development project officer for the Nike Hercules surface-to-air missile. As such, he was involved in the engineering, production, testing, and deployment of the system. Chen enjoyed this type of work, and it would eventually become the cornerstone of his military career. In 1967, he was charged with developing requirements for all new missile systems. He was specifically responsible for developing requirements for what the military called SAM-D, or surface-to-air missile deployment.

Chen has also served the military overseas. In 1964, he was posted in Korea, where he served as first assistant chief—later becoming chief—of the missiles and weapons branch of the Eighth Army depot command. In 1966, he was sent as a captain for a tour of duty in Vietnam, where the United States was fighting on the side of South Vietnam in a long and bloody civil war. He served as an ordnance (military supply) and logistics advisor to the South Vietnamese infantry division. As such he was responsible for the management of huge amounts of equipment and supplies that had to be deployed in the jungle.

The Sergeant York

In 1984, Chen was brought in by the army to help manage what was becoming a very controversial missile system called the division air defense gun, or the Sergeant York. By the time Chen took over the project, it had failed to pass the required technical and operational tests that would allow it to continue receiving funding from

Congress. This was during President Ronald Reagan's massive arms build-up of the 1980s—the largest peacetime build-up in American history—and critics were questioning the need for many of the military's weapons systems. When the Sergeant York failed its tests, the media seized on the system and began labeling it a failure. Chen's job was to bring his long years of experience as a systems developer to the project to either help it pass the required tests or to recommend it be scrapped. Chen eventually came to the belief that the system should be scrapped, and he reported that finding directly to the secretary of defense, Caspar Weinberger, a rare privilege for a project manager.

Chen believes that this highly controversial system was doomed because of overly high expectations about its capabilities. In fact, Chen had worked on the system, then in its infancy, earlier in his career. He had run an affordability analysis on it and determined that it would eventually run into just the sorts of problems that ultimately emerged. His report was ignored, however, teaching Chen that the special political interests behind a weapons system often prevail over considerations of its military capability.

A first

On May 1, 1987, Chen was promoted to brigadier general; then, on October 1, 1989, he was promoted again, this time to major general, making him the first Chinese American to reach that rank. With that promotion, he became commanding general of the U.S. Military Missile Command at Redstone Arsenal in Alabama, a base where he had served several times during his career. This posting—the top in his field—was in recognition of a career of highest achievement. Chen described it as the highlight of his military career.

Chen believes it is important for Americans—nearly all of whom are descended from immigrants—to acknowledge the impact their ethnic cultures have had on their lives and careers. He told *AAB,* however, that Asian Americans should "go into and be a part of the mainstream of America, that we should tend to avoid being stereotyped, but be all you can be to be a part of the mainstream." Even, he added, when that means abandoning traditional aspects of one's culture.

Chen is married and has two sons. In September 1993, he retired from the military after 33 years and took a job in private industry as a division vice president for Nicholls Research, a high technology engineering services company. In 1994, he took a similar vice presidential position at United Defense, where he oversees the Armament Systems Division Advanced Field Artillery System (AFAS) program.

Sources:

Chen, William Shao Chang, telephone interview with Jim Henry, May 17, 1994.

Defense Daily, http://www.defensedaily.com (accessed March 2003).

U.S. Army, biographical materials and press releases.

Doug Chiang

Art and special effects director in film
Born February 16, 1962, Taipei, Taiwan

"I've always dreamed of working for ILM [the special effects company founded by George Lucas]. Star Wars totally changed my life. I have been a science-fiction geek since grade school."

Doug Chiang

Doug Chiang is one of the most sought-after special effects directors in Hollywood. (Special effects are visual or sound effects that are added into a film by experts.) He has provided the special effects for some of the most popular movies of the 1990s, among them *Forrest Gump, The Mask,* and *Terminator II.* He also worked on the 1992 film *Death Becomes Her,* starring Meryl Streep, for which he won an Academy Award.

Chiang worked on all these films as associate creative director of Industrial Light and Magic (ILM), the special effects company founded by George Lucas, the director of *Star Wars*, one of the great special effects films of all time. ILM was a pioneer in the use of computer-generated animation in conjunction with live-action film. (Animated movies or cartoons have traditionally been made by photographing a series of drawings or inanimate objects such as clay figures or puppets. The illusion of motion is achieved by rapidly filming the images, in which there are slight, progressive changes. The use of computers to create the images makes the process more efficient and gives the artist more freedom.) ILM has set the standard for special effects in contemporary Hollywood moviemaking.

Backyard filmmaker

Chiang was five years old when he and his family left their native Taiwan and moved to the United States. His father, now a designer with the Ford automobile company, had been studying engineering at the University of Alabama when the family was finally able to join him. Eventually, the Chiangs settled in Westland, Michigan, where Chiang first started to cultivate his interest in film. He was especially fascinated by what he saw as the unlimited potential of special effects.

When he was 15, Chiang used his father's video camera to make a four-minute clay animation short film called *Gladiator*. The film won the grand prize at the Michigan Student Film Festival and drew the attention of John Prusak, a teacher at a local vocational school, the William D. Ford Vocational/Technical School in Westland. *Gladiator* displayed a high degree of technical competence in the difficult style of animation known as "claymation." Prusak described the process in an article in *Vocational Education Journal:* "The backgrounds were crude, but the movements in Doug's film were especially sophisticated. It's painstaking work that's difficult even for professionals to grasp. You're breaking movement down into fractions of seconds. For every second in a motion picture there are 24 movements."

Unconventional film education

After Chiang graduated from high school he wasn't sure what he wanted to do, other than study film somewhere. He had no idea where to begin until he was approached by Prusak, who offered him a position as his teaching assistant at William D. Ford. Chiang took him up on the unconventional offer. The young artist discussed this decision in *Vocational Education Journal:* "I refined my skills in photography and film production. It was the first time I was exposed to professional equipment, like the 16-millimeter camera.... Realistically, from

William D. Ford you could expect to go out to Hollywood and get a job assisting on film productions and then work your way up."

After studying with Prusak, Chiang transferred to the University of California at Los Angeles (UCLA) film school. There he won a school-wide contest in the experimental/animation category for his four-and-a-half-minute film *Mental Block*. The film presents a variety of facial expressions, from anger to sadness to joy, and was shot over a ten-week period in Chiang's living room. Winning the contest allowed Chiang to participate in a number of seminars, where he became familiar with production and design crews, and which proved to be an invaluable experience for the young film student. In his third year at UCLA, Chiang switched his major from film directing to art directing and design. He told *Asia, Inc.,* "I'd always been interested in drawing, and it was easier to get freelance jobs as an artist."

Chiang graduated from UCLA in 1986 with a bachelor's degree and quickly immersed himself in numerous freelance projects. He landed a job with Digital Productions in 1986, and while there worked as a design director for such shows as *Oprah Winfrey* and *Good Morning America*. In 1987 he worked as a designer and key animator for CBS's innovative and now-legendary Saturday morning television show *Pee-Wee's Playhouse*.

Industrial Light and Magic

ILM was founded by George Lucas, the filmmaker behind such pioneering works as *Star Wars*. Chiang discussed the impact of that film on his early life in *Asia, Inc.,* revealing, "I've always dreamed of working for ILM. *Star Wars* totally changed my life. I have been a science-fiction geek since grade school." ILM has mounted over 80 films. It employs 250 people and has won 12 Academy Awards, six British Academy Awards, and two Emmys. Chiang has worked on such films as *Back to the Future II, Ghost, Switch, The Doors, Terminator II, The Mask, Forrest Gump* (for which he won a British Academy Award in 1995), and *Death Becomes Her* (which earned him Academy Awards in both the U.S. and Britain). *Vocational Education Journal* described some of the work Chiang did for that film: "In [the film] audiences saw Meryl Streep's character walk and talk with her head twisted backward, after a fall down the stairs breaks her neck. It looks impossibly real, but Streep's neck is a 3-D computer graphic with [her] real head imposed above it." Chiang created this striking and much-discussed image.

In 1995 Chiang became design director for *Star Wars: The Phantom Menace* and in 1999 he worked on *Star Wars: Attack of the Clones*. Chiang told *Asian American Biography (AAB)* in an interview that he uses a "mixture of stop motion photography, multiple film exposures, animatronics, and computer graphics to play tricks on the audience." As an art director, Chiang is responsible for numerous tasks in the production of a film. He typically handles everything from estimating the viability of a writer or director's vision of a scene—whether or not the technology exists to film what is envisioned—to set designs, special effects techniques, and even budgeting.

Some fans will be sorry to hear that after Episode II, Chiang has retired from *Star Wars* to pursue other projects. Since 1993 he has been working on what he calls an illus-trated "film book," *Robota: Reign of Machines,* with a story that explores the relationship between nature and technology. The book was scheduled to be published by Chronicle Books in late 2003. And he expanded into online video games in 2002, when he worked on animations for Electric Arts' "Earth and Beyond." Chiang was also part of the team producing the film version of the Chris Van Allsburg book, *The Polar Express.*

A chief inspiration to Chiang, as he related in an article in *Asia, Inc.,* was the teasing he experienced as a self-described "science-fiction geek." "I remember being picked on," he said. "I think that's why I've worked so hard to prove them wrong." Chiang is married and has two sons.

Sources:

Chiang, Doug, telephone interview with Abby Warren, July 7, 1994.

Doug Chiang Studio, http://www.dchiang.com (accessed March 2003).

Dykman, Ann, "Oscar Winner Learned the Ropes in Vo-Tech School," *Vocational Education Journal,* October 1993, p. 16.

Gandel, Cathy, "Special Effects Magician," *Asia, Inc.,* March 1994, pp. 58-59.

Industrial Light and Magic, "Doug Chiang," professional resume, 1994.

Leroy Chiao

Astronaut, scientist
Born August 28, 1960, Milwaukee, Wisconsin

"The education I have gotten is bringing me something I have dreamed about since I was seven years old.... Education can take you to the most unlikely places. It took me to NASA."

In July 1994, Leroy Chiao fulfilled a lifelong dream when he flew aboard the space shuttle *Columbia* as a mission specialist. On board the shuttle, Chiao conducted experiments in life and material sciences in the International Microgravity Laboratory II, or Space Lab, as it is commonly called. The flight had been his goal since he was a child of seven, watching television coverage of the Gemini and Apollo missions of the 1960s and early 1970s.

A child of scientists

Although Chiao was born in Wisconsin, his family moved to California when he was young, and he spent most of his childhood in Danville. His father, Tsu Tao, is a chemical engineer, and his mother, Cherry Chao, holds a Ph.D. in material sciences and engineering. Both parents continually stressed to their children the importance of education in getting the most out of life. It was advice the young Chiao took to heart. After graduating from Monte Vista High School in 1978, he enrolled in the University of California at Berkeley, where he studied chemical engineering.

In an article in *College Digest,* Chiao reflected on the challenges he faced while working toward his bachelor's degree. He explained, "The philosophy at Berkeley is that they take more students than they plan to graduate, especially in the chemical engineering program. Only about 55 percent of the students who started actually graduated. My engineering friends and I hardly had time to do anything but study just to keep afloat." It was a grueling program but one that had its benefits, which the young man recognized. "We learned to look things up for ourselves," he said, "and to discover things on our own. This ability has become crucial to me in my career."

Chiao graduated from Berkeley with a bachelor of science degree in 1983 and enrolled immediately in graduate studies at the University of California at Santa Barbara. There, the atmosphere was less competitive but still very demanding academically. Chiao stated, "In graduate school... we were able to focus our attention on specific areas of study. Professors were no longer trying to weed us out, although we were expected to put in just as much work as we did at Berkeley." After completing his master's degree in 1985, Chiao stayed on at Santa Barbara and earned his doctorate two years later.

From private industry to NASA

Chiao's first job after earning his doctorate was with Hexcel, a medium-sized supplier of material to the aerospace industry.

There he was afforded the opportunity to work on a project in conjunction with the Jet Propulsion Laboratory (JPL), a branch of the National Aeronautics and Space Administration (NASA), developing materials for future space telescopes. The work was interesting and Chiao enjoyed participating in aerospace science, but what was most exciting to him was the fact that working with NASA and JPL brought him a step closer to fulfilling his dream of becoming an astronaut.

From Hexcel, Chiao moved to the Lawrence Livermore Laboratory, a government-funded research institution administered by the University of California and located on the Berkeley campus. At Livermore, Chiao worked on processing research for the manufacture of technologically advanced aerospace composites. In 1989 he applied to the astronaut training program at NASA.

In an interview with *Asian American Biography (AAB),* Chiao described the application process for the astronaut program. NASA receives thousands of applications for astronaut training every year, of which roughly 2,500 applicants are chosen as worthy of consideration by the agency. Of these, 100 are interviewed and, ultimately, 23 are chosen. In terms of percentages, one percent of the total applicants are chosen. Chiao was selected in 1990, becoming an astronaut in 1991.

Mission specialist

On his first mission in 1994, aboard the *Columbia,* Chiao conducted his experiments in a pressurized module within the cargo

Leroy Chiao

bay of the shuttle. Research on that mission was on microgravity. On his second mission, in 1996, aboard the *Endeavor,* Chiao took two spacewalks to demonstrate the use of tools and hardware, and to evaluate the techniques that would later be used in construction of the International Space Station. His third mission aboard *Discovery* in 2000 featured four space walks to configure the elements of a newly attached hardware to the Space Station.

In addition to his work as an astronaut, Chiao is a respected scientist who has been published widely in scientific journals, beginning in 1987. He said in *College Digest,* "If I were ever to leave NASA, I might turn to teaching. I enjoyed those few lectures I gave as a teaching assistant while I was earning my doctorate. For now, however, the education I have gotten is bringing me something I have dreamed about since I was seven years old.... Education can take you to the most unlikely places. It took me to NASA."

Sources:

Chiao, Leroy, telephone interview with Jim Henry, March 2, 1994.

Chiao, Leroy, "Your Rocket to the Stars," *College Digest,* special edition, 1993-94, pp. 2-3.

Johnson Space Center, http://www.jsc.nasa.gov (accessed March 2003).

National Aeronautics and Space Administration, biographical data, Houston, 1994.

Margaret Cho

Comedian, actor
Born December 5, 1968, San Francisco, California

"I think part of my journey has to be illustrating my experience, showing what you can do. I feel like I've gotten to a great place in my life. I just want to do it for a long time."

Margaret Cho has risen to the top of the highly competitive stand-up comedy field in a relatively short time. As an Asian American woman in a field dominated by white males, she has broken barriers and stereotypes by performing on such shows as the *Bob Hope Special,* *Evening at the Improv, The Arsenio Hall Show,* and *Star Search.* In 1994, Cho became the first Asian American to star in her own television show, *All American Girl,* a short-lived sitcom on ABC about a Korean American family.

In a press release marking the premiere of the series, Cho wrote about her hopes for the groundbreaking show. "The most important thing about the show is that... the Kims are an identifiable, individual family, with the same problems, communication barriers, and the same love [as any other family]. I think the show takes away some of the mystery about Asian Americans, and demonstrates that we're like everybody else."

An early desire to perform

Cho was born into a liberal, yet religious, Korean American family in the Sunset District of San Francisco. In a press release, Cho said that her father "writes Korean books like *1,001 Jokes for Public Speakers,* real corny stuff." As a child her parents encouraged her to study voice, dance, and piano but stopped short of supporting her decision, at age 13, to pursue a career in acting. Cho was not dissuaded from her dream, however, and won acceptance to San Francisco's prestigious High School of the Performing Arts. After graduation she enrolled in the theater department of San Francisco State University, but she dropped out before graduating. She had hoped to continue her acting studies at Yale or Juilliard but was discouraged by the lack of serious roles available to Asian women. It was then that she turned to stand-up comedy at the suggestion of a friend.

Cho developed her stand-up routine when she was 16 at a club above the bookstore her parents owned in San Francisco, where she worked part time. She would go upstairs and perform a set during her breaks. Her material revolved around aspects of her own life, mainly addressing generational and cultural conflicts. In her early career, Cho was uncertain about doing comedy; she didn't know that much about it, having studied theater. Over time, though, she realized that she had found her niche. "Stand-up is a way of acting, but it's also its own art form. I've grown to love and respect comedy," she told the *Daily Bruin.*

Cho's parents were dismayed by their daughter's course, especially after she dropped out of college and began performing in nightclubs, but she persisted. Discussing the conflict in her family over her choice of career in the *Daily Bruin,* Cho said, "Stand-up goes against every typical Asian aesthetic. It's too personal. You have to reveal yourself. It's not what a woman should do." As Cho has become more and more successful at what she does, her parents have come around and now support her. Many in the Asian American community view her popularity as mainstream acceptance of an Asian in a non-stereotypical role.

Margaret Cho

Rising above the fold

In 1991, Cho became the West Coast division champion of the U.S. College Comedy competition, which led to a billing with Jerry Seinfeld, then perhaps the top-drawing stand-up comic in the country. After that exposure she began to appear with increasing regularity as the host of television shows spotlighting stand-up comedy, including MTV's *Half-Hour Comedy Hour,* Lifetime's *Six Comics in Search of a Generation,* and Fox's *Comic Strip Live.* Cho has also made the break into films. In a small role, she played a Brooklyn nurse in *Angie,* which starred Geena Davis. She also played a featured role in *The Doomed Generation* with Dustin Nguyen.

Cho's routine focuses heavily on her generation. "Slacking off is the main art form of my generation, the only pleasure we have left," said Cho. "We have so many restrictions—no sex, no drugs—the only vice left was greed, but where did that take us? 'Just

Say No' has become the 'Keep on Truckin' of my generation." Cho's ethnicity and gender are fodder for her comedy as well. "Men look at me and think I'm going to walk on their backs or something," she joked. "I tell them the only time I'll walk on your back is if there's something on the other side of you I need." In 1994, she won the American Comedy Award for Female Comedian.

All American Girl

Soon after came the ABC sitcom *All American Girl*. Cho spoke to *Asian Week* about the idea behind her show. "*All American Girl* is basically about me and the people in my life," she said. "It's the first show that sees Asian Americans as they really are. These days there are more extraterrestrials on shows than Asians—even if you include reruns of *Kung Fu*," which, she noted, should be renamed *That Guy's Not Chinese*. "I want to continue the trend [the 1993 film] *The Joy Luck Club* started. We're the first layer of generational culture," Cho noted. "This is important because we are on the ground floor of things for the future of Asian Americans in this country. I want to be a part of that."

All American Girl was created by Cho and television producer and writer Gary Jacobs. It also starred **B. D. Wong,** the Tony Award-winning actor, as Cho's older brother and Clyde Kusatsu as Cho's father. That the entire cast was not ethnically Korean—Wong, for instance, is Chinese American—caused some controversy, but the show's executive producer, Pat Dougherty, insisted at a press conference that actors should be allowed to play characters of different ethnicities, that to do so is part of being an actor. A Korean cultural consultant was on the payroll to make sure the show's portrayals were accurate.

All American Girl was cancelled after its first season, but the show's airing brought home to television audiences the prior lack of Asian American themes and faces on TV.

Moving on

After the show, Cho tried her hand at movies, starring in *Faceoff* with Nicolas Cage, and reading the voice of the detective in *Rugrats*. Live performances seem to be Cho's greatest strength, however. In 1999, she toured the country with her show "I'm the One that I Want," which was then made into a movie and a book, released in 2001.

In 2000, Cho won the Gracie Allen Award from the American Women in Radio and Television organization and the first-ever Golden Gate award from the Gay and Lesbian Alliance Against Defamation (GLAAD), which honored her for making a significant contribution in promoting equal rights for all, regardless of sexual orientation or gender identity.

In 2001 Cho began a second tour, "The Notorious C.H.O.," which ended in 2002 before a sold-out crowd at Carnegie Hall. This performance was recorded and released on compact disk that year. Cho also received the Media Award from the National Organization for Women in 2002. As of 2003, Cho planned to keep going strong, with another book and a new tour, "Revolution."

Sources:

Cho, Margaret, press releases and biographical materials, summer 1994.

Lee, Elisa, "Margaret Cho Brings Asian Pacific American Twenty-some-things to Television," *Asian Week,* November 19, 1993, p. 19.

Lim, Gerard, "What Makes the First Asian American Sitcom So Special? It's Cho's Show...," *Asian Week,* July 1, 1994, p. 1.

Margaret Cho, http://www.margartcho.com (accessed March 2003).

Polkinghorne, Rex, "Comic Cho Proves Laughter Can Sever Racial Stereotypes," *Daily Bruin,* February 22, 1994, p. 21.

Provenzano, Jim, "It's Cho Time," *Advocate,* July 1994, p. 54.

Vernon Chong

Military surgeon
Born November 13, 1933, Fresno, California

As command surgeon at the headquarters of the Air Training Command and as commander of the Joint Military Medical Command at Randolph Air Force Base, Chong is responsible for managing 7,500 people and overseeing health care at various military hospitals in Texas.

Major General Vernon Chong was the command surgeon at the headquarters of the Air Training Command and the commander of the Joint Military Medical Command at Randolph Air Force Base in Randolph, Texas. He was responsible for managing 7,500 people and overseeing health care at various military hospitals in Texas.

During his long, distinguished medical and military career, Chong has earned many awards and honors. He also has participated in the space program as a member of the launch site recovery team for all of the Apollo, Skylab, and Apollo-Soyuz manned missions.

Medicine and military

Vernon Chong was born on November 13, 1933, in Fresno, California. He attended public schools and graduated from Fresno High School in 1951. He earned a bachelor of arts degree in basic medical sciences from Stanford University in 1955. He then enrolled in the Stanford University School of Medicine, from which he graduated in 1958. Chong interned at the General Hospital of Fresno County, California, where he completed his internship in 1963.

Chong entered the air force in 1963. His first assignment was as chief of general surgery at the U.S. Air Force Hospital at Scott Air Force Base in Illinois. In June of 1965 he was transferred to the air force hospital at Tachikawa Air Base in Japan, where he served as a staff general surgeon and, later, as director of intern and resident education for Japanese physicians.

In 1968, Chong returned to the United States and was assigned as a staff general surgeon and instructor for the surgical residency training program at the David Grant USAF Medical Center at Travis Air Force Base in California. From July 1970 to June 1974, he served at the air force hospital of the U.S. Air Force Academy in Colorado. He worked as a staff general surgeon and then as chair of the department of surgery before becoming director of hospital services. He also helped advise cadets who were students in the premedical program and was the team physician for the air force hockey team.

Chong became deputy commander and director of hospital services at the U.S. Air Force Regional Hospital at March Air Force Base in July 1974. Two years later, he returned to Travis Air Force Base and served as deputy commander and director of hospital services at the base's David Grant Medical Center. He became commander there in 1978.

Command posts

In November of 1981, Chong was assigned as commander of the Malcolm Grow Medical Center at Andrews Air Force Base in Maryland. Three and a half years later, he became the command surgeon for the Military Airlift Command at Scott Air Force Base, and in 1987 was assigned as commander of the Willford Hall Medical Center at Lackland Air Force Base in Texas. He also earned the rank of major general in 1987. He assumed his position as commander of the Joint Military Medical Command at Randolph Air Force Base in May of 1990. In August 1991, he became command surgeon at the Headquarters U.S. European Command in Stuttgart, Germany, a position he held until his retirement in 1994.

In addition to his work in the space program, Chong has served as a member of the governing board of the National Library of Medicine and as an adviser to the governing board of the Uniformed Services University of Health Sciences. He is a fellow of the American College of Surgeons and a member of the Pan Pacific Surgical Association, the Association of Military Surgeons of the United States, the Aerospace Medical Association, the Society of Air Force Clinical Sur-

Vernon Chong

geons, the Society of Air Force Flight Surgeons, the Society of NASA Flight Surgeons, and the American College of Physician Executives. In the 1990s, he was the U.S. Air Force representative to the board of governors of the American College of Surgeons.

Chong's military awards and decorations include the Distinguished Service Medal, the Legion of Merit with oak leaf cluster, the Meritorious Service Medal, the Air Force Commendation Medal, the Air Force Outstanding Unit Award with four oak leaf clusters, the Air Force Organizational Excellence Award, the Naval Unit Citation, the National

Defense Service Medal, the Vietnam Service Medal with service star, the Air Force Overseas Ribbon, the Air Force Longevity Service Award Ribbon with five oak leaf clusters, the Order of Merit (Brazil), and the Gold Cross of Honor (Germany).

Sources:

United States Air Force, http://www.af.mil (accessed March 2003).

U.S. Air Force, biographical information, July 1990.

Deepak Chopra

Physician, author
Born 1946, New Delhi, India

"You know, we are all participants in the whole process of illness. There are two levels of responsibility: one is individual and the other is shared."

Deepak Chopra is a prominent physician who has written several bestselling books presenting new ways of looking at health, fitness, disease, and aging. His theories incorporate Eastern (Asian) ideas about spirituality with Western (primarily European and American) notions about health care, arriving at a unique perspective for addressing modern ailments. His most celebrated—and most controversial—contribution to the literature of alternative health theories concerns aging. Chopra believes that what we have for thousands of years understood as the natural process of aging is, in fact, a process within our control. In his 1993 internation-

ally bestselling book *Ageless Body, Timeless Mind: The Quantum Alternative to Growing Old,* he asserted, "Because the mind influences every cell in the body, human aging is actually fluid, changeable; it can speed up, slow down, stop for a time, and even reverse itself." Radical statements such as this have gained Chopra international fame, but along with this fame has come a certain amount of skepticism, and even scorn, from the established medical community, of which he used to be a part.

The American doctor as drug dealer

Chopra was the son of a prominent cardiologist in New Delhi, India. He studied medicine at the All India Institute of Medical Science, where he became interested in Western medicine. He left India for the United States in 1970 and completed residencies in internal medicine and endocrinology. (Endocrinology is the science that deals with the endocrine glands, which secrete hormones, or chemical messengers, in the body.) From there he went on to teaching posts at major medical institutions such as the Tufts University and Boston University schools of medicine, while establishing a very successful private practice. By the time he was 35 years old, Chopra had become chief of staff at New England Memorial Hospital. He had arrived at, or very near, the top of his profession; he was successful financially and professionally and he was still a very young man.

But there was something disturbing to Chopra about the traditional practice of medicine in the West. He was especially

Deepak Chopra

the culture and environment in which he or she lives. Alternative medicine also tends to concentrate on prevention and treating underlying causes.

As for Chopra, he told *People* magazine that by 1980 he had begun to see himself as a "legalized drug pusher, dispensing antibiotics and sleeping pills" at what he had come to see was an alarming rate. He began to search for alternatives and discovered one in the teachings of a Hindu priest named Maharishi Mahesh Yogi. The Maharishi was a prominent Indian spiritualist who had gained a cult following in the 1960s and early 1970s teaching his brand of meditation, called Transcendental Meditation (TM), to such celebrities as the Beatles.

Chopra began practicing TM fervently, and within a couple of years he had the opportunity to meet the Maharishi. The meeting proved to be beneficial for both Chopra and the Maharishi, who saw in Chopra a well-established medical professional with impeccable Western credentials who could introduce ancient Eastern philosophies of medicine and lifestyle into American culture. Chopra viewed the Maharishi as a great source of ancient wisdom that he could use to better treat his patients. The Maharishi asked Chopra to help him bring Ayurvedic medicine to America. Developed in India, Ayurvedic medicine, Chopra explained in *USA Today,* "is an ancient holistic system of medicine that takes into account all aspects of a patient's life and includes the environment, the body, the mind, and consciousness." In 1985, Chopra founded the Ayurvedic Health Center for Stress Management and Behavioral Medicine in Lancaster, Massachusetts. There he established what would become a sort of empire, one of the most successful

distressed about trusting the prevailing wisdom and relying heavily on pharmaceuticals to treat patients. One of the main complaints of the alternative medicine movement as it has evolved since the 1970s is that American doctors are far too eager to prescribe drugs and recommend surgery. Alternative health-care practitioners view this as a feeble approach to a larger problem. They prefer to look at illnesses holistically, taking into consideration the whole human being who is sick—not only the body but the mind and the spirit and even integrations of Eastern and Western medicine in the United States.

The doctor as healer, writer, and star

In an era when books on healing and recovery are granted their own sections in bookstores, Chopra's contributions to the genre stand out. One reason is just what the Maharishi envisioned: his undeniable expertise as a traditional doctor. He can accurately portray himself as someone who ran up against the limitations, excesses, and abuses of traditional medicine firsthand. When he tells *USA Today* that "eighty percent of all the drugs we use in Western medicine are 'optional' or of marginal benefit," he has the weight of his degrees and former positions of authority to back him up.

Chopra, and many of the other new gurus of alternative medicine, have hit a resonant chord with the American public, which in large numbers has become frustrated with what many perceive as the arrogance of traditional medicine. Doctors are often seen as uncaring, unsympathetic, and vastly overpaid. Chopra began writing books, giving speeches, and organizing seminars. His first book, *Creating Health,* published in 1987, and his next, *Return of the Rishi: A Doctor's Search for the Ultimate Healer,* published in 1988, were both bestsellers. They preached holistic approaches to health and wellness and established Chopra as one of the premier writers in this new field.

Chopra kept his name on the bestseller list with his 1990 contribution, *Perfect Health: The Complete Mind/Body Guide,* and *Unconditional Life: Discovering the Power to Fulfill Your Dreams,* which was published in 1991. Then in 1993 he published two books that not only put him back on the bestseller list, but brought him stardom via television talk shows like *The Oprah Winfrey Show,* where he became a regular and popular guest. The first of these was *Creating Affluence: Wealth and Consciousness in the Field of All Possibilities.* The second was the enormously successful *Ageless Body, Timeless Mind.* In this book, Chopra presented his most radical hypothesis, perhaps the most radical medical theory of the century: that aging is not, after all, the inevitable deterioration of organs and mind as we have been traditionally taught. Rather, he suggests, it is a process that can be influenced, slowed down, and even reversed with the correct kind of therapies. These therapies, according to Chopra, are simple and self-administered and can be learned by anyone. He asserts that getting rid of "toxic relations, emotions, [and] foods can influence your life span by 30 years."

His proclamations have attracted a lot of attention from a culture obsessed with youth and terrified of old age. Chopra says that following his regimen can lead to increased life spans of up to 120 years. And he claims that these additional years do not have to be spent wasting away in nursing homes, as many of the elderly are today, but could be productive, creative years.

In 1995, Chopra worked with his friend and colleague David Simon, M.D., to open the Chopra Center for Well-Being in La Jolla, California, which served as the first formal facility dedicated to a healing process that integrates Western medicine with natural healing traditions.

In 2001 Chopra worked with the American Health Research Institute to open the alternative therapy spa, Moksha, in Alabama. In 2002, he opened a second Chopra Center at La Costa Resort and Spa in Carlsbad, California, and partnered with Memorial Health, a hospital in Savannah, Georgia, to create a Chopra Center as part of that healthcare system.

Controversy

Chopra's ideas have caused considerable controversy within the established medical community, which generally regards most alternative medicine as faddish at best and dangerous at worst. His most controversial positions are his assertions about the nature of aging, which have drawn ridicule from his detractors, and his notions about the causes of disease and the level of responsibility the afflicted must assume for their illnesses. He defended these principles in *Psychology Today:* "You know, we are all participants in the whole process of illness. There are two levels of responsibility: one is individual and the other is shared. If I smoke cigarettes then I am to a great extent responsible for the carcinoma that is statistically more likely to occur. But what about the innocent 12-year-old with leukemia? That is where collective responsibility comes in." In Chopra's view, the collective responsibility for illness in innocent people is actually the culmination of generations of negative emotions processed incorrectly. He believes that a longer view needs to be incorporated so that we can correct our relationship with disease and illness and thus spare future generations from being the victims of our collective misdirected emotions.

Chopra and his teachings have struck a chord around the world. His clients include such celebrities as musicians George Harrison and Michael Jackson. Chopra's books have sold in the millions and have been translated into 25 languages. He lectures around the world and is commonly featured in newspapers and magazines and on television shows.

Sources:

Bromberg, Craig, "Doc of Ages: Deepak Chopra Offers a Fountain of Youth," *People,* November 15, 1993, pp. 169-70.

Chopra Center at La Costa Resort and Spa, http://www.chopra.com (accessed March 2003).

Chopra, Deepak, *Ageless Body, Timeless Mind: The Quantum Alternative to Growing Old,* New York: Harmony Books, 1993.

Mauro, James, "From Here and Now to Eternity: An Interview with Deepak Chopra," *Psychology Today,* November/December 1993, pp. 36–37.

Reynolds, Barbara, "Treat Whole Person, Not Just the Disease: An Interview with Deepak Chopra," *USA Today,* January 4, 1990.

Connie Chung

Television journalist
Born August 20, 1946, Washington, D.C.

"To me, Watergate was the story of the decade. It was the unraveling of the presidency, a textbook course in responsible reporting and a lesson in truth."

On June 1, 1993, Connie Chung made television history when she became the permanent co-anchor, with Dan Rather, of *The CBS Evening News.* CBS's decision to end white male dominance of the nightly network newscasts generated a lot of publicity, both positive and negative. In addition to her role as anchor, Chung was the host of *Eye to Eye with Connie Chung,* a popular prime-time television newsmagazine that highlighted interviews with controversial newsmakers, a specialty of Chung's. Over the course of her 20 years in broadcast journalism, Chung has become one of the most recognizable personalities in American culture—and one of the most sought after and highly paid broadcasters in contemporary media.

The youngest of ten

Chung was the last child born to Margaret Ma and William Ling Chung—and the only one of their ten children to be born in the United States. Chung's father had been an intelligence officer in China's Nationalist Army, the forces fighting against the revolutionary insurgency of Mao Zedong. As the war worsened in their homeland, the Chungs fled to the United States, but not before five of their children—all the Chung sons—died in the violence. Constance Yu-hwa was their last child, born in 1946 in suburban Washington, D.C.

Chung earned a bachelor's degree in journalism from the University of Maryland in 1969. Her first job was as a copy person and secretary at WTTG-TV, an independent television station in the nation's capital. It was not the kind of work that most interested her, but she put in her time until a reporting position opened up. Then, in 1971, she became an on-the-air reporter. After working for nearly a year at WTTG,

Connie Chung

covering fires, murders, and airplane disasters, Chung was hired by CBS to work in its Washington bureau.

Her network career begins

In her early years with CBS, Chung covered issues of national importance, such as the presidential campaign of George McGovern, anti-Vietnam War protests, and the presidency of Richard Nixon. While covering Nixon, she traveled with him to the Middle East and Soviet Union. Later in the Nixon presidency, as Congress began looking into the Watergate scandal, Chung covered the historic, nationally televised hearings on the break-in at Democratic National Headquarters, a break-in that was later revealed to have been funded by the Committee to Reelect the President. Reflecting on those days almost 20 years later for *Redbook* magazine, Chung said, "To me, Watergate was the story of the decade. It was the unraveling of the presidency, a textbook course in responsible reporting and a lesson in truth."

In 1976 Chung moved to Los Angeles to become an anchor at the local CBS affiliate KNXT (now KCBS). She anchored three broadcasts a day, and the show's ratings began to climb, as did Chung's salary. By 1983 she was the highest-paid local anchor in the country. She also won several honors, including local Emmy awards in 1978 and 1980 and a citation from the Los Angeles Press Club for outstanding television reporting.

A switch in networks

In 1983 Chung decided to take an offer to become a reporter with NBC. It meant a drastic cut in pay, but she would be reporting again, rather than just anchoring, and that had become her first priority. She covered both the Democratic and Republican national conventions in 1984. Her work at NBC catapulted Chung to celebrity status, and the network began seeking formats to exploit her popularity. She began substituting for anchor Jane Pauley on the *Today Show* and in 1985 was named the chief correspondent for a new newsmagazine, *American Almanac.* Hosted by Chung and NBC reporter and anchor Roger Mudd, the

show was NBC's fourteenth failed attempt to launch a successful newsmagazine.

In 1986 Chung began substituting for anchor Tom Brokaw on *The NBC Nightly News,* becoming the first Asian American to anchor an evening network newscast. She also hosted a new newsmagazine, *1986.* This show failed too, however, and Chung began working on a series of one-hour prime-time documentaries focusing on social and political issues of the time; among the shows produced were *Life in the Fat Lane, Scared Sexless, Stressed to Kill, Everybody's Doing It,* and *Guns, Guns, Guns.*

Return to CBS

When Chung's contract at NBC expired in 1989, she announced that she would be open to bids from other networks. CBS, the network where her career had started, won the bidding war, offering a reported $1.5 million annually for Chung's services. Her initial duties with CBS included hosting *West 57th, The CBS Sunday Night News,* and serving as the principal replacement for Dan Rather on *The CBS Evening News.* After *West 57th* was canceled, Chung began hosting *Saturday Night with Connie Chung,* another one-hour newsmagazine. The show generated controversy when it became the first network news show to use dramatic recreations of news events, a staple of so-called tabloid television thought by many to be unduly sensational and thus beneath network journalism. The show did not last. But in 1990 she tried again with *Face to Face with Connie Chung,* which featured exclusive interviews, including interviews with Joseph Hazelwood, captain of the *Exxon Valdez,* and Magic Johnson of the L.A. Lakers after he announced he was

HIV-positive. For her report on the controversial subject of testing rapists for AIDS, she was awarded the Silver Gavel Award from the American Bar Association.

In 1991 Chung also served as rotating anchor and contributing correspondent for CBS's coverage of the Persian Gulf War, in which the United States entered into a conflict supporting the Middle Eastern state of Kuwait against aggression from its neighbor Iraq. The next year Chung co-anchored *America on the Line,* an experiment with interactive television that broadcast viewer responses to President George Bush's 1992 State of the Union address. Then, in 1993, she became co-anchor of *The CBS Evening News* and was once again named anchor of a prime-time newsmagazine, *Eye to Eye with Connie Chung.* In the spring of 1995, however, Chung was dismissed from her anchoring duties on *The CBS Evening News,* sparking rumors of discrimination within the network. Detractors blamed her questionable journalistic techniques, but other observers speculated that Chung became a scapegoat for CBS's declining ratings problems.

Chung spent the year of 1996-1997 teaching and lecturing as a fellow in the Hoan Shorenstein Center on the Press, Politics and Public Policy at the John F. Kennedy School of Government. Then in 1997, she joined ABC news as a co-anchor for 20/20. In the 1999–2000 season of the show, Chung received the Amnesty International Human Rights Award for a report on attacks against women in Bangladesh who speak out on women's rights. These women were attacked by men who threw acid in their faces, causing permanent disfigurement. She also received an award from the National Association of Black Journalists for a report enti-

tled "Justice Delayed." This investigation produced new evidence in the 1966 Ku Klux Klan murder of Ben Chester White. As a result, the case was reopened and Klansman Ernest Avants was indicted for the murder.

In 2002 Chung moved to CNN to host her own show, *Connie Chung Tonight.* In April 2003, the program was suspended to allow for expanded news coverage of the United States' war with Iraq. Chung's show was cancelled a few days later, and Chung then left CNN.

Awards

Chung has received numerous awards for her work, including three national Emmy awards (two for best interview/interviewer) and a Peabody Award. In 1990 she was chosen by *U.S. News and World Report* as favorite interviewer in its annual "Best of America" reader survey. She has also received the Edward R. Murrow Award, the National Educational Media Networks Golden Apple Award, CINE Golden Eagle Award, and the U.S. International Film and Video Festivals Gold Camera Award. In 1991, she received the Ohio State Award, National Headliner Award, two American Women in Radio and Television National Commendations, and a Clarion Award, and, in 1999, the Chicago International Television Competition's Silver Plaque for investigative reporting and the Communicator Award's Crystal Award of Excellence.

On December 2, 1984, Connie Chung married fellow television journalist Maury Povich, then the host of Fox Television's tabloid news program *A Current Affair.* Povich went on to host *The Maury Povich Show,* a syndicated daytime television talk show.

The couple live in Manhattan with their adopted son, Matthew.

Sources:

Cable News Network, http://www.cnn.com (accessed March 2003).

Romano, Lois, "Stories That Changed Their Lives: Connie Chung, Witness to Truth," *Redbook,* October 1991.

Yang, Jeff, and Betty Wong, "Power Brokers," *A. Magazine,* December 15, 1993, pp. 25-34.

Eugene Chung

Football player
Born June 14, 1969, Prince George's County, Maryland

"When I was growing up I would watch sports and say, 'Wait a second, How come there are no Korean guys playing basketball? How come they're not out there slamming the ball and tearing down the rim? How come they're not playing pro baseball and hitting that home run? What's going on with that?'"

In the 1992 college draft, Eugene Yon Chung was chosen by the New England Patriots, becoming the first Asian American football player to be drafted in the first round. The offensive lineman played his college ball at Virginia Tech, where he was a first team All-American and All-Big East after his senior year. As a Patriot, Chung has distinguished himself as an important anchor in the offensive line. He was named to the All-Rookie team following his first year.

Early interest in sports

Eugene Chung's father, Choon Chung, came to the United States in 1956. An ambitious man, he studied public administration at the City College of New York, political science at Columbia University, and law at Yale. He settled in the Washington, D.C., area where he worked primarily as an attorney. Based on his own experience, the elder Chung taught his three sons that there were no limitations in life.

Eugene Chung was athletic as a child and played most sports fairly well. He was small, though, so his father pushed him toward baseball, where his size would not be an issue. As a fan of professional sports, Chung noticed that there were few, if any, Asian American athletes to whom he could look as a role model. He told the *Washington Post,* "When I was growing up I would watch sports and say, 'Wait a second, How come there are no Korean guys playing basketball? How come they're not out there slamming the ball and tearing down the rim? How come they're not playing pro baseball and hitting that home run? What's going on with that?'"

At Oakton High School in Oakton, Virginia, Chung was an all-around athlete. He began playing football after years of having been considered too small for the sport. By his senior season he was a starting defensive lineman and was selected All-District and All-Region after recording 86 tackles, eight sacks, and six fumble recoveries. He went on to earn three letters in two sports: football and track. He also competed in judo, winning the Virginia State Judo Championship in 1990. He is currently a brown belt in the sport.

An outstanding college career

As a freshman at Virginia Tech, Chung was moved to offensive lineman. He made it to the starting lineup seven games into the season, playing first at guard before being moved to tackle just prior to the end of the season. As a sophomore he was voted best offensive lineman, and as a junior he allowed only one sack and received an 84 percent grade for blocking consistency. Following his senior year, Chung was named an All-American and All-Big East player.

Off the playing field, Chung experienced little racism, despite breaking long-held stereotypes about Asian Americans. He told the *Washington Post,* "I really didn't get hassled at all being a Korean here." Nonetheless, Chung's high profile and the fact that very few Asian Americans have made it in professional team sports make him aware of his status as a role model. "I think having a chance to play in the NFL is going to do a lot for the Korean community. I'd like to be somewhat of a spokesman for that.... I think by [playing] well it will let people know back in Korea and in the United States... that we are able to do this. We're not a meek people."

The New England Patriots

Chung is the third Asian American to play professional football, the second in contemporary times. His predecessors were Walter Aichu, a running back for the Dayton Triangles in the 1920s, and John Lee, a field goal kicker who was one of the most successful in NCAA history, but who didn't make it in the pros. Chung shares the spot-

Eugene Chung

light with San Diego Chargers linebacker **Junior Seau** as the two most prominent Asians playing in the NFL today.

Chung's rookie season with the New England Patriots was less than stellar; by the beginning of training camp, he was still a holdout over contractual matters and so had a late start. Then personal tragedy struck when Chung's father died. Chung's mother had died when he was a young child, and the loss of his father took a heavy emotional toll. Throughout his first season Chung was bothered by recurring injuries and was bounced from position to position on the offensive line. With each new spot, he had to learn new moves and strategies. The Patriots compiled a dismal record for the 1992 season, losing 14 of 16 games.

During the 1993 season things began to look up for Chung. Mending both physically and emotionally, the young man began living up to his early promise and performing well enough to justify his status as a first-round draft pick. Speaking to the *Boston Herald* about his first two seasons, Chung said, "Last year there were a lot of things I had no control over, things going on at home and I think those things are behind me. Now I can concentrate on what's at hand. Having that rookie year under the belt also helps with the experience. I think I'm doing better." His teammates seem to agree. Right tackle Pat Harlow said, "He just had a rough year. Nobody thought that was the real Eugene Chung. Now he's just playing the way he's supposed to be playing."

Sources:

Conroy, Steve, "Chung Strong on Rebound," *Boston Herald,* September 25, 1993.

Freeman, Mike, "For Chung, NFL Dream Has Special Glow," *Washington Post,* April 15, 1992, pp. D1, D3.

Mannix, Kevin, "Pats Pick Their Spots," *Boston Herald,* April 27, 1992, p. 74.

Mannix, Kevin, "Vote of Confidence for Chung," *Boston Herald,* August 20, 1992.

May, Peter, "Chung Is Starting to Feel Comfortable," *Boston Globe,* October 11, 1992.

Ann Curry

Journalist
Born, November 19, 1956, Agano, Guam

"People who are disenfranchised will reach so far to find an opening in that door."

Ann Curry is a high-profile television journalist who has risen steadily in her profession, earning the respect of peers and viewers. From the start, her reporting has shown that she cares about others. "I sought stories about people who needed help," she has written. She looked for assignments where she could report on the "suffering of homeless people, the rise of the AIDS crisis, the struggle of immigrants, the humanitarian disaster in Kosovo." Curry frequently speaks out on racial issues, expressing pride in her mixed Asian American heritage, and emphasizing the need for ethnic role models in the news media. She has also been an influential advocate for health issues.

From small-town girl to local newscaster

Curry grew up in the southern Oregon college town of Ashland, where a renowned Shakespeare Festival is held each summer. Her Japanese mother married her white American father when he was serving in the military. Her mother tried to make sure that Ann was completely assimilated into American culture. Ann noted, "She wouldn't even let me speak Japanese!" Her mother was worried about anti-Japanese prejudice that lingered after World War II, when the United States and Japan fought each other. But her father always encouraged her to identify with what he called her Asian "samurai" side, telling her, "Never forsake [turn away from] either world."

Although her father wanted her to follow his footsteps into the military as did two of her brothers, Curry went to the University of Oregon. Driven by the conviction that "knowledge was power" she graduated from the School of Journalism in 1978. From then on, her path in television newscasting did not waver.

As a young journalist, Curry started on her way with a job as a news reporter at local NBC-affiliate television station KTVL in Medford, a southern Oregon town. She worked there from 1978 to 1981. From Medford she moved on to the state's largest city, Portland. There she gained prominence as a reporter and, eventually, news anchor for KGW television from 1981 to 1984. The next step was the "major market" city of Los Angeles, where Curry earned praise as an intrepid reporter with television station KCBS from 1984 to 1990. This CBS station was the only time Curry worked for a network other than NBC. While at KCBS Curry won an Emmy Award for reporting live on the Los Angeles earthquake of October 1987. She won a second Emmy for her on-the-scene coverage of a gas pipeline explosion in an outlying town. In 1990, she returned to work for NBC. The NBC network of stations would lead, like stepping stones, to the coveted rank of national NBC news anchor.

Ann Curry

A Morning Star

Curry joined NBC's national news team in 1990, becoming their Chicago correspondent. Next, she served as anchor of NBC's *News at Sunrise* from July 1991 to July 1996. Although this may be viewed as the lowest rung on the ladder of national news anchoring, it put Curry right in line for the move to a very high visibility slot later. She joined the venerable NBC *Today* show as its news anchor in 1996. *Today*'s decades-old blend of talk-show, news, and weather had been stretched into a three-hour format. Ann Curry's hard-news stories were aired between segments featuring celebrity interviews, cooking demonstrations, and informal banter by hosts Katie Couric and Matt Lauer.

On the *Today* show, viewers might think Curry just reads reports that are given to her by a writer. But she does more than that. "My job is to read, edit and fact-check every single news story that comes in each day and I take great pride in keeping our country on the forefront of any pivotal news. The first thing I do (at about 5:00 A.M. every morning) is check the wires for breaking news stories."

Curry's *Today* news coverage of the September 11 attacks in New York was intensive, as she tirelessly reported from the "Ground Zero" World Trade Center site. Other noteworthy *Today* assignments have included her reports from Albania and Macedonia during the Kosovo refugee crisis in 1999. In 2001, she reported during an Arabian Sea tour aboard the USS *Roosevelt* aircraft carrier, and conducted an exclusive interview with General Tommy Franks at the Ramstein Air Force Base in Germany.

Curry is also a correspondent for *Dateline NBC,* a weekly magazine show. For *Dateline* she obtained exclusive coverage of the birth of septuplets to the McCaughey family in Iowa. She reported on their birth in 1997, and returned for yearly follow-up reports. Curry also has served as a substitute anchor on the evening news, and has fearlessly revealed her ultimate ambition for the top rung of national news: "I want Tom Brokaw's job."

Anchor and advocate

Popular with viewers, Curry has a professional yet sympathetic on-the-air style. She always appears relaxed, and has an authoritative, slightly deep voice. She won Emmy Awards for reporting in 1987 and 1989. She has also garnered Four Golden Mike awards from the Radio and Television News Association of Southern California, Associated Press Certificates of Excellence, the AmeriCares Humanitarian Medal, and an Award for Excellence in Reporting from the National Association for the Advancement of Colored People (NAACP.)

In 1987, Curry married Brian Ross, a computer consultant. They have a daughter and a son. She has written that she encourages her children to be proud of their mixed ethnic heritage, using her own father's words: "You are the best of both worlds."

As a woman of Asian American background, Curry has consciously served as a television journalism role model for non-whites. She had found such role models noticeably lacking when she was growing up. "When you're a child and you don't see people like you doing something, it doesn't enter your mind you could do it. It's like looking through a shut glass door into a room that seems so tantalizing, but the door isn't open to you," she has observed. Curry has noted that viewers sometimes guess about her ethnic heritage. Viewers have thought she might be "Iranian, Eskimo, or Hispanic." Curry wonders if they were projecting their own hopes for television representation onto her appearance.

Curry works to make people aware of health issues. She uses her status as a public figure to promote education and preventive measures to fight diseases that have affected her own life. Curry advocates for breast cancer early detection and treatment. (Her sister is a survivor of breast cancer.) She also lends her name to awareness and research on gallbladder cancer. (Her mother died of this disease.) Curry also works on behalf of those individuals with AIDS. She publicizes all these health issues through a variety of charitable works, and by presenting news stories about them. Curry wrote the introduction for *Fighting for Our Future,* an authoritative book about breast cancer as it affects younger women like her sister. In a 2002 article about gallbladder cancer, Curry commented: "Before my mother died, she said 'I wish I had taken better care of myself.' Now I do what my mother wished she had done for herself. I drink water, do yoga, and eat an unbelievable amount of vegetables. That's the gift she left me."

Sources:

"Ann Curry" biography, *MSNBC News,* http://www.msnbc.com/onair/bios/a_curry.asp (accessed April 12, 2003).

Berman, Marc, "News Is a 'Ball' for Curry," *Daily Variety,* January 14, 2002, vol. 274, no. 31, p. B6.

Hack, Richard. *Madness in the Morning: Life and Death in TV's Early Morning Ratings War,* Beverly Hills, CA: New Millennium Press, 1999.

Slaughter, Adele, "Ann Curry Reports on Gallbladder Cancer," *Spotlight Health,* June 21, 2002, http://www.spotlighthealth.com/nasp/daily_article/daily_article2.asp?article_id+680 (accessed April 12, 2003).

Victoria Manolo Draves

Olympic diver
Born December 31, 1924, San Francisco, California

V icki Manolo Draves was formerly a national champion diver and the winner of two Olympic gold medals. In the 1948 Olympic Games she became the first woman to win gold medals in both the ten-meter platform and three-meter springboard events. After her Olympic victory she performed in aquacades (water shows) in Minnesota and Chicago, Illinois, and then toured Europe in an exhibition show with Buster Crabbe, the great Olympic swimmer and Hollywood film star.

Victoria Manolo was born on December 31, 1924, in San Francisco, California. Her parents were immigrants. Her father was born in the Philippines and her mother was born in England. While a high school student, Manolo became interested in diving and swimming and used to practice in downtown San Francisco at the Fairmount Hotel and at the Crystal Bath Plunge, both of which had public pools with diving boards. Manolo was already a gifted diver and she caught the attention of Phil Patterson, a well-known coach of an amateur swimming and diving team.

After graduating from high school in 1938, Manolo briefly attended San Francisco State Junior College, but ultimately withdrew when World War II broke out. She then began competing in earnest on the amateur diving circuit.

In 1941 Jack Lavery, who was associated with the Fairmount Swim Club, took an interest in Manolo. Because many Americans were prejudiced against all Asians during the years of World War II, Victoria used her mother's name (Taylor) to disguise her Filipino background when competing.

Sammy Lee as mentor

In 1943 **Sammy Lee** was a national diving champion. When he first saw Manolo dive in competition, he reports that he "was stunned by her natural abilities." After watching her dive, Lee introduced himself and told her that she would become a champion diver.

Manolo's first national competition was in 1944 in Shakemack, Indiana. She placed in the top four in her two events, the ten-meter platform and the three-meter springboard. The next year, Sammy Lee suggested she should find a more experienced coach. Coach Lyle Draves was coaching some of the world's best divers at the Athens Swim Club in Oakland, California. In 1945 Manolo began working with Draves and at that year's national championships placed in the top four again.

Their partnership went beyond the diving pool. In 1946 Manolo and Draves were married. That year, Victoria won the ten-meter platform competition, her first national championship.

A first for women Olympians

In 1948 Manolo Draves qualified for the Olympics, but just barely. The competition

Victoria Manolo Draves

was fierce, and Manolo Draves seemed to thrive on the pressure. She won gold medals in both of her events, becoming the first woman to win both diving events at the same Olympics.

When she returned to the United States after the 1948 Olympics, she was treated like a celebrity. She gave up competition, performing around the country in extravagant aquacades (swimming exhibitions), similar to the ice skating shows that are popular today. In 1952 she traveled to Europe to perform in a traveling aquacade there.

Victoria then gave up diving. She and Lyle began to raise a family. They had four children.

In 1969, Victoria Manolo Draves was inducted into the International Swimming Hall of Fame in Fort Lauderdale, Florida. After retiring from diving, she continued to make her home in California.

Sources:

"Victoria Manolo Draves," *International Swimming Hall of Fame,* http://www.ishof.org/HonorD.html#vdraves (accessed April 12, 2003).

March Fong Eu

Politician, ambassador
Born 1922, Oakdale, California

"I think a desire to change my circumstances, rather than any people, motivated me to do well in school. I recall having a very strong desire to succeed and to do some good to help others who might be situated similarly to me."

March Fong Eu is a longtime California politician who has broken new ground in nearly every position she has held. In the mid-1950s, she was the first woman and first Asian American member of the Alameda County Board of Education. In 1966, she became the first Asian American woman to serve in the California state legislature. After a distinguished career as a legislator, she went on to become California's first female secretary of state. In 1994, as she was serving her fifth term at that post, President Bill Clinton chose her to become U.S. Ambassador to Micronesia, a small island nation in the South Pacific. Eu has served in each of these positions with professionalism and grace, and in 1988, she was recognized for her long years of public service when *Ladies Home Journal* named her one of America's 100 Most Important Women.

Growing up in poverty

Eu was born March Fong in the back of the laundry her parents owned in the farming community of Oakdale, California. As a small child, Eu, the youngest of four, moved to Richmond, California, where hers was the only family of Chinese ancestry. The family was very poor, yet Eu was a highly motivated young girl in spite of obstacles she faced because of her race. "Two instances stand out in my mind," she told *Asian American Biography (AAB)*. "One was a discussion with my high school counselor during which I indicated that I wanted to become a teacher. He responded that that was not such a good choice since it would be very difficult for me to get a job because I was Chinese. The second instance was in a conversation with my high school bus driver. I recall very vividly... the bus driver talking to me about what I was going to be when I grew up. I remember saying something like, 'I sure like chemistry and I'm pretty good at it.' He replied that would be very good... because when I finished my studies I could go back and help my people in China.... The implication was that I was not American."

After graduation from high school, Eu attended Salinas Junior College for one year, then went on to the University of California at Berkeley, where she earned a bachelor of science degree. Following that she enrolled in Mills College in Oakland, where she earned a master's degree in education. She completed her education at Stanford University, earning a doctorate.

Commenting on the motivation behind her achievements, Eu said, "I don't recall having any [role models] as a youngster. In many ways I believe I was a self-made person in that I did not receive any encouragement to excel or strive for improvement from my parents or older brothers and sister.... I think a desire to change my circumstances, rather than any people, motivated me to do well in school. I recall having a very strong desire to succeed and to do some good to help others who might be situated similarly to me."

The beginnings of a political life

Eu worked for several years in the health care field before entering politics. Her first jobs were as a dental hygienist, a field in which she excelled, eventually being elected the first Asian American president of the American Dental Hygienist Association in 1956. She then worked as a professional health educator before taking an extended leave of absence from the professional world to raise her children. Her interest in the welfare of her children eventually led her to become active in political affairs, especially in working toward bettering their educational opportunities.

In 1956, Eu was elected to the Alameda County Board of Education. She served on that board for the next ten years, holding the office of president from 1961 to 1962. In

March Fong Eu

1966, she ran for the California State Assembly, becoming the state's first Asian American assemblywoman. She was reelected in 1968, 1970, and 1972. While in the legislature, Eu worked on behalf of women's rights, and lobbied for the creation of the California Commission on the Status of Women and worked on passing bills that improved child care facilities, established fair standards for pregnancy leave, and eliminated the requirement that women state their marital status when registering to vote. At the end of her fourth term, in 1974, Eu ran for secretary of state, winning the election by a record-setting margin.

Secretary of State

Eu's tenure as secretary of state made her an immensely popular public official. She organized and streamlined the management of the office. (Hers was one of the few state offices that generated more revenue than was required to run it.) Perhaps Eu's most celebrated reforms have been in the area of voting laws. In an effort to increase voter participation, she instituted a number of measures, including voter registration by mail, availability of bilingual (in two languages) ballots, accessibility of voting sites to the elderly and the handicapped, and cassette tapes of state ballot pamphlets for visually impaired voters. In 1986, Eu hired an elections investigator to look into allegations of misconduct on the part of petitioners, voter registration drive workers, and local election officials. In her later years as secretary of state, Eu devoted her considerable energy to working on crime and victims' rights issues. These efforts were prompted in part by an attack she suffered in her own home in 1986. She also worked hard to promote the export of California-made products and sponsored the creation of the California State World Trade Commission, serving as that organization's first chair.

Eu resigned from the secretary of state position in 1994 to accept an appointment from President Bill Clinton as the U.S. ambassador to the Federated States of Micronesia. Her responsibilities then focused on promoting cultural understanding between nations. She held that position until 1996, when she returned to California and continued working on trade and voting issues. In 2002 she campaigned unsuccessfully to return to the office of secretary of state for California, losing the election to Kevin Shelley.

Other interests

While her list of accomplishments as a government official is extensive, Eu's capabilities extend beyond this realm. She is also an artist of considerable skill, cultivating a talent she discovered during a trip to Taiwan in 1988. To relieve the stress of an intensive Mandarin language program, she took up brush painting and calligraphy. Since that time she has exhibited her work at several galleries, including the Pacific Asia Museum in Pasadena.

Eu is married to businessman Henry Eu, and the couple has two children. Eu's son, Mark, is an attorney and her daughter, Suyin, is a homemaker.

Sources:

Hirano, Steve, "March Fong Eu," *RICE,* November 1988.

Lyons, Steve, "March Fong Eu, Ed.D.: Breaking Barriers to Serve," *ACCESS,* July 1992.

Office of the Secretary of State (California), "Eu Hosts Groundbreaking Ceremony for New Building," news release, June 24, 1992.

Wong, Jerrye, "Friends and Supporters Clamoring for Eu Originals," *Asian Week,* May 24, 1991.

Wong, Jerrye, "Supporters Gather to Hear Eu Take Oath for Fifth Term," *Asian Week,* January 1, 1991.

Hiram Fong

Politician, attorney, gardener
Born October 1, 1907, Honolulu, Hawaii

From the time he was four until he was seven, Fong worked on a plantation picking beans, which were sold as cattle feed. He was paid ten cents for each 30-pound bag. From age seven to age ten he shined shoes and sold newspapers on the streets of Honolulu.

W hen Hiram Leong Fong was chosen as Hawaii's first senator in 1959, he became the first American of Asian descent to be elected to the U.S. Senate. A Republican, Fong went on to serve Hawaii for three terms. His position as senator was the crowning achievement of a lifetime of civic, political, and business leadership.

Before becoming a senator, Fong had served in Hawaii's territorial legislature from 1938 to 1954, including four years as vice-speaker of the house of representatives and six years as speaker. He was vice president of the Hawaii State Constitutional Convention held in 1950, and was a longtime, enthusiastic supporter of Hawaiian statehood. Since his retirement from the U.S. Senate in 1977, Fong has established himself as a very successful businessman.

A childhood in poverty

Fong was born in the Kalihi district of Honolulu, Hawaii, on October 1, 1907, the seventh of eleven children. Both his parents were immigrants from Kwangtung Province, China. His father, Lum, was a laborer on a sugar cane plantation who had left China for Hawaii at age 15. His mother immigrated to Hawaii at age ten and worked as a maid.

The family was poor, and the neighborhood they lived in was "rough and tumble," Fong told *Asian American Biography (AAB)*. From the time he was four until he was seven, he worked on a plantation picking beans, which were sold as cattle feed. He was paid ten cents for each 30-pound bag. From age seven to age ten he shined shoes and sold newspapers on the streets of Honolulu. Later he caught and sold fish and crabs, delivered poi (a Hawaiian food made from the root of a tropical plant), and caddied at a local golf course, where he was paid 25 cents for nine holes.

Fong graduated from McKinley High School in Honolulu and then went on to study at the University of Hawaii. There he was the editor of the school newspaper, associate editor of the yearbook, and on the debating, volleyball, and rifle teams. (He competed at the National Rifle Championships in 1929.) In 1930, after only three years of study, he graduated with honors with a bachelor of arts degree.

Fong continued his education at Harvard University, where he studied law. He had to leave school twice temporarily to save money to continue his studies, but in 1935, after working to support himself since the age of four, Fong earned his law degree from Harvard.

The beginning of a distinguished career

After graduating from Harvard, Fong formed the multi-ethnic law firm of Fong, Miho, Choy, and Robinson. He also began his career in public service by serving as the deputy attorney for the city and county of Honolulu. He held that post until 1938, when he was elected to the territorial legislature. He served in the legislature for 14 years, all the while working for Hawaiian statehood. And in 1959, when the territory became the forty-ninth state, he was elected to the U.S. Senate as its first senator.

In the Senate, Fong worked hard for the people of his newly established state. He demanded that Hawaii get its fair share of federal funds for the national highway construction programs of the 1960s. The federal government reasoned that since Hawaii didn't have any roads connecting it to other states, it didn't qualify for funds. Fong challenged this thinking and won $50 million to build highways that would connect military installations.

Fong also worked to improve civil rights. He helped pass laws that would make it easier for native islanders and immigrants to vote. He voted in favor of the Civil Rights Act of 1964 and played a major role in the passage of sweeping immigration reforms in 1965. In an interview with *AAB*, Fong said he was generally in favor of President Lyndon Johnson's sweeping social welfare legislation known as the Great Society programs. He described his own political beliefs as liberal when it came to social policy and as conservative when it came to the military and to financial policy, especially taxes.

Fong describes himself as having been generally "hawkish" on the Vietnam War; he believes that the war could have been won if the Democrats had not blocked more financial support. During the Nixon administration, Fong worked closely with the

Hiram Fong

Republican White House—the first of his Senate career—in the areas of minorities and hiring, and he helped to bring about several high-level minority appointments.

Fong founded and serves on the board of many corporations. He is an honorary consultant to China Airlines and an honorary member of the board of directors of the Lincoln University Foundation.

Fong served in the U.S. Army Air Corps from 1942 to 1944, where he achieved the rank of major. He continued serving in the reserves for 20 years and currently holds the rank of retired colonel. He has 11 honorary degrees and dozens of other honors.

Gardener

Many people take up gardening when they retire, but not so many go to the extent that Fong has. In 1950, Fong purchased a plot of land near the Ko'lau Mountains to serve as a ranch area for his children's horses. But with an interest in gardening and nature, he kept adding on to his purchase. The result is the current 725-acre park known as Senator Fong's Plantation and Gardens. The park is open to tourists, and features landscaped gardens, tropical forests with more than 75 varieties of edible fruits and nuts, and a panoramic view of the Koolau Mountains and Kaneoho Bay.

Fong tries to find time each day to work in his gardens and is always considering new additions and improvements to what he considers to be a work in progress.

Sources:

Financial Factors, Ltd., "Biographical Sketch: Hiram Leong Fong," promotional material, Honolulu, Hawaii, June 1, 1993.

Fong, Hiram, telephone interview with Jim Henry, April 4, 1994.

Senator Fong's Plantation and Gardens, http://www.fonggarden.com (accessed March 2003).

Ben Fong-Torres

Author, journalist
Born January 7, 1945, Oakland, California

"It was a dream job. Rock and Roll—and no more suits."

Ben Fong-Torres was a founding editor of *Rolling Stone* magazine, the counterculture music magazine that helped define the 1960s and is still influential today. As a writer and editor at the magazine, he interviewed some of the biggest names in the history of popular music, including Bob Dylan; the Beatles; Crosby, Stills, Nash and Young; Jefferson Airplane; and the Rolling Stones. He was a disc jockey at KSAN in San Francisco, one of the pre-eminent FM stations in FM radio's heyday, wrote a column on radio and regularly contributed features to the *San Francisco Chronicle*, and has been published in such magazines as *Playboy, GQ, Esquire,* and *Sports Illustrated.* Fong-Torres has written three books and served as editor of a third. His 1994 book, an autobiography, is titled *The Rice Room: Growing Up Chinese American, From Number Two Son to Rock 'N' Roll.* It received excellent reviews as a landmark chronicle of the 1960s and as evidence of an Asian American making a significant mark on American popular culture.

Mai fong

Fong-Torres was the third of five children born to Fong Kwok Shang and Soo Hoo Tui Wing, both Chinese immigrants.

Fong-Torres's father, Kwok Shang, had immigrated by way of the Philippines, where he paid $1,200 for the birth certificate of a dead Filipino named Ricardo Torres. (He then combined his real surname with his assumed surname.) He was forced to do this to get around the infamous 1882 Chinese Exclusion Act, a law that barred Chinese immigration into the United States except in very limited instances. When Fong-Torres was born in 1945, the family owned a Chinese restaurant in Oakland's Chinatown called the New Eastern Cafe. As a child, Fong-Torres and his siblings would spend hours every day at the restaurant, marveling at the hectic pace and playing in the back room, known as the *mai fong,* or the rice room.

Fong-Torres was educated in the public schools and from the time he was eight, his parents saw to it that he was also schooled in Chinese culture at the local Chinese Community Center. Still, Fong-Torres and his older brother Barry were enraptured by America and its popular culture. They secretly read comic books and listened to the burgeoning phenomenon known as rock and roll. In high school, where he was a B student, Fong-Torres became interested in journalism and broadcasting and got a part-time job with a local top-40 radio station. He also filled several posts in student government.

In 1962, Fong-Torres enrolled in San Francisco State College. In his junior year he joined the college paper and the radio station. Through the school, he became host of a public affairs show about comedy on a local FM station and was selected to be one of 12 student hosts of "Records at Random," a live, one-hour show on the most

Ben Fong-Torres

popular radio station in town, KFSO. During his senior year in college, Fong-Torres was named editor of the school newspaper and took a job with a local community paper, the *Oakland Times.*

Rock and roll–and no more suits

The 1960s were very intense years on college campuses in America, and San Francisco State emerged as one of the most politically radical campuses in the country. The school newspaper reflected this radicalism, and Fong-Torres went through major changes in his views about politics and the U.S. government during these years. After graduating from college in 1967, he took a job as a midnight-to-dawn disc jockey on easy listening station KFOG, where, sometimes at night—to amuse himself—he would play music of his own choosing. From there he took a job at a new television station as a writer. Then, in late 1967, one of his roommates brought home a copy of a new magazine called *Rolling Stone*.

At first, Fong-Torres wrote small stories for the new journal and didn't really think much would ever come of it. As he wrote in *The Rice Room*, "I thought of *Rolling Stone* more as an entertaining side job than as any kind of a career." But within two years he was writing for the magazine regularly, and in May of 1969, *Rolling Stone*'s legendary founder, Jann Wenner, offered Fong-Torres a job at about $150 less a month than he was making at the time. He wrote in *The Rice Room*, "It was a dream job. Rock and Roll—and no more suits."

Fong-Torres took the title of news editor, though there was little formality at the magazine and everybody chipped in on all aspects of production. As a reporter he covered a variety of music events in the San Francisco Bay Area, then the international center of the rock music scene. He reported the comings and goings of the Grateful Dead, the Jefferson Airplane, Janis Joplin, Joni Mitchell, the concert promoter Bill Graham, and all sorts of other rock and roll legends. Through it all he maintained close ties to his family, still helping out at the family restaurant, though there were occasional confrontations with his parents over his lifestyle and the length of his hair. It was at this time that Fong-Torres

started work as a disc jockey at KSAN; it was supposed to be a temporary assignment, but he ended up staying for eight years. While there, he wrote and narrated the syndicated show, "San Francisco: What a Long Strange Trip it's Been."

Family tragedy

In the summer of 1972, Fong-Torres's brother Barry, who was working as a youth counselor in San Francisco's Chinatown, was mysteriously murdered outside of his apartment. It was widely assumed to be the work of one of the gangs that were beginning to terrorize the neighborhood. The murder, of course, devastated the family, and Fong-Torres especially. The brothers had been very close; Barry had introduced Ben to rock and roll. From the tragedy, though, came a little light, when Fong-Torres received a sympathy card from a girl he'd known in high school, Dianne Sweet. In 1974, they moved in together and in 1976, they were married. His parents were scandalized by his marrying a white woman, but they eventually came to accept her.

In 1977, *Rolling Stone* moved its offices from San Francisco to New York. Fong-Torres stayed behind and became West Coast editor. He also worked on many of Wenner's other projects, including anthologies, radio shows, and, in 1977, a television special that aired on CBS entitled *Rolling Stone–The Tenth Anniversary Special*. He even tried his hand at screenwriting. By 1981, Fong-Torres felt that his time at *Rolling Stone* was coming to a close. Anything he wanted to write was published in the magazine, but, he wondered, how would he fare on his own? Would his writing be good enough to sell to other magazines?

He quickly found out that it would be. He wrote features for such magazines as *Esquire, Playboy, GQ,* and *Parade.* And then, in 1982, he got what he called "the assignment of a lifetime" when he was invited by a film producer to "go to China for three weeks, to either write about or help write the script for a TV documentary called *Cycling Through China.*" In preparation for this assignment he went to his parents to find out all they could tell him about China. They told him about their lives there and suggested that while he was there he visit some of his relatives. He had never really heard of any of these people before, but his parents had been keeping them abreast of events on the American side of the family.

During the trip, Fong-Torres took time out to find his mother's village and to visit many relatives living there. In his autobiography he wrote of his mother's cousin's house in a small village: "On the back wall was a large, framed photograph of my grandmother. It was the same picture I'd seen so often as a child in Oakland. And along a side wall, several long frames held montages of photos, one of them devoted to my immediate family. There we were—in grade school, graduating from high school, getting married— our life histories hanging on a wall in southern China." In discussing this experience later with *Transpacific* magazine he said, "They were strangers and they had a better collection of my life's story than I did.... It forces you to sit back and gives you a whole new idea of what family's all about."

From 1983–1992, Fong-Torres was a feature writer and radio columnist for the *San Fransisco Chronicle.* He then worked as managing editor for *Gavin,* a San Francisco trade weekly for the radio and recording industries. He took time out to write *The Hits Just Keep on Coming: The History of Top 40 Radio,* published in 1998. The next year he became editorial director of myplay.com, an Internet music site. He still contributes articles to the Web site, Asian-Connections.com, and is an advisor to the Rock and Roll Hall of Fame.

The freelance writer

Fong-Torres continues to write for major magazines and newspapers across the country. In 1991 he wrote his first book, *Hickory Wind: The Life and Times of Gram Parsons,* about the legendary pioneer of country rock. A new edition was published in 1998. Commenting on his 1994 autobiography, *The Rice Room,* writer Amy Tan noted, "Ben Fong-Torres gives us a wonderfully poignant and sometimes hilarious portrait of growing up American—from Chinatown kitchens and talent shows of the '50s to the Age of Aquarius in San Francisco and the hotel rooms of the rock stars."

In 1999, Fong-Torres completed his book *Not Fade Away: A Backstage Pass to 20 Years of Rock and Roll,* a compilation of past articles.

Sources:

Ben Fong-Torres, http://www.benfongtorres.com (accessed March 2003).

Collabrys, http://www.collabrys.com (accessed March 2003).

Fong-Torres, Ben, *The Rice Room: Growing Up Chinese American, From Number Two Son to Rock 'N' Roll,* Westport, CT: Hyperion Press, 1994.

Tuber, Keith, "Rolling Writer," *Transpacific,* June 1994, p. 26.

John L. Fugh

Military officer, attorney
Born September 12, 1934, Beijing, China

Fugh was the first Chinese American to be pro-moted to general officer status in the history of the military, and he served a distinguished term as judge advocate general of the army—the ser-vice's top uniformed attorney.

Major General John L. Fugh spent more than 30 years in ser-vice to the United States as an officer in the U.S. Army. He was the first Chinese Ameri-can to be promoted to general officer status in the history of the military and he served a distinguished term as judge advocate gen-eral of the army—the service's top uni-formed attorney—from 1987 until his retirement in 1993. Since his retirement, Fugh has joined the prestigious Washing-ton, D.C., law firm of McGuire, Woods, Battle, and Boothe, one of the nation's 40 largest firms.

A childhood of war

When Fugh was born, China was par-tially occupied by the Japanese, who were in the midst of an expansionist drive across much of Asia. It was a bloody and defiantly resisted occupation that ended in 1945 when the United States defeated the Japanese in World War II with the dropping of atomic bombs on the civilian populations of Nagasaki and Hiroshima in Japan. The retreat of the Japanese, however, did not bring a sustained peace to mainland China.

A civil war broke out between the postwar government of Chiang Kai-shek and the communist insurgency led by Mao Zedong. In 1948, one year before Mao's final victory, the Fugh family fled the mainland via Hong Kong, where they were able to obtain visas to immigrate to the United States.

The family settled in the Washington, D.C., area, where Fugh attended the public schools. After graduation from high school he went to Georgetown University, where he studied at the school of foreign service. He graduated with a bachelor's degree in inter-national relations in 1957. He then became an American citizen and enrolled in the George Washington University Law School. After graduating from law school he enlisted in the army and was commissioned as an officer in the judge advocate general corps.

The judge advocate general corps

The judge advocate general corps, where Fugh spent the entirety of his military career, consists of thousands of attorneys and other legal professionals stationed all over the world who represent the U.S. mili-tary's legal interests. Fugh completed train-ing as an infantry officer and then graduated from the Judge Advocate General School. In 1961 he was appointed an assistant staff judge advocate at the Presidio of San Fran-cisco. He held this position until 1964. Since this first assignment, Fugh has served four tours of duty in California, Europe, Viet-nam, Taiwan, and Washington, D.C. He went on to graduate from the Army Com-mand and General Staff College, the Army War College, and Harvard University's John F. Kennedy School of Government.

John L. Fugh

In 1984 Fugh was promoted to brigadier general and became assistant judge advocate general for civil law, where he created the Procurement Fraud and Environmental Law divisions to help minimize purchasing abuses and environmental damage. He then consolidated the administration of all army litigation functions in the newly established Army Litigation Center.

Army's number-one lawyer

In 1987 Fugh was promoted to the judge advocate general (TJAG). In that capacity,

he served as the legal advisor to the chief of staff of the army and the military legal advisor to the secretary of the army and the army secretariat. Fugh was widely credited with advancing the reputation of the corps and increasing the army's role in addressing environmental concerns. Indeed, the impact of military operations on the environment was a primary concern of Fugh's throughout his career. The seriousness of the problem was underscored by the unprecedented environmental catastrophe caused by the Kuwaiti oil well fires set by retreating Iraqi soldiers in the Persian Gulf War (in which the United States supported Kuwait in defending its interests against Iraq).

After the Gulf War, Fugh established legal assistance for families of veterans of the conflict. In other areas, he founded a program for human rights training in developing countries and published the *War Crimes Report,* the first documentation of worldwide war crimes since World War II. He also successfully led the army through controversial lawsuits involving promotion policies, its homosexual exclusion policy, and its conscientious objector policy. (Conscientious objectors refuse to serve in the military because of their moral or religious beliefs.) Another of Fugh's career achievements was the establishment of a legal support system to protect military doctors in malpractice suits.

Recognition

In recognition of all that he accomplished in three decades of service, Fugh has received many awards and military commendations. Among these are the Defense Superior Service Medal, the Legion of Merit with oak leaf cluster, the Meritorious Service Medal with oak leaf cluster, the Air Medal, the Joint Service Commendation Medal, and the Army Commendation Medal with oak leaf cluster. At his retirement ceremonies in 1993, the chief of staff of the army awarded Fugh the Distinguished Service Medal. In addition, Fugh was selected Man of the Year in 1994 by the Chinese American Planning Council of New York City, a major social service organization.

Since his retirement, Fugh has held key positions. Fugh worked for the law firm of McGuire, Woods, Battle, and Boothe as a partner in its Washington, D.C., offices. He also served McDonnell Douglas China, and Enron China. Since 2000, he has been working with the Spectrum Group, a consulting services organization that works with federal agencies.

Fugh is married to the former June Chung of Washington, D.C. They have two children, both of whom are attorneys.

Sources:

Spectrum Group, http://www.spectrumgrp.com (accessed March 2003).

U.S. Army, "Major Fugh Retires," press release, Washington, D.C., 1993.

Roman Gabriel

Professional football player
Born August 5, 1940, Wilmington, North Carolina

"I've never quit; I've never given up on anything, and I think that's the way it should be. I don't know any other way."

R oman Gabriel is known as one of the greatest, most dynamic quarterbacks of the National Football League (NFL). He played for the Los Angeles Rams from 1962 until 1973, during which time he was chosen as the team's most valuable player three times. He was named to the All-Pro Team four times, was voted Most Valuable Player (MVP) of the 1969 Pro-Bowl game, and was named the league's most valuable player that year as well. After the Rams let him go, Gabriel signed with the Philadelphia Eagles, with whom he played for five years. In his first year with the Eagles he was named Comeback Player of the Year in the NFL. Since retiring from professional football, Gabriel has done some acting and worked as a sports broadcaster. He is currently president and general manager of the Charlotte Knights Class AA baseball team in Charlotte, North Carolina. He also breeds Arabian horses and operates a series of sports training centers.

The son of an immigrant

Gabriel's father was a Filipino immigrant who supported his family by working as a cook for the Atlantic Coast Line Railroad. Gabriel attended New Hanover High School

Roman Gabriel

in Wilmington, North Carolina, where he became an excellent all-around athlete. He was an All-State, All-American quarterback on the football team, an All-Conference baseball player, and a conference MVP in basketball. Gabriel graduated from high school in 1958. He was so talented in baseball that he was offered a contract with the New York Yankees. He decided against that, however, when he was offered a football scholarship to attend North Carolina State University.

In college, Gabriel continued playing several sports but concentrated his efforts on football. When he was a sophomore, he led the nation in pass completions, throwing with a 60.4 percent accuracy rate. In 1960 and 1961, he was named Athlete of the Year in the Atlantic Coast Conference, an All-American, and Football Player of the Year. In addition to distinguishing himself in three sports, Gabriel, an excellent student, was named a Scholastic All-American. He also received the Teague Award as Carolina's most outstanding amateur athlete and was a two-time recipient of the Governor's Award. His college career passing yardage was 2,951 yards, and as a junior and senior he accounted for more than 50 percent of his team's offensive yardage. He graduated in 1962 with a degree in physical education and high hopes for a career in professional football.

Early problems

Many college coaches considered Gabriel one of the greatest college passers of all time. In the 1962 NFL draft, he was a highly sought-after player, and there was great speculation about where this remarkable young athlete would land. He was finally drafted by the Los Angeles Rams and became their backup quarterback. That he played backup instead of starting became a point of contention between Gabriel—who, along with many observers, felt that a quarterback (QB) of his caliber should be used regularly—and the Rams coaching staff, who were solidly behind starter Zeke Bratkowski. There were also problems with the team's performance. In 1962, the team compiled a dismal 1-12-1 record, and in November, the coach, Bob Waterfield, retired. Gabriel did manage to start four games and was selected as the quarterback of the NFL's All-Rookie team. He also established an NFL record for fewest interceptions (two) in more than a hundred passing attempts.

The next year the Rams' problems continued. A new coach, Harland Svare, was hired, and Heisman Trophy-winning quarterback Terry Baker was drafted, making Gabriel third string. *Peterson's Pro Football Annual* wrote, "Baker was nurtured as the coming Ram quarterback though his long passes were floaters compared to Gabriel's cannonades." Gabriel was quoted as saying, "When you have a coach come in with a different system, he doesn't know you and you don't know him. So you really never have a chance to be accepted. You have no chance to build confidence with one guy... or even with the same team, because we had players being shipped out as well as coaches."

Gabriel started nine of fourteen games in the 1963 season and eventually beat out Baker for the starting QB job. In the off-season, however, the Rams used their first-round draft choice to pick another quarterback, Bill Munson of Utah State, further undermining Gabriel's sense of security and confidence. In the second exhibition game of the 1964 season Gabriel suffered a knee injury that would keep him sidelined until October. Munson started the first few games and, after Gabriel's knee healed, he and Gabriel alternated in the starting post. Munson's play excelled toward the end of the season, and he was given the permanent nod as the starter. Gabriel discussed these early, discouraging years in *Peterson's,* admitting, "All of these things add up and become hardships, and it's easy to say to yourself, 'Maybe I should get out... maybe I should quit.' But I've never quit; I've never given up on anything, and I think that's the way it should be. I don't know any other way."

A new coach, a new chance

In 1966, the Rams hired George Allen as their new head coach, and he made Gabriel starting quarterback. That year the Rams had their first winning season in years, going 8-6. Gabriel set a Rams' single-season record with 217 completions in 397 attempts, passing for 2,540 yards. The next season, 1967, the Rams' startling turnaround became even more startling: they finished with a record of 11-1-2 and made it to the National Football Conference (NFC) Championship game, losing to the Green Bay Packers. Gabriel again had a remarkeable season, completing 196 of 371 passes for 2,779 yards. He set another Rams' single-season record with 25 touchdown passes.

By 1968, Gabriel had proven himself to such an extent that he began calling his own plays. The team was hungry from losing in the NFC Championship game the season before, and they wanted to go all the way. Although they didn't make it, Gabriel considers the season one of the most important of his career. That year the team posted a 10-3-1 mark, and Gabriel completed 184 of 366 passes for 2,364 yards and 19 touchdowns.

The 1969 season was Gabriel's finest. The team finished with an 11-2-1 record and lost to the Minnesota Vikings in the Western Conference Championship game. Gabriel tied his passing record of 217 completions and set a new record for attempts at 399. He passed for a total of 2,549 yards and scored 24 touchdowns. He was given the NFL's Most Valuable Player Award—the Jim Thorpe Trophy—by the Associated Press, United Press International, the Columbus Touchdown Club, and the Maxwell Club of Philadelphia.

During the next three seasons Gabriel continued delivering outstanding performances. In 1970, he broke his own club record for passing attempts and maintained a completion record of over 50 percent, averaging 2,272 yards and 15 touchdowns per season.

Traded to Philadelphia

In 1973, after 11 seasons with the Rams, Gabriel was traded to the Philadelphia Eagles. It was thought that he was nearing retirement and the Rams needed a younger quarterback. In his first season with the Eagles, however, Gabriel set a personal record of 270 completions of 460 attempted passes for 3,219 yards and 23 touchdowns, numbers far exceeding even his MVP year with the Rams. Gabriel transformed the Eagles from one of the worst offensive teams in the NFL into the league's second most powerful. For this he was named Comeback Player of the Year. Gabriel played well in 1974 and 1975, but injuries plagued him as he approached his mid-thirties, an advanced age for football players. In 1976, he underwent his fifth operation on his knee and played in only the last four games of the season. Gabriel retired from professional football after the 1977 season with 201 touchdown passes, 30 rushing touchdowns, 149 interceptions, and 2,366 completions in 4,498 attempts for 29,444 yards.

Life after the NFL

Since retiring from the NFL, Gabriel has been active in coaching both at the college and professional levels. He was the quarterback coach of the Arizona Wranglers and offensive coordinator of the Boston Breakers—both of the short-lived World Football League—and head coach of the Raleigh-Durham (North Carolina) Skyhawks of the World League of American Football, another now-defunct challenger to the NFL. He also spent three seasons as head coach at the California Polytechnic Institute in Pomona. He has served as a sports analyst for CBS television and radio and has even done a little acting, appearing on such television shows as *Sheriff Lobo, Wonder Woman,* and *Ironside,* and in the John Wayne film *The Undefeated.*

Later in his retirement, Gabriel returned to his home state of North Carolina, where he serves as president and general manager of the Charlotte Knights Class AA baseball team. He is also active in the community as a board member of the Greater Carolinas Chapter for Multiple Sclerosis, the Center for the Blind in Phoenix, Arizona, and the Onslow County Charities in Jacksonville, North Carolina. In addition, he has served as vice president of the Carolinas Chapter of the National Football League's Alumni Association.

He was inducted into the College Football Hall of Fame and the North Carolina Sports Hall of Fame. He currently owns and operates the Roman Gabriel Sports Connection. In 1997, his hometown honored him as the first inductee to have a star on the Celebrate Wilmington! Walk of Fame.

Sources:

Baker, Hugh, "It Takes Six Years," *Peterson's Pro Football Annual,* 1970.

Charlotte Knights Baseball Club, "Biography, Roman Gabriel," press release, Charlotte, NC.

Los Angeles Rams, press release, Los Angeles, CA.

South East Public Interest Network of North Carolina, http://www.spinnc.org (accessed March 2003).

Twentieth Century Fox, "Biography of Roman Gabriel," press release, Beverly Hills, CA.

Lillian Gonzalez-Pardo

Physician
Born February 5, 1939, Manila, the Philippines

"When I arrived in this country to start my post-graduate training with a few dollars in one pocket and a stethoscope in the other, the only dream in my heart was to be the best neurologist I could be."

L illian Gonzalez-Pardo was the first Asian American woman to serve as president of the American Medical Women's Association. A clinical professor of pediatrics and neurology (the study of the nervous system) at the University of Kansas Medical Center in Kansas City, Kansas, she has worked to promote better health care for women and children, both nationally and internationally.

Gonzalez-Pardo was born February 5, 1939, in Manila, Philippines. Her maternal grandmother's influence during her early childhood helped Lillian learn responsibility, organization, good manners, and proper conduct. Her parents, especially her father, a lawyer, encouraged her to pursue education as a means to higher achievement in life.

Following her father's advice, Gonzalez-Pardo enrolled in the University of the Philippines in Quezon City. She graduated with an associate of arts in premed in 1957 and a doctor of medicine in 1962. In 1961 she served an internship at Philippines General Hospital in Manila. She received her certifi-

Lillian Gonzalez-Pardo

until 1967, Gonzalez-Pardo was a resident at UKMC, first in neurology, then in child psychiatry. In 1967 she became a fellow in pediatric neurology at Children's Mercy Hospital in Kansas City, Missouri. After taking time off to teach in the Philippines, she returned to UKMC, where she was a fellow in developmental pediatrics from 1972 until 1973 and a resident in pediatrics, beginning in 1974.

Physician and teacher

Gonzalez-Pardo returned to the Philippines in 1969. She was an instructor of medicine at the University of the Philippines College of Medicine in Manila from July 1969 to April 1971. She also was a consultant in neurology at three Manila hospitals: Philippines General Hospital, Metropolitan General Hospital, and Quezon Institute.

She continued her teaching in 1975, when she became an assistant professor of pediatrics and neurology at the University of Kansas School of Medicine. From 1979 until 1981 she also worked as the medical director of the Children's Rehabilitation Unit/University Affiliated Facility at UKMC. In 1980 she was granted American citizenship. Gonzalez-Pardo became a full clinical professor at UKMC in 1992. While continuing in this position, she earned a master's degree in health services administration at the University of Kansas.

Apart from her teaching duties, Gonzalez-Pardo has also been active in many medical and community associations. She has served on the board of directors of several medical organizations. Her greatest dedication, however, has been to the American Medical Women's Association (AMWA).

cation from the Philippines Medical Board in May 1962.

Gonzalez-Pardo then traveled to the United States to pursue her postgraduate training at the University of Kansas Medical Center (UKMC) in Kansas City, Kansas. She recalled, "When I arrived in this country to start my post-graduate training with a few dollars in one pocket and a stethoscope in the other, the only dream in my heart was to be the best neurologist I could be."

When she arrived in Kansas City to begin her residency, she met Dr. Manuel Pardo, whom she married a year later. From 1963

American Medical Women's Association

Since 1979 Gonzalez-Pardo has held many positions with AMWA on both the local and national levels. In 1992 she became national president, the first Asian American to serve as president in the history of the association. In her president's address before the 1992 Midwest Regional Conference of AMWA, she stated, "AMWA is committed to the development of an advanced women's health curriculum for physicians to provide improved and integrated health care to women patients." She called for the AMWA to be involved in politics, public and professional education, and worldwide conferences. She believes in increased biomedical research for women, reproductive rights, and sharing resources with other countries to improve the health care of women and children globally.

Gonzalez-Pardo also used her term as AMWA president to promote cultural diversity, especially drawing attention to Asian Americans. She developed the Asian American Women Physicians Project, in cooperation with the Archives and Special Collection on Women in Medicine of the Medical College of Pennsylvania. The goal of the project is to develop educational materials about Asian American women physicians, both past and the present.

Despite her many professional commitments, Gonzalez-Pardo has been active in numerous community organizations. She has been a member of the Asian Council of Greater Kansas City, the Filipino Association of Greater Kansas City, and one of the founders of the Filipino Cultural Center. Moreover, she has been involved with the Mid-Continent Regional Educational Laboratory Project, which encourages girls to pursue careers in science, engineering, and mathematics, and the National Research Council's Committee on Women in Science and Engineering, among many other groups.

For her dedication as a physician and a citizen, Gonzalez-Pardo has received several awards. She was named the Outstanding Alumnus of the University of the Philippines College of Medicine in 1991. The same year, the University of the Philippines Alumni Association bestowed on her the Outstanding Alumnus Community Service Award. And in May 1993 she was given the Excellence 2000 Award as Outstanding Asian American by the U.S. Pan Asian American Pacific Chamber of Commerce in Washington, D.C.

A role model both as a woman physician and an Asian American, Gonzalez-Pardo said at the close of her term as president of AMWA: "It is my hope that others like me will follow, that I have paved the way to promote the cultural diversity that this country needs to recognize. Be challenged, as I was, with these words from [First Lady] Eleanor Roosevelt, 'You must do the things you think you cannot do.'"

Gonzalez-Pardo and her husband have three children: Manuel, Jr., who is also a doctor, Lillie, and Patrick. The couple resides in Mission Hills, Kansas.

Sources:

Asian American and Pacific Islander Journal of Health, vol. 2, no. 1, winter 1994.

Gonzalez-Pardo, Lillian, M.D., "The Heart of the Matter," Third Midwest Regional Conference on Women in Medicine.

Gonzalez-Pardo, Lillian G., M.D., professional resume, 1994.

Journal of the American Medical Women's Association (JAMWA), May-June 1992; September-October 1992; November-December 1994.

Philip Kan Gotanda

Playwright, filmmaker
Born December 17, 1951, Stockton, California

"Artistic expression by Asian Americans is here to stay. I sense the passion."

Acclaimed playwright Philip Kan Gotanda has found success in the cultural mainstream despite the prejudice many Asian Americans experience as they try to express themselves in the United States. Gotanda, whose career as a writer for the theater came about "by accident," has won much praise for plays such as *The Wash* and *Fish Head Soup*. In 1993, he was awarded a three-year grant from the prestigious Lila Wallace-*Reader's Digest* Fund. He also has been honored with Guggenheim, Rockefeller, National Endowment of the Arts, and McKnight fellowships, and received the Pen/West award for writing in 1996.

Elvis as role model

Born in Stockton, California, on December 17, 1951, Gotanda was the youngest in a family of three boys. He is a third-generation Japanese American, descended on both sides from immigrants from Hiroshima, Japan. Gotanda told *Asian American Biography* *(AAB)* that he had "a very good childhood" and claimed that an early role model was rock and roll pioneer Elvis Presley. "I *really* liked him when I was growing up," he remarked with a chuckle.

In 1969, Gotanda began studying at the University of California at Santa Cruz, where he remained for only a couple of years. He traveled to Japan, then returned to California, this time to the University of California at Berkeley. But he didn't stay long, moving on to the University of California at Santa Barbara, where he earned a degree in Japanese art in 1974. He went on to law school and eventually found work as a legal aide in San Francisco.

Gotanda also began to write music, completing a musical titled *The Avocado Kid.* He sent the script to East West Players, and in 1980, his first production was staged. Suddenly, he found himself writing for the theater. Gradually, he moved away from musicals to plays. "I became more interested in the spoken word, in hearing characters talk," he explained.

The following year, Gotanda wrote *Song for a Nisei Fisherman,* the saga of a Japanese American family that featured some elements of Gotanda's own life. It was first produced by San Francisco's Asian American Theater Company. He followed up with *The Dream of Kitamura,* a fantasy/fairy tale set in ancient Japan, which premiered in 1984.

Gotanda earned national praise for his next play, *The Wash,* an emotional depiction of the troubled marriage of an older couple. First staged at San Francisco's Eureka Theater in 1987, the play was made into an American Playhouse film for public television in 1988, and two years later it was staged by the Manhattan Theater Club in a coproduction with Los Angeles's esteemed Mark Taper Forum.

Yankee Dawg You Die, a play about two actors, opened at the Berkeley Repertory Company in 1988 and went on to New York's Playwrights Horizon in 1990. In 1992, Gotanda received some of his best reviews for *Fish Head Soup,* which also premiered at the Berkeley Repertory Company. In this portrait of a Japanese American family, a long-lost son returns to his home, bringing with him a variety of emotional problems that he and his family must face.

Branched out to film

For a period after *Fish Head Soup,* Gotanda stopped writing plays. In the meantime, he wrote, directed, and starred in a short film, *The Kiss.* It was about a downtrodden, harassed office worker who, during his lunch hour in a crowded restaurant, quietly, heroically saves a person's life with a single kiss. *The Kiss* played at the 1993 Sundance, Berlin, Edinburgh, and Asian American film festivals to favorable reviews.

Gotanda wrote his next work, *Day Standing on Its Head,* in just two and a half weeks. "Sometimes you have to get out of the way of the writing and not worry so much about being in control. Writing *Day* was a process of just letting it come out of me, to put it out there and not worry," he told *AAB.* Next, Gotanda wrote *The Ballad of Yachiyo.* Set on the Hawaiian island of Kauai, the play is based on the life of an older aunt who died tragically in the early 1900s.

In 1996, Gotanda returned to the Sundance Film Festival to present his 30-

Philip Kan Gotanda

minute film *Drinking Tea.* Following this success, he set his mind to producing a feature-length film. First, though, he studied more about screenwriting and film production as a Sundance Film Fellow in 1998. The result of his labors was the feature length film *Life Tastes Good,* presented at the Festival in 1999 to great reviews. In 2002, Gotanda stepped back to play writing to complete *Wind Cries Mary,* an adaptation of the Henrik Ibsen play *Hedda Gabber.*

Sisters Matsumoto, another Gotanda play, is about three sisters and how they pieced their lives together after their stay in an Arkansas internment camp during World War II.

Gotanda is optimistic about the way Asian American arts have developed in the 1990s. "Artistic expression by Asian Americans is here to stay. I sense the passion. There is a need to express ourselves. There are people literally trying to kill you out there, so you must answer that need to speak and be heard... to say 'Hey, we're here, look at us, we're not going away and you're not going to make us disappear.' What we're doing as a community is to rethink, to re-envision who we are as Asian Americans, to figure out how we're all going to live together and still have our own community."

The success of his first film, *The Kiss*, has inspired Gotanda to pursue a new feature-length endeavor: "It's about a man, similar to the guy in *The Kiss*. He works in an antique store, surrounded by old things. He discovers that he's dying, goes on a journey, and in the process, his life becomes transformed."

Sources:

Gotanda, Philip Kan, telephone interviews with Terry Hong, October 10, 1993 and January 25, 1994.

Philip Kan Gotanda, http://www.philiphangotanda.com (accessed March 2003).

James Hattori

Journalist
Born in Los Angeles, California

"There's no doubt that being of Japanese heritage is a part of the success I've enjoyed. It's what makes me distinctive—apart from the crowd, at least superficially. But inside it makes a difference too. Growing up feeling like something of an outsider has made me tougher. It constantly challenges me to assess myself and where I am and where I want to be."

J ames Hattori is one of the few prominent Asian American television journalists working at the network level. As a correspondent for CNN and the anchor reporter for *Next* at CNN, he has covered important stories all over the world.

Reading and travel

Hattori was born and raised in the Los Angeles area, the youngest of three children. He spent his early years in the inner-city neighborhood of Crenshaw, which had a large Japanese American community. His parents were dedicated to their children, and Hattori told *Asian American Biography (AAB)* that they had a profound influence on him. "I didn't realize it or fully appreciate it at the time," he said, "but they are hardworking, honest people who live modestly. I feel very lucky to have parents who care so much about their children, and who unselfishly dedicated so much of their lives [to them]." One thing he got from his parents that was especially important to him was a love of reading. His mother used to read to him at bedtime and, Hattori explained, "It exposed me to new worlds and possibilities beyond everyday life, which I came to realize were not just 'out there,' but really attainable if seriously pursued."

When Hattori was in junior high school, his family moved from the inner city to the Los Angeles suburb of Torrance. The family began traveling a lot, and Hattori has many fond memories of visiting national parks like Yosemite and the Grand Canyon. He also did a lot of camping and hiking with the Boy Scouts. "I loved to travel," he told *AAB,* "and I still do. I'm fascinated by seeing new places and people. It's one reason why my job is so great."

Studying journalism

After graduating from high school in Torrance, Hattori enrolled in the University of Southern California's school of journalism. His first interest in this area was in broadcasting management, but while he was in college, the management and journalism programs merged and he became more interested in reporting. "I really decided after taking a course from two well-regarded reporters in Los Angeles," Hattori told *AAB.* "They were award-winning, serious journalists whose jobs seemed challenging and meaningful. That's when it struck me that this was a career that was not only interesting but could also serve the public interest."

Hattori graduated *cum laude* (with honors) in 1977. His first job was as a weekend assignment editor and writer at KGTV-TV in San Diego. He later took a position with KREM-TV in Spokane, Washington, as a reporter and midday anchor. Hattori spent

James Hattori

four years at KREM. In 1982 he joined KING-TV in Seattle as a reporter, legislative correspondent, and weekend anchor. After five years there, Hattori left the West Coast for a job in Houston, Texas, with KPRC-TV as a reporter in the special projects unit. While he was in Houston, CBS News offered him his first network post, that of Dallas correspondent. As a national correspondent, Hattori reported on significant events for the evening newscasts and was a regular contributor to the CBS weekly newsmagazine *48 Hours.* These stories were on such diverse topics as animal rights, abuse of the elderly,

Alzheimer's disease, dieting fads, the fight to save the rhinoceros, fire fighting, and juveniles on death row. He has covered stories including the Persian Gulf War, the U.S. invasion of Panama, the *Exxon Valdez* oil spill, drug trafficking in Colombia, and National Aeronautics and Space Administration (NASA) space shuttle flights. In the area of national politics, Hattori covered Texas billionaire H. Ross Perot's initial bid for the presidency in 1992 and that year's Republican National Convention in Houston. After his coverage of the 1992 presidential race, Hattori was offered the position of Tokyo correspondent.

He was with CBS for a total of eight years, but by 1996 he had accepted a position as weekend anchor for KRON-TV, an NBC news affiliate. Then in 1999, Hattori took a position as sole anchor for the CNN weekly program CNNdotcom. This program was originally a half-hour show covering general stories on science and technology. The popularity of the show grew so much that CNN created the one-hour news magazine program *Next* at CNN, with Hattori as science correspondent. In 2002, Hattori still held that position and continued to work as a CNN correspondent on other news topics. In 1999, Hattori received the National Headliner Award for the coverage of Hurricane Floyd.

Reflections on success

Hattori has risen to prominence in a very competitive field, attaining a level of achievement to which many aspire. Asked what led to his success, Hattori told *AAB*, "There's no doubt that being of Japanese heritage is a part of the success I've enjoyed. It's what makes me distinctive—apart from the crowd, at least superficially. But inside it makes a difference too. Growing up feeling like something of an outsider striving to be in the mainstream—whether or not that's a mistaken notion—has made me tougher. More resourceful. More independent. It constantly challenges me to assess myself and where I am and where I want to be." Hattori also very much believes in the power of the mind. "Anything can happen if you put your mind to it," he insisted. "No one can do all things or be everything to everyone. We all choose what we want most. If we're inspired and committed, things work out."

Sources:

Cable News Network, http://www.cnn.com (accessed March 2003).

CBS News, biographical information and press releases, 1994.

Hattori, James, written interview with Helen Zia, May 1994.

David D. Ho

Medical doctor, AIDS researcher
Born November 3, 1952, Taiwan

"If you look at the whole picture [of the AIDS virus] the task is daunting. You've got to approach it one step at a time–pick a topic and do one experiment at a time."

Dr. David D. Ho is one of the pioneer researchers in the field of Acquired Immune Deficiency Syndrome (AIDS). As the chief resident at Cedars-Sinai Medical Center at the University of California,

Los Angeles (UCLA) School of Medicine, Ho has been treating AIDS patients since 1981, when the mysterious disease first appeared. Throughout the 1980s, Ho was at the forefront of medical research exploring the properties of AIDS. In 1984, for instance, he isolated HIV—the virus that is generally believed to cause AIDS—in semen; one year later, he assured a panicked public that the disease could not be spread through casual contact when he proved that the virus was not present in saliva. Also in 1985, Ho demonstrated that HIV can invade the central nervous system and induce brain dysfunction, opening up a new area of inquiry.

In 1991, Ho was named the head of New York City's Aaron Diamond Research Center, one of the largest AIDS research facilities in the world. The committee that recruited Ho cited his combination of research skills, his history as a practicing physician, and his scientific mind as the key factors in their choice. Under Ho's leadership the center has earned an international reputation for excellence and has attracted top scientists from around the world.

David D. Ho

A young immigrant

Ho's father immigrated to the United States in the late 1950s to attend graduate school in electrical engineering. In 1964, the rest of the family joined him, settling in the Los Angeles area. Ho was 12 years old at the time, and though he spoke only a few words of English, he was three years ahead of his class in math. Ho described his early educational experiences in America in an interview with *Asian American Biography (AAB).* "It was rough at the beginning," he admitted, "but kids learn fast, and after a

three-month period I was [speaking English] reasonably well. After a year it was no problem and I was doing fine. That was a real dramatic change and I would hate to go through that adjustment now."

After catching up in language skills, Ho excelled at school. He had an especially thoughtful ninth grade math teacher who saw to it that he was placed in the advanced mathematics course, where he quickly became a top student. After graduating from high school, Ho enrolled in the California Institute of Technology, where he earned a bachelor's degree in 1974, graduating *summa cum laude* (with highest honors). He then went on to medical school at Harvard, where he was one of four Asian Americans in a class of 140. It was at Harvard that Ho's interest in research was solidified. "Harvard is very research oriented," he told *AAB*. "The faculty really emphasizes medical research. That's what nailed it down for me."

Return to Los Angeles

After graduation from Harvard Medical School, where he studied all four years on an academic scholarship, Ho returned to Los Angeles, needing a change of scenery. During the last year of his three-year residency in the UCLA hospital system, Ho saw his first case of AIDS, then an unknown disease. "It was an experience I will never forget," he told *AAB*. "Two young gay men with fulminant [sudden and severe] pneumonia came in. We knew they were dying, their immune systems were depleted. We didn't know the cause, but the cases looked similar. We couldn't find any literature on anything like it. It was something new, something that wiped out the immune system. Even though the cases were isolated, it was exciting because it was something new. My interest in the disease was formed from that stage on."

After his initial exposure to patients suffering from this disease, Ho began seeing it more and more often. His interest as a medical researcher was stimulated. Aside from his obvious concern for the suffering of his patients, Ho was fascinated by the prospect of studying the appearance of a disease that, evidently, had not affected human beings before. By mid-1981, Ho and his colleagues realized that it was growing rapidly and that cases were doubling every few months. "It was *dramatic*," Ho said.

AIDS is named

By mid-1982, the disease that had been puzzling doctors for several years was named Acquired Immune Deficiency Syndrome (AIDS). Ho, meanwhile, had returned to Harvard and Massachusetts General Hospital to focus on research into viruses. He began to look for a viral origin for AIDS and studied people suffering from the disease. Ho's work during this period was groundbreaking, and in recognition of this the National Institutes of Health awarded him a Clinical Investigator Award for three consecutive years. In 1987, Ho left Massachusetts to return to Los Angeles, where he had been offered a position as a researcher at Cedars-Sinai and, more importantly, as co-chair of their AIDS task force. In 1988, Ho was named to the AIDS advisory committee of the Centers for Disease Control, further evidence of his stature among researchers.

In 1991, Ho assumed the directorship of the newly established Aaron Diamond AIDS Research Center with a mission to focus on the basic sciences of AIDS and HIV. In 1996, the Center joined with Rockefeller University. Ho and his partners worked on understanding how a patient acquires AIDS from HIV, how the disease is passed from an infected mother to her child and from an infected person to a sexual partner, and on the creation of a vaccine to prevent the disease. Research conducted by Ho's team led to the discovery of the AIDS "cocktail," a combination of drugs that has reduced the death rate of AIDS patients in the United States. Ho is optimistic that a vaccine will be developed within the next five to ten years. A cure, however, is unlikely in the short term.

Running a marathon

In addition to his work at the Diamond Center, Ho serves on the President's Task Force on AIDS and as a member of the national HIV Vaccine Working Group. He described his work as "running a marathon. If you look at the whole picture," he told *AAB*, "the task is daunting. You've got to approach it one step at a time—pick a topic and do one experiment at a time."

In 1996 Ho was selected as *Time* magazine's Man of the Year. In 1999 he received the Hoechst Roussel Award for outstanding accomplishments in research and in 2001, Ho was among the 28 recipients of the Presidential Citizen Medal presented by then-president Bill Clinton.

In *New York Newsday,* Ho expressed gratitude to his wife, Susan, for "taking care of the home front" while he is occupied with his research. The couple met while Ho was in medical school and married shortly thereafter. They have three children and live in upstate New York.

Sources:

Ho, David D., interview with Terry Hong, March 10, 1994.

Rockefeller University. http://www.rockefeller.edu (accessed March 2003).

Woodard, Catherine, "Unraveling AIDS: City Lab and Its Director Work at the Cutting Edge," *New York Newsday,* September 7, 1993.

Yang, Jeff, and Betty Wong, "Power Brokers: The 25 Most Influential People in Asian America," *A. Magazine,* vol. 2, no. 3, December 15, 1993, p. 30.

David Henry Hwang

Playwright, screenwriter
Born August 11, 1957, San Gabriel, California

"I don't feel I have to express the Asian American aesthetic anymore. One person can't represent a whole community. That there are so many voices now is the hopeful direction of the future."

David Henry Hwang was thrust into the national spotlight in 1988 when his play *M. Butterfly* opened and became one of the most successful nonmusical works in Broadway history. The story of a French diplomat and his relationship with a male Chinese spy, *M. Butterfly* won a Tony Award and eventually was produced in three dozen countries around the world. In 1989, *Time* magazine referred to Hwang as "potential[ly]... the first important dramatist of American public life since Arthur Miller, and maybe the best of them all."

Hwang has written many plays during his career, some commercially successful and some not. Because many of them deal with his experiences as a Chinese American, he is considered a spokesperson for the Asian American community.

Meshing East and West

Hwang was the only son of a Shanghai-born banker who founded the first Asian American-owned national bank in the United States. His mother was a Chinese pianist raised in the Philippines. Growing up in San Gabriel, California, Hwang describes himself as a "Chinese-Filipino-American, born-again-Christian kid from suburban Los Angeles" who had always thought of his Chinese heritage as an interesting detail, "like having red hair."

Hwang's father, Henry, was determined that his children become comfortable with Western culture. At the same time, his mother, Dorothy, brought to the family a strict Protestant tradition. Although the Hwang family seemed westernized, David still absorbed much of the ancient Chinese culture with its myths and fables. His grandmother told him stories about an ancestor sold into slavery and other tales from China. When he was ten, Hwang wrote a 90-page "novel" based on his grandmother's memories.

Hwang attended the Harvard School, a private institution for privileged children in Los Angeles. Later, at Stanford University, Hwang first tried journalism and instrumental music before he attempted play writing. More and more, he was exploring what it meant to be Chinese American. He lived in an Asian American dormitory and played in an all-Asian American rock band, Bamboo.

David Henry Hwang

Writing begins

Hwang's first play was about a musician. When he showed it to a professor, he was told that he obviously knew nothing about writing plays. Later he found a teacher who was willing to work with him and wrote *FOB*, which tells the story of the cultural clash between a new immigrant and a westernized Asian American. (The term FOB referred to a new immigrant, someone who was "fresh off the boat.") It was first performed in 1979 by students in Hwang's dormitory, under his direction. Then, only weeks before Hwang's graduation, the Eugene O'Neill Theater Center in Waterford, Connecticut, called to say they wanted *FOB* for their National Playwrights' Conference. "Of all the moments in my career so far," says Hwang, "that's probably been the most exciting." A few months later, *FOB* was staged in New York at the Public Theater. In the spring of 1981, barely two years after Hwang graduated from college, *FOB* won an Obie Award for best new play.

More success and a flop

Hwang's second play, *Dance and the Railroad,* was inspired by the experiences of Chinese railroad workers in the United States in 1867. It was nominated for a Drama Desk Award in 1982. He then wrote *Family Devotions,* a play in which Hwang questions Christian traditions. In 1983, the Public Theater produced a pair of his one-act plays, *The House of Sleeping Beauties* and *The Sound of a Voice.*

For the next two years, Hwang found himself unable to write. When he finally started composing again, he created his first non-Asian play, *Rich Relations.* The play was his first flop, and he said it taught him a great lesson. "I realized, it's okay. I'm still alive. It's not the end of the world."

Later, with *M. Butterfly,* Hwang became an international phenomenon at age 32. *M. Butterfly* debuted on Broadway in March 1988 and grossed more than $35 million. In addition to the Tony Award, the play received the Drama Desk, Outer Critics Circle, and John Gassner awards in 1988, and the 1991 L.A. Drama Critics Circle Award.

New paths, new plans

The worldwide success of *M. Butterfly* brought Hwang many new opportunities. A few months after its opening, he and composer Philip Glass produced *1000 Airplanes on the Roof,* a multimedia extravaganza. Hwang would later write the words for Glass's opera *The Voyage.*

Hwang also began to write for films. He completed a script for the screen version of *M. Butterfly,* which was released in late 1993. Another of his screenplays, *Golden Gate,* a mystical tale about an FBI agent who falls in love with the daughter of a Chinese American laundryman, was released in early 1994.

His 1997 off-Broadway play, *Golden Child,* earned Hwang an Obie award and when the play moved to Broadway in 1998, it received three Tony nominations. Also in 1997, Hwang wrote the libretto for *The Silver River,* which was first presented at the Santa Fe Chamber Music Festival in 1997, with music written by Bright Sheng. It was presented at the Lincoln Center Festival in 2002. Other screenplays by Hwang include *The Lost Empire* (2001) and *The Possession,* which he co-wrote in 2002.

Hwang said he is heartened by the recent progress made by other Asian American writers. "I don't feel I have to express *the* Asian American aesthetic anymore. One person can't represent a whole community. That there are so *many* voices now is the hopeful direction of the future."

In 1994, Hwang was appointed by President Bill Clinton to serve on the Presidential Committee on the Arts and the Humanities. In 2000–2001, Hwang served as the Artist-in-Residence at New York University's Asian Pacific American Studies Institute, which produced a twenty-year retrospective of his work. Hwang lives in New York City with his wife, actress Kathryn Layng, and their two children.

Sources:

Gerard, Jeremy, "David Henry Hwang: Riding on the Hyphen," *New York Times Magazine,* March 13, 1988, pp. 44-45 and 88-89.

Henry, William A. III, "When East and West Collide," *Time,* August 14, 1989, pp. 62 and 64.

Hwang, David Henry, telephone interview with Terry Hong, February 9, 1994.

Playscripts, Inc., http://www.playscripts.com (accessed March 2003).

Smith, Dinitia, "Face Values: The Sexual and Racial Obsessions of Playwright David Henry Hwang," *New York Magazine,* January 11, 1993, pp. 42-45.

Daniel K. Inouye

U.S. Senator
Born September 17, 1924, Honolulu, Hawaii

In 1959, when Hawaii was admitted to the United States as the fiftieth state, Inouye was elected as its first representative to the House. In that election Inouye won the largest number of votes ever cast for a candidate in a Hawaiian election.

Senator Daniel Ken Inouye was the first American of Japanese descent to serve in the U.S. Congress. He has represented Hawaii in Congress since the territory was made a state in 1959, first in the House of Representatives and then in the Senate, where he has served continuously since 1962. Inouye is a highly decorated World War II hero, who served in an all-Japanese army unit while many Americans of Japanese descent were imprisoned in relocation, or internment, camps during the war.

Inouye first came to public prominence in 1968 at the Democratic National Convention, where he made the keynote speech and called for greater racial understanding. In 1973 and 1974 he once again drew the national spotlight as a member of the Senate Watergate Committee, which investigated the wrongdoings of Republicans during Richard Nixon's 1972 reelection campaign—and the cover-ups that followed their exposure.

A child of immigrants

Inouye was the oldest of four children born to Hyotaro and Kame (Imanaga) Inouye, who immigrated to the United States from Japan. The elder Inouye worked as a file clerk to support his family. Inouye was educated at a special Japanese-language school as well as the Honolulu public schools. As soon as he was old enough, he began working part-time jobs, including parking cars at Honolulu Stadium and giving haircuts to his friends. He spent most of his money from these jobs on his youthful hobbies of stamp collecting, chemistry, electronics, and keeping homing pigeons. In 1942 he graduated from McKinley High School in Honolulu and enrolled in the premed program at the University of Hawaii. He dropped out of college within a year, however, to enroll in the U.S. Army.

War heroics

Inouye enlisted in the army in 1943, joining the 442nd Regimental Combat Team, an all-volunteer unit made up of Japanese Americans eager to prove their loyalty to the U.S. government. The 442nd fought for nearly three months in the bloody Rome-Arno campaign, then went on to France, where they rescued an American battalion surrounded by Germans. The Battle of the Lost Battalion, as it is known, is listed in the annals of U.S. military history as one of the most significant and heroic military battles of the twentieth century.

The 442nd returned to Italy in the closing months of the war, when the regiment again saw action. Inouye was hit in the abdomen

Daniel K. Inouye

was made a captain and awarded a Distinguished Service Cross (the second-highest award for military valor), a Bronze Star, a Purple Heart with cluster and 12 other medals and citations.

In 2000, President Bill Clinton upgraded Inouye's Distinguished Service Cross to the Medal of Honor.

Return to civilian life

Inouye used the GI Bill to return to college after being discharged from the army. He enrolled in the University of Hawaii, and instead of returning to premed he took up the study of government and economics. In 1950 he earned a bachelor's degree and went on to law school at the prestigious George Washington University Law School in Washington, D.C. He was elected to the professional law fraternity Phi Delta Phi, served as editor of the *George Washington Law Review,* and did volunteer work for the Democratic National Committee, helping to get his foot in the door of the world of politics.

Inouye earned his law degree in 1952 and on his return to Hawaii he was appointed deputy public prosecutor for the city of Honolulu. In 1954 he won election to the territorial house of representatives, where he served for four years. In 1958 he was elected to the territorial senate. In 1959, when Hawaii was admitted to the United States as the fiftieth state, Inouye was elected as its first representative to the House. In that election Inouye won the largest number of votes ever cast for a candidate in a Hawaiian election. Three years later, when Hawaii's first senator, Orrin E. Long, retired, Long endorsed Inouye as his successor. Inouye easily won both the primary

by a bullet that exited through his back, barely missing his spine. In spite of his injury, Inouye continued leading his platoon and advanced alone against an enemy machine-gun nest that had his men pinned down. He tossed two grenades into the nest, crippling the machine-gunners before his right arm was shattered by a rifle grenade fired at close range. Inouye, now suffering multiple, serious injuries, continued his assault, throwing his last grenade with his left arm. He was finally knocked down the hill by a bullet to the leg. For this remarkable display of bravery and selflessness, Inouye and general elections and assumed his seat in the U.S. Senate in 1963.

Inouye's legislative record

Since his election to Congress in 1958, Inouye has voted in the liberal tradition on most social issues, such as civil rights, and has taken moderate positions on economic and defense issues. He is a staunch defender of abortion rights, desegregation of public institutions, and tough gun control. He champions consumer rights and has voted in favor of public works programs to put the unemployed to work. Inouye was a strong supporter of the Civil Rights Act of 1964 and its subsequent provisions and was an equally strong supporter of President Lyndon B. Johnson's "Great Society" era, in which many federal assistance programs, such as Head Start, Medicaid and Medicare, and the Food Stamp Program, were introduced as part of a massive effort referred to as the "War on Poverty."

In matters of national defense Inouye's voting has been less partisan. During his first term he was in favor of continued military involvement in Southeast Asia. By his second term, however, when popular support for the Vietnam War had nearly disappeared, Inouye changed his position and supported the Cooper-Church and McGovern-Hatfield amendments to end it. He also cosponsored the historic War Powers Act of 1973, which was intended to limit a president's power to commit American military forces overseas by giving Congress the right to establish time limits for their deployment. The law was passed in large part because of the public's disgust over America's nearly 15-year battle against three countries in Southeast Asia (Vietnam, Cambodia, and Laos), which had been fought without a formal declaration of war.

More recently, Inouye voted in favor of many Cold War military systems. (The Cold War marked the post-World War II period in American history when tensions between the Soviet Union and the United States fostered an arms race, each side amassing enough weapons to allegedly prevent the other from launching a devastating offensive strike.) Among these was funding for the controversial neutron bomb, a nuclear device designed to kill populations while leaving structures intact.

Inouye opposed many Ronald Reagan-era defense programs, however, most notably the Strategic Defense Initiative, also known as Star Wars, an elaborate, expensive (and, many thought, scientifically impossible) scheme meant to protect the United States from intercontinental nuclear attack through a system of space-based laser beams and nuclear devices.

Crucial congressional investigations

In 1973 Inouye was named to sit on the Senate Select Committee on Presidential Campaign Activities, commonly known as the Watergate Committee. The committee had been set up to investigate allegations that President Richard Nixon's administration had engaged in—or conspired to cover up for others who had engaged in—illegal activities on behalf of Nixon's 1972 reelection campaign. The committee's hearings were nationally televised and widely watched, and Inouye distinguished himself as a nonpartisan investigator. At the conclusion of the hearings, which ultimately led to the resignation of President Nixon, a Gallup Poll gave the young senator favorable ratings of 84 percent.

In 1976 Inouye sat on another investigative committee when he chaired the Senate Select Committee on Intelligence, which was established to formulate regulations governing secret operations in other countries, and internal operations against American citizens by the intelligence divisions of the government. Until that time, the CIA and the FBI had operated with few restraints around the world or at home, engaging in practices that horrified most Americans when they were exposed in the mid-1970s.

In 1987 Inouye was again appointed chair of a committee looking into executive abuse of power, the Senate Select Committee on Secret Military Assistance to Iran and Nicaraguan Opposition, commonly known as the Iran-Contra Committee. This committee was set up to look into allegations that members of Ronald Reagan's National Security Staff had sold arms to Iran—in violation of international law and official U.S. policy—and then sent the profits to a band of resistance fighters seeking to overthrow the Communist government of Nicaragua through a campaign of terror. This band of guns-for-hire, known as the Contras, had been specifically denied funding by the U.S. Congress.

In the mid-1990s, the senior senator from Hawaii chaired the Committee on Indian Affairs, the Appropriations Subcommittee on Defense, and the Commerce, Science, and Transportation Subcommittee on Communications, where he had a major impact on the formation of national computer-based information delivery systems, often referred to as the "information superhighway."

In 1993, Inouye helped to restore the island of Kahoolawe to the government of the state of Hawaii. Previously, that island had been used for U.S. military target practice. In the past few years, Inouye has continued to be involved with a variety of concerns and committees within the Senate, always looking to the health, education, and economy of his constituencies as his main priorities.

Sources:

Inouye, Daniel, "Biography, Daniel K. Inouye, United States Senator," Washington, D.C., May 1994.
"Senator Daniel Inouye," http://www.senate.gov/ ~inouye/ (accessed March 2003).
Yang, Jeff, "Power Brokers," *A. Magazine,* vol. 2, no. 3, December 15, 1993, pp. 25-34.

Paul Isaki

Business executive and political appointee
Born June 6, 1944, Topaz, Utah

"I relish the opportunity to make Washington state the nation's business leader."

In 1992, Paul Isaki became the vice president of business development for the Seattle Mariners baseball team. Before and after his time with the Mariners, Isaki served in various positions in the Washington state government. Beginning in 1985 he has held posts that make use of his background as a savvy business executive. From 1985–1992 he served under Governor

Booth Gardner, first as the special assistant for international trade and economic development and then as director of the state of Washington's department of trade and economic development. From 1992–99, he took a break from politics to serve as vice president of business development for the Seattle Mariners baseball team. Isaki returned to state service under Governor **Gary Locke,** first as the governor's special trade representative, then as the chief of staff. In November 2001, he was appointed as the governor's special assistant for business.

Born in a camp

Isaki was born in the internment camp set up by the U.S. government in Topaz, Utah. His family, like 120,000 other Americans of Japanese descent, had been rounded up during World War II and sent to isolated camps on the pretext that in the event of a Japanese invasion of the West Coast, they would be security risks. No such action was taken against German or Italian Americans. (Germany and Italy were also U.S. enemies during the war.) When the war ended and the prisoners were allowed to resume their lives, the Isaki family returned to Oakland, California, where Isaki's father started a trucking company. Isaki grew up in Oakland and attended the public schools there, which were predominantly populated by black students. Experiencing the economic injustice of the inner city had a profound impact on the young boy, more so, even, than his parents' experiences in the camps, which he did not begin to appreciate until later in life.

After graduating from high school, Isaki enrolled in the University of California at Berkeley, planning to become a dentist, as his parents wished. The Berkeley campus at the time abounded with student activism over a variety of concerns about social justice, and the civil rights movement had begun. Isaki remembers hearing James Farmer, then the head of the Congress for Racial Equality (CORE), give a speech on campus. He told *Asian American Biography (AAB),* "He was speaking on a street corner in Berkeley. This was before the Voting Rights Act of 1964, but that was how things were in Berkeley then."

The birth of an activist

Isaki graduated from Berkeley in 1965 and became involved in President Lyndon B. Johnson's War on Poverty. His first jobs were with various community agencies serving migrant workers in rural central California and in the San Francisco Bay area, and working with impoverished African American communities. In 1971 he moved to Seattle to take a job with the Seattle Opportunities Industrialization Center, a skills-training center for federally funded job training programs. In 1973 he left to take a job with the city of Seattle.

In this new position, Isaki began the activities that would eventually become his life's work. His first big development project was a $3.1 million job training center in the inner city. His next post was as assistant director of a four-county, public/private economic development project, with which he stayed until 1979. It was then that Isaki decided to capitalize on his experience with both public and private concerns in real estate development. The company he started, a real estate development firm, was very successful, and in 1981 it was pur-

Paul Isaki

ultimately leading to his directorship of the department of trade and economic development, a vital department in Washington, which is the most trade-dependent state in the country. In that post he worked on such diverse projects as instituting the "Clean Washington" recycling program and developing the Everett Navy Homeport.

It was in this position that Isaki first crossed paths with major league baseball. Isaki was on the governor's staff in charge of business and economic issues when a dispute erupted over the Mariners' lease with the Kingdome, the enclosed stadium where they play their home games. The impasse was so severe that the owners of the Mariners were threatening to move the team out of Seattle if favorable terms could not be reached. The governor assigned Isaki to work full time on resolving the conflict, and his critical role in settling the dispute was universally appreciated.

Working for the Mariners

In 1992 Isaki was offered a position with the Mariners that had been created for him by the team's owners, that of vice president of business development. His assignment was to expand the Mariners' business interests in the Pacific Northwest, especially tapping markets in Vancouver, Canada, and Japan. The Mariners' objective of increasing exposure in Japan, where baseball was extremely popular, was seen as an exciting new venture for the sport.

The team's link with the Japanese drew national attention in 1992, when a majority ownership in the Seattle club was bought by Hiroshi Yamauchi, president of Nintendo, the entertainment game conglomerate head-

chased by a national corporation, making Isaki and his partner a lot of money.

Government service

In 1984 Isaki left the corporation that had bought him out, intending to work as a developer on his own. During this period he was approached by a friend heading the transition team for Washington's new governor, Booth Gardner, who had been elected on the theme of economic development—Isaki's area of expertise. Isaki joined the new administration, serving in a variety of posts quartered in Redmond, Washington. This move spurred some protest around the country against the loss of the "American" nature of baseball, similar to the controversy aroused when the Rockefeller family sold a controlling interest of Rockefeller Center in New York City to a Japanese firm. Isaki claims that such protests are misdirected and believes that without the money put in by Yamauchi there would be no baseball in the Pacific Northwest today. Isaki worked to expand the team's market in an effort to bring in more money, allowing it to compete with wealthier teams.

Isaki's plans for the team were inventive—some would say radical. For instance, he wanted to play a yearly regular season game in Japan against another American team, possibly the Detroit Tigers, who are well known in Japan.

With Isaki's leadership and business strategies the team and the city were able to build the brand new Safeco Field, which has served as home to the Mariners since 1999. Soon afterward, however, Isaki chose to step back into the political field to serve as a special trade representative to Governor Gary Locke. In this position he was the governor's main advisor on all matters of international trade and policy, helping the governor to work toward removing unfair trade barriers with foreign markets. In January 2001, he was promoted to chief of staff. But in November of the same year, Locke asked him to take the post of special assistant for business. When he accepted the position, Isaki told the press that he looked forward to handling the "tough challenges that this latest assignment brings." He commented further, "I relish the opportunity to make

Washington state the nation's business leader."

Sources:

"Editorial: Step 1 for Regional M's: Hiring New Business Veep," *Seattle Times,* December 4, 1992, p. A16.

"Gary Locke," *State of Washington Governor's Office,* http://www.governor.wa.gov (accessed March 15, 2003).

Isaki, Paul, telephone interview with Susan Gall, August 2 and 18, 1994.

Lim, Gerard, "Paul Isaki Lands Front Office Job with Mariners," *Asian Week,* January 22, 1994, p. 4.

Mochizuki, Ken, "Paul Isaki: Seattle Mariners VP Hustles for Major League Support," *Northwest Nikkei,* vol. 5, no. 4, April 1993, p. 1.

Seattle Mariners, professional biography and press releases, 1994.

Lance Ito

Judge
Born August 2, 1950, Los Angeles, California

"Be cautious, careful, and when in doubt, keep your mouth shut. When tempted to say something, take a deep breath and refer to rule one."

Lance A. Ito is a Los Angeles County superior court judge, and one of the most respected jurists in the state of California. After serving for ten years as a county prosecutor, he spent two years as a municipal court judge before being elevated to his present post. In 1992 the Los Angeles County Bar Association named him trial judge of the year.

In 1994 Ito was appointed to preside over the high-profile murder trial of former football star O. J. Simpson, who was accused of killing his former wife, Nicole Brown Simpson, and her friend Ronald Goldman. Through the fanatical media coverage of the trial, the judge became a familiar face to the millions of Americans glued to their television sets watching the drama unfold. The judge became a refreshing presence in the courtroom, at times apparently the only one not interested in how he looked to the cameras. In fact, he routinely expressed contempt for the obsessive voyeurism of the media in covering the case, frequently threatening to remove the cameras from his courtroom.

The son of schoolteachers

Ito is the son of Jim and Toshi Ito, second-generation Japanese Americans who were both born in California. Jim Ito's father came to the United States from Kyushu, a southern Japanese island, where he could trace his ancestry back to the samurai—Japan's disciplined, aristocratic class of warriors. Before Lance Ito was born, his parents, along with nearly 120,000 other Americans of Japanese descent, were relocated from their home to an internment camp as part of the executive order to place all West Coast Japanese Americans in confinement during World War II. This unconstitutional and inhumane internment of American citizens was based largely on anti-Japanese hysteria after the Japanese bombing of Pearl Harbor, Hawaii. The U.S. government called into question the loyalty of many Japanese Americans by claiming that they might help the Japanese troops should Japan invade the West Coast. The Itos were sent to Heart

Lance Ito

Mountain Relocation Camp in northwestern Wyoming. Ito's uncle, Bill Ito, who was at Heart Mountain as well, described the experience in *U.S. News & World Report*, "It wasn't a pretty sight, those GIs with their rifles pointing at us. But we had *gaman* [perseverance]—just grin and bear it."

Lance Ito learned about the wartime internment camps from his parents, both of whom became schoolteachers in Los Angeles after their release from Heart Mountain. Many people attribute Ito's powerful sense of justice to the profound effect the memories of his parents had upon him. "The tragic circumstances his parents went through, essentially being imprisoned in their own country, simply increased his sense of fairness," said former Los Angeles district attorney Robert Philibosian in *U.S. News & World Report.* Ito expressed some of his own concerns in regard to his parents in a television interview: "One of the reasons I try to do as good a job as I can [is that] I don't want to cause problems for my parents." He continued that when critical things are said about him as a judge, it "wounds my parents very deeply."

Ito was educated in the Los Angeles public school system and graduated from John Marshall High School in 1968, where he had been an honors student and president of one of his classes. From there he went to the University of California, Los Angeles, where he studied political science. He parked cars at a student lot to earn money for his schooling. In 1972 he graduated *cum laude* (with honors). Following his graduation, Ito enrolled in the Boalt Hall School of Law at the University of California at Berkeley, graduating in 1975. He was admitted to the California Bar on December 8, 1975.

Ito's first job after law school was with the firm of Irsfield, Irsfield, and Younger, where he practiced for two years. In 1977 he left private practice to work for the L.A. district attorney's office as a prosecutor. During the ten years he stayed in this position, he volunteered to be on a team assigned to prosecute cases involving street gangs and organized crime. His high conviction rate as well as his tireless efforts received notice. From 1984 to 1987 he served on the board of directors of the Los Angeles County Association of Deputy District Attorneys. He also served as vice

chair of California's State Task Force on Youth Gang Violence (in 1986 and again in 1989) and on the state's Task Force on Victims' Rights.

Career as a judge

In December 1987 Republican California governor George Dukmejian appointed Ito, a Democrat, to fill the newly created position of municipal court judge of the Los Angeles Judicial District of Los Angeles County. In 1989 Ito was appointed, again by Dukmejian, to the Los Angeles County Superior Court. The next year, he ran unopposed in an election to retain his seat. In 1992 Ito presided over the trial of Charles Keating, a key financial manipulator behind the fall of several savings and loan companies. After this trial, Ito was named trial judge of the year by the Los Angeles County Bar Association. Ito's position in 1995 was assistant presiding judge of the Los Angeles Superior Court.

Prior to being named to the Simpson case, Ito taught a course for judges called "Media and the Courts—Handling High Profile Cases." Working in the Los Angeles area, with its high concentration of money and celebrities, judges are often confronted with such cases. Ito, quoted in the *New York Times,* taught that there were two rules for handling such cases: "Be cautious, careful, and when in doubt, keep your mouth shut. When tempted to say something, take a deep breath and refer to rule one." Before he was selected as the judge hearing the Simpson case, Ito was quoted as saying that a judge "would have to be crazy" to want to sit on that case.

The intense media scrutiny of the Simpson case is often justified by the fact that it spotlighted the problem of domestic violence. Ito has presided over several cases involving this charge and has expressed discouragement at how difficult it is to prosecute abusers. He told the *Los Angeles Times,* "Often there are serious injuries and implausible explanations as to how [they] happened. The problem is, 75 to 90 days later, when the case comes to trial, emotions have cooled down, economic realities have set in, and victims often become reluctant [to prosecute]."

Spotlight on the judge

In the Simpson trial, probably the most highly publicized case of the twentieth century, Ito received his inevitable share of criticism. His relationship with the jury went through many changes, the defense at times found him unyielding, critics suggested that he did not exercise enough control in the courtroom, and he was engaged in a battle with the media. As one reporter for *Newsweek* noted, "Judge Ito, ready or not, is on trial."

Considering how fully in the limelight this case was, the response to the judge has generally been quite favorable. At the outset of the case, Robert Shapiro, one of Simpson's attorneys, said that Ito was "an excellent choice because he is one of the finest judges in the state of California." Blair Bernholz, a Los Angeles-area defense attorney, said that Ito "is very sensitive to the needs of trial lawyers and allows them to do their work. But there's never any question who is in control of the courtroom. He keeps a firm hand." Janet Kerr, a law professor at Pepperdine University in Malibu, California, said, "I believe him to be a brilliant judge who's willing to listen to many different sides of an issue and who makes very well-reasoned decisions. He does have a dry sense of humor. I think he adds a lot of personality in the courtroom."

Many observed the great balance between Ito's disciplined, even-handed administration of justice and his engaging personal manner. In his days in the district attorney's office he was known as a workhorse as well as a mischievous practical jokester who frequently relieved the enormous tensions of the office by pulling such pranks as loading a colleague's office furniture into the freight elevator or putting a goldfish into an attorney's water cooler.

Early in the Simpson trial, while trying to fight the mania of media coverage, Ito was hit in the head with a TV microphone, and he once again showed humor and graciousness in the face of a very tense situation. Ito is married to Captain Margaret York, the highest-ranking female officer in the Los Angeles Police Department. He still presides over the Superior Court at the Clara Shortridge Foltz Criminal Justice Center, L.A. County, California.

Sources:

Los Angeles Superior Court, press release and publicity materials, Los Angeles, California, 1994.

Miller, Mark, and Jeanne Gordon, "The Celebrity on the Bench," *Newsweek,* November 28, 1994, p. 35.

Mydans, Seth, "Judge in Simpson Case Goes by the Rules," *New York Times,* July 23, 1994, p. 9.

Tharp, Mike, "Ito's Fairness Doctrine: How His Parents' World War II Internment Shaped His Life in the Law," *U.S. News & World Report,* October 31, 1994, pp. 80-81.

Philip Jaisohn

Physician, civil servant, newspaper publisher
Born November 28, 1864, Kanaeris, Korea
Died January 5, 1951, Media, Pennsylvania

At age 13, the youngest of the 19 candidates taking the kwago (government service examination), Jaisohn had the distinction of receiving the highest score.

Philip Jaisohn is a remarkable figure in history for many reasons. He was fiercely devoted to political reform in his native Korea *and* a patriotic American citizen. He founded the first newspaper in Korea to be published in a conversational form of Korean, so that it was accessible to all who read it. (Until then, all official business in Korea was conducted in Chinese, which only the elite and the educated classes could read and understand.) In 1884, Jaisohn was a leader of the first reformist uprising in Korea's history, a failed coup d'etat that lasted only three days. In 1888, Jaisohn became the first Korean to become a U.S. citizen. Even so, Jaisohn remained devoted to reforming his country throughout his life, and his efforts continue to serve as an example to reformers.

Early years

Jaisohn was born in Kanaeris, in the Tong-Bok District of South Cholla Province, Korea. His Korean name was Suh Jae-pil, which he anglicized when he moved to the United States. At the time of Jaisohn's birth, Korea was a feudal monarchy, a largely agricultural society where a class of royalty ruled over a class of peasantry with no, or very limited, rights. This rigid social structure was known in Korea as *yangban,* a word that over time came to identify the upper class. The peasantry worked the land owned by the royalty and paid them in crops for the right to do so. At this time, Korea was a very isolationist country, rejecting contact with the outside world—so much so that it was known as the Hermit Kingdom. By the 1860s, this rejection of foreigners had reached the point where the government had outlawed any contact between its citizens and foreigners.

Jaisohn was born into the yangban or upper class, the second son of the magistrate of the Tong-Bok District. His parents were descended from two of the richest, most prominent families in Korea. As a child, Jaisohn was carefree and precocious. Then, at the age of seven, he was sent by his family to live as the adopted son of one of his family's clansmen who had produced no male heir. Jaisohn was treated well by his new family, but he was sternly instructed not to play with children of the peasantry, and he was groomed to assume his role in the traditional social hierarchy.

When he was eight, Jaisohn went to live with a wealthy uncle in the capital of Seoul, where he attended a private school established by his uncle to study for the *kwago,* the government service examination. Entering government service was viewed as a very honorable profession in those days, and children of the yangban were expected to bring honor to their families. At age 13, the youngest of the 19 candidates, Jaisohn not only passed the kwago, but had the distinction of receiving the highest score.

Philip Jaisohn

Revolutionary thought

As a young man, Jaisohn began to meet members of the yangban who found fault with both the strict order of their society and with Korea's place in the world. They also were opposed to the influence of the Chinese, who had been taking more and more control of the country, with the Korean royal family's apparent cooperation. In 1882, Jaisohn and several young reformers traveled to Japan to study at a military institute there. When they returned to Korea in 1884, they were excluded from society for leaving the country, and this treatment, combined with their resentment about Chinese influence, inspired them to stage a revolt that December. The young revolutionary reformers—Jaisohn was the youngest at 20—captured the royal palace and the royal family and held power for three days, until the Chinese military intervened and restored order. Jaisohn and his fellow reformers fled Seoul and, soon after this, left Korea.

Life in exile

Jaisohn arrived in the United States in April 1885 after living briefly in Japan. He first settled in San Francisco, California, where he supported himself distributing advertising circulars for a furniture store. He studied English at the YMCA and attended Bible study classes. A man Jaisohn met at church took an interest in him and sent the young exile to Harry Hillman Academy in Pennsylvania. There he was to study for the ministry with the goal of returning to Korea as a Christian missionary.

Jaisohn completed four years of courses in two years and graduated in 1888 with high honors. Also that year, he became the first Korean to be naturalized as an American citizen. By this time, however, he had lost interest in returning to Korea as a missionary and instead took a job at the Army Surgeon General's Library in Washington, D.C. He then enrolled in medical school and in 1892 graduated from what is now George Washington University, becoming the first U.S.-educated Korean to earn a medical degree. In 1894, he met and married Muriel Armstrong.

Returning home

In 1895, Jaisohn decided to return to Korea to work for Korean independence, which was greatly threatened by a war then being fought between China and Japan. He and his wife arrived in Korea on New Year's Day, 1896. As a former leader of a failed coup, Jaisohn was unsure of how he would be viewed by the government, but when those in power learned of his return, he was granted a government post. Later that year, with a small grant from the government and his own money, Jaisohn began publishing *The Independent (Toknip)*, Korea's first newspaper. The four-page, nonpartisan paper was made up of three pages written in Korean and one page in English. By 1897, the paper had doubled in size.

Jaisohn was buoyed by the success of *The Independent* and sought to spread the idea of Korean freedom in other ways as well. To this end he formed the Independence Club, a reformist political movement. These measures were not viewed sympathetically by the royal family, however, and in 1898 Jaisohn was stripped of his government post and once again fled the country.

Back in the United States, Jaisohn conducted medical research at the University of Pennsylvania for several years. Then, in 1905, he founded a printing and office equipment business. The company became very successful, earning Jaisohn financial independence, which enabled him to devote himself more fully to the cause of Korean independence. In 1910, Japan invaded and annexed Korea, establishing a brutal occupation that would last until the Japanese defeat in World War II. In 1919, Jaisohn organized the First Korean Congress, held in Philadelphia, Pennsylvania, where two hundred Koreans from all over North America convened to discuss the situation in their homeland.

Meanwhile, Jaisohn had neglected his business, and in 1924, it failed. In 1927, he returned to medicine and took a research position in Washington, D.C. Seven years later, he established a private practice, which eventually thrived. During World War II, he volunteered his services as an examining physician to the Draft Board. His beloved wife died in July 1941.

A final journey home

In June 1947, after Korea had been liberated by the United States (which took control of the southern half of the Korean peninsula, the Chinese having secured influence over the North—a circumstance that would eventually result in U.S. involvement in the Korean War), Jaisohn returned to his home. It had been 50 years since he was first exiled. He returned in the position of chief advisor to the commanding general of the U.S. Army Forces in Korea and as a special counselor on Korean affairs. The country was being prepared for its first-ever elections, and Jaisohn, despite vowing not to get involved, found himself in the midst of the chaos of the election. On July 19, 1948, the Korean people elected Syngman Rhee president. Jaisohn had once worked with Rhee but now considered him corrupt, so he left the country rather than take part in the Rhee government.

In 1949, Jaisohn established a medical practice in Media, Pennsylvania, remaining keenly interested in Korean politics. He was a particularly outspoken critic of the Rhee government as it became more and more like a dictatorship. In 1950, as war broke out between the North and the South, Jaisohn was diagnosed with cancer. He died on January 5, 1951.

During a lifetime devoted to Korean independence, Jaisohn remained true to his given Korean name, Jae-pil, which means "assumer of service."

Since his death, the Philip Jaisohn Memorial Foundation has been established with a mission to fulfill the ideals of humanity that Dr. Jaisohn held so dear by offering support to Korean American communities, as well as others in need, through medical, social, educational and cultural services. In 1990, the foundation opened the Jaisohn House in Media (the doctor's former residence). The house serves as a museum and a library with resources on Korean history and culture as well as books written by Korean Americas and books written in Korean.

Sources:

Liem, Channing. *Philip Jaisohn: The First Korean American,* Kyujang Publishing Company, 1984.

The Philip Jaisohn Memorial Foundation, "Philip Jaisohn," biographical information, Elkins Park, PA, 1994.

The Philip Jaisohn Memorial Foundation, http://www.jaisohn.org (accessed March 2003).

Gish Jen

Writer
Born August 12, 1955, Queens, New York

"Since I wrote Typical American, *honors have fallen out of the sky. It's all so far beyond my wildest expectations."*

Gish Jen cites her husband, David O'Connor, as "the liberator" who helped her write again. Newly married after completing her master's degree in fine arts, Jen had put her writing aside to become, as she said in an interview with Terry Hong, "a dutiful wife," a role that eventually frustrated and enraged her. The turning point came when she and her husband were preparing to move. "We had this set of fancy glasses that I had just finished packing up to bring to California and now I was going to have to pack them all up again to bring to Massachusetts. And I didn't even like them! But they were a wedding gift, and I felt I had to do it. So my husband just picked up one of the glasses and threw it out the window. It was such a liberating experience. Then we had a huge garage sale and got rid of all these things that were tying me down, and I started to write again," Jen remembered. "I wrote a short story, 'In the American Society,' which later became *Typical American*," Jen's first novel. It was published in 1991 and was a resounding success. It was a finalist for a National Book Critics' Circle Award. *Time* magazine called it an "engaging tale of one immigrant family's pursuit of the American Dream."

The dutiful daughter

Born in Queens, New York, on August 12, 1955, to immigrant parents from Shanghai, China, Lillian Jen was the second of five children. She would later adopt the name "Gish"—as in the actress Lillian Gish. "It was part of becoming a writer," she told the *New York Times* in 1991, " . . . not becoming the person I was supposed to be."

From her earliest memories, Jen was the one person in her family with an insatiable interest in books. "My parents were very academically inclined. My mother was a schoolteacher and my father a professor of civil engineering....Although my parents were educated, they were struggling so much as newcomers in this country that there was no room in their lives for leisurely things like reading. I think my book was the first nontechnical book that my father ever sat down to read."

Growing up, Jen moved from the predominantly working-class neighborhood of Yonkers, New York, to the more affluent town of Scarsdale. She quickly discovered the Scarsdale school library. She told Hong, "I felt like a kid in a chocolate factory. I must have read every book. I read indiscriminately, whether it was Albert Camus or Walter Farley. They all made me say 'wow.'"

In class, Jen was more interested in math and sciences than in English. "By eighth grade, I had decided to get a Ph.D. in math. But by high school, it was socially unacceptable for girls to be science-and math-types.

...I think that social pressure helped me switch over to English," said Jen.

In 1972, Jen entered Harvard University where she majored in literature. But she also took the required courses to be designated premed. During her junior year, Jen took her first writing class taught by famed translator Robert Fitzgerald. Fitzgerald saw great potential in her writing. He pulled Jen aside and asked her if she had ever thought about writing as a career. She replied that she loved writing, but she had never known anyone who became a writer of any sort. A career in writing "just seemed like a crazy idea."

In search of the writer

After graduating from Harvard in 1977, Jen worked for the book publisher, Doubleday. In such literary surroundings, she became more and more interested in writing and took further writing classes paid for by Doubleday. But she felt confused about which career path to take. With three siblings who went to business schools (and a fourth who went to medical school), Jen decided she would apply to business school.

Jen struggled through the first year in Stanford University's Graduate School of Business. Jen told Hong, "I knew the first day that I was not in the right place. I read more than 100 novels that first year and took as many writing courses as I could. I should have dropped out but I couldn't because I was being the dutiful daughter." The next year, she dropped out of business school.

Her parents were not happy about her decision to leave Stanford, and they did not speak to her for almost a year. "I was on the verge of a nervous breakdown. What I real-

Gish Jen

When she returned to the United States, Jen headed to the University of Iowa's Writers' Workshop. After she graduated in 1983, she returned to San Francisco and married David O'Connor, whom she had met during orientation week at Stanford. "My parents' worst fear was that I would become a writer. Their second worst fear was that I would marry a writer. At least I didn't do that," she laughed.

Author, author

Married life for Jen was initially trying. "I was married to a very successful businessman and I didn't know what it meant to be a wife." When she finally freed herself—with her husband's supportive encouragement—from the pressure of trying to be a dutiful wife, Jen threw herself wholeheartedly into writing. But she was still uncertain about her future. "I was writing, but nothing particularly was happening for me as a writer."

In 1986, Jen finally succeeded. Awarded a year-long fellowship from the prestigious Radcliffe Bunting Institute, Jen now had both the motivation and the means to write full time, without distraction. At the Bunting Institute, Jen found herself surrounded by ambitious women. "I came in expecting to do a collection of short stories. But after a week of being around that kind of ambition, I thought—no, I'm going to write a novel."

Jen began to publish short stories in magazines like *Atlantic Monthly*, *The New Yorker*, and *The Southern Review*. Her stories were also published in anthologies (collections of short stories by different authors) such as Norton's *Worlds of Literature, The*

ized was that I had to become a writer. People say that no one becomes a writer who can do anything else, and I think that's true."

Leaving California, Jen spent a year in China, teaching English to coal-mining engineers slated to study in the United States. "It was a wonderful experience in every way," she recalled. "Not only was it a discovery of my roots, but it was also the first time that I really felt I was contributing to something larger than myself. It was the first time that I understood what culture was. . . . I couldn't have written *Typical American* without that trip."

Heath Anthology of American Literature, and *Best American Short Stories 1988.*

"Beyond my wildest expectations"

Typical American is the often comic, at times tragic, story of the immigrant Chang family. Each of the characters must learn enough about his or her own self in order to come back together as a family. "Since I wrote *Typical American,* honors have fallen out of the sky," Jen marveled. "It's all so far beyond my wildest expectations." Having achieved success, Jen is often asked about the key to success by aspiring writers. Her answer is simple: "Develop your own voice."

As a sequel to *Typical American,* Jen wrote *Mona in the Promised Land* (1996), a novel continuing the story of the Chang family. In it, the teenage daughter, Mona, struggles with identity and cultural diversity as she converts to Judaism. Her next major work, a collection of short stories entitled *Who's Irish* (1999), examined the issues of multicultural marriage and identity.

Coming off the publication of *Who's Irish*, Jen was awarded another fellowship at the Radcliffe Institute for 2001–02. She spent the year working on a new novel about a Chinese American family with both adopted and biological children. And Jen's short story, *Birthmates* (1995), was chosen by author and editor John Updike to be included in his anthology, *Best American Short Stories of the Century.*

Jen lives in Cambridge, Massachusetts, with her husband and their children, son Luke and daughter Paloma.

Sources:

Jones, Malcolm, and David Gates, "Newsmakers," *Newsweek,* January 13, 2003, p. 71.

Mojtabai, A.G. "The Complete Other Side of the World," *New York Times Book Review,* March 31, 1991, pp. 9–10.

Roxe, Hilary, "Asian Balancing Act: Gish Jen Mends Conflicting Aspects of Immigrant Culture with Candor, Humor and Poignancy, " *Time International,* August 9, 1999, vol. 154, no. 5, p. 48.

Simpson, Janice C., "Fresh Voices Above the Noisy Din," *Time,* June 3, 1991, vol. 137, no. 22, pp. 66–67.

Duke Kahanamoku

Olympic athlete, surfer, actor
Born August 24, 1890, Honolulu, Hawaii
Died January 22, 1968

"It took Tarzan to finally beat me."

Duke Kahanamoku was one of the great Olympic athletes of the twentieth century. His astonishing skills as a swimmer took the world by storm at the 1912 Olympics. Prior to that performance, however, the media was already taking notice of him. The *New York Times* wrote glowingly of Kahanamoku, describing him as "a wonder at 100 yards... a giant, ebony-skinned native about twenty years old standing over six feet in stockings, weighing about 190 pounds, and a magnificent specimen of manhood, straight, well-muscled and perfectly formed. He... goes through the water with shoulders high above the surface,

Bobby Jones to golf. He has been Mister Surfer and Mister Swimming rolled into one incredible giant of a man."

Born into a royal family

A full-blooded Hawaiian, Duke Paoa Kahinu Mokoe Hulikohola Kahanamoku was born in the palace of Princess Ruth in Honolulu. A descendent of the early nineteenth-century King Kamehameha, Kahanamoku could trace his given name to the British Duke of Edinburgh, whose 1869 visit to the Hawaiian islands coincided with the birth of Kahanamoku's father, Duke Sr., who passed the name on to his first-born son. Young Duke grew up in a family of five brothers and three sisters near the ocean in a section of Waikiki now occupied by the Hilton Hawaiian Village resort. He always loved the ocean, and he left school after the eleventh grade to pursue a life in the water by concentrating on his swimming.

Shortly before the Olympic trials in August 1911, the first Amateur Athletic Union (AAU) swim meet was held in Hawaii. When young Kahanamoku broke the world record for the 100-yard freestyle event by an incredible 4.6 seconds and tied the 50-yard freestyle world record, mainland officials refused to believe the times were accurate. They first asked if the Hawaiian timekeepers had been using alarm clocks for stopwatches and then claimed that the ocean currents had aided the swimmer. Eager to prove that Kahanamoku's performance was not a fluke, Hawaiian locals raised the funds to send the swimmer to the mainland. In Chicago, Kahanamoku swam for the first time in a pool, dominating the 50-yard and 100-yard freestyle events. At the Olympic

Duke Kahanamoku

moving at fast speed." The young swimmer would go on to compete in four Olympic Games, altogether winning three gold and two silver medals.

Kahanamoku is also credited as the father of modern surfing, taking the sport that had once been the private pastime of Hawaiian kings and transforming it into an international sensation. Shortly after the athlete's death in 1968, Reed McQueen wrote in the *Honolulu Advertiser,* "[Kahanamoku] had been to both sports exactly what Babe Ruth was to baseball, Joe Louis to boxing, Red Grange to football, and qualifying trials in Philadelphia, Pennsylvania, Kahanamoku won the 100-meter freestyle and was the top qualifier for the 800-meter relay team.

In Stockholm, Kahanamoku tied the world record in a qualifying heat for the 100-meter freestyle. At the time of the final, however, he was nowhere to be found. The story is a favorite of Sergeant Kahanamoku, Duke's younger brother: "Brother Duke slept 99 percent of the time. He could sleep while he was sitting there talking to you. And I always thought that was what made him a great swimmer. He was clear in the head. So at the Olympic finals, they found him asleep under a bridge, snoring. He got up, said sorry, got in the water to loosen up, and then won the race. His mind was clear." So clear was Kahanamoku's mind that at the halfway mark, he took the time to look back and survey the pool. Realizing he had a comfortable lead, he allowed himself a more leisurely pace, and still won by two yards.

The Stockholm Games made Kahanamoku an international sensation. Although the 1916 Games were canceled because of World War I, he spent the following eight years traveling extensively, defending his titles at AAU meets and demonstrating the powerful "Kahanamoku kick." It was also during this time that Kahanamoku began to spread surfing throughout the world. He would often carry with him one of his longboards made from Hawaiian koa wood. His 1915 visit to Australia is remembered in Australian surfing lore as a historic moment. And during a 1916 Red Cross fund-raising tour of the East Coast, Kahanamoku stopped for surfing exhibitions in Atlantic City, New Jersey, and Coney Island, New York. In New York, officials even named a Brighton

Beach thoroughfare after him. At the 1920 Olympics in Antwerp, Belgium, Kahanamoku broke his own world record for the 100-meter freestyle just in time for his thirtieth birthday. He was also the anchor for the world-record-setting 800-meter relay team.

A movie star

During the 1920s, Kahanamoku split his time between Honolulu and Hollywood as he began a movie career that would span 28 years and dozens of films, in which he usually appeared as a bare-chested Hawaiian king. Perhaps the highlight of his film career was a role as a Polynesian chief in the 1948 adventure film *Wake of the Red Witch*, which starred John Wayne.

At the same time, Kahanamoku was unofficially designated Hawaii's greeter; he welcomed almost every well-known person who came to visit the islands. Photos collected over the years show Kahanamoku in a boat with Babe Ruth, on the beach with child star Shirley Temple, holding comedian Groucho Marx on his shoulders, chatting with statesman John F. Kennedy, and giving an impromptu hula lesson to Britain's Queen Mother Elizabeth.

Olympic defeat

Kahanamoku's first defeat was in 1924 at the Paris Games, in which he was beaten in the 100-meter event by 19-year-old Johnny Weissmuller, who would later play Tarzan in several Hollywood movies. During the final, Weissmuller swam between Kahanamoku on one side and Kahanamoku's 19-year-old brother, Sam, on the other. The young Weissmuller remembered Kahanamoku's encouraging words: "Johnny, good luck. The most important thing in this race is to get the American flag up there three times. Let's do it." When the race was over, Weissmuller had won, leaving Kahanamoku with a silver, and Sam with the bronze. (Sam reportedly had slowed down in deference to his older brother.) Years later Kahanamoku would joke, "It took Tarzan to finally beat me."

A hero for life

Despite his defeat at the Olympics, Kahanamoku will always be remembered as a hero. In 1925, he and a group of friends saw a boat capsize during a fierce storm off the coast of southern California. Without hesitation, Kahanamoku grabbed his surfboard and, making three trips through violent waves, personally saved 8 people in a disaster that claimed 17 out of 29 lives. The local chief of police was later quoted in newspapers as saying, "Kahanamoku's performance was the most superhuman rescue act and the finest display of surfboard riding that has ever been seen in the world."

Kahanamoku did not compete in the 1928 Games in Amsterdam, the Netherlands, due to illness. In 1932, at the age of 42, he missed qualifying for the Los Angeles Games, though his trial times were faster than the world records he had set 21 years earlier. He did earn a spot as an alternate on the bronze-winning water polo team, though he did not play.

From Hollywood, Kahanamoku returned to Hawaii to settle down. He first operated two gas stations. But soon after, he began his 26-year career as Honolulu's sheriff. Nonetheless, the spirit of competition remained with him well into his fifties—under his guidance, Hawaii's Outrigger Canoe Club won seven straight championships.

Kahanamouku passed away in 1968 at the age of 77, but he was not soon forgotten. In 1963, a number of his friends had worked together to establish the Duke Kahanamoku Foundation to encourage and support youth interested in water sports and international relations. In 1986, the foundation merged with the Outrigger Canoe Club to form the Outrigger Duke Kahanamoku Foundation, which is dedicated to encouraging athletes and scholars in the state of Hawaii. In 1990, Hawaii commemorated the 100th anniversary of his birth by dedicating a nine-foot bronze statue on Waikiki Beach. Standing with his back to the Ocean, a 12-foot surfboard at his side, the "Bronze Duke of Waikiki" continues to greet all visitors to his island, his arms outstretched in a grand welcome.

In 2002, the U.S. Postal Service issued a commemorative stamp in Honolulu bearing Kahanamoku's picture.

Sources:

Gullo, Jim, "The Beloved Duke of Waikiki," *Sports Illustrated,* September 17, 1990, p. 97.

Outrigger Duke Kahanamoku Foundation, http://www.dukefoundation.org (accessed March 2003).

Wallechinsky, David, *The Complete Book of the Olympics,* New York: Little, Brown, 1991, p. 475.

Ken Kashiwahara

Broadcast journalist
Born July 18, 1940, Waimea, Hawaii

"I think the media has to realize that Asian Americans are part of America. We are Americans. Asian Americans ought to be used in stories that have to do with general things in the country, whether it be the economy, or politics, or how Americans feel about the Middle East. What's wrong with asking an Asian American about that? Nothing."

Ken Kashiwahara was a correspondent for ABC News and one of the first Asian Americans to work in network television. He became a correspondent for ABC in 1974 and served as Los Angeles bureau chief from 1978 to 1998. Kashiwahara is also a vocal commentator on Asian American issues, especially as they are reflected in the media. He told *A. Magazine,* "I think we've come a long way, but we have an even longer way to go. Even most people in the media don't really understand and are not educated about Asian Americans. It's our responsibility to be watchdogs, to see what is happening in our communities and the media and to point out to our superiors what we see as unjust and wrong."

Born just before Pearl Harbor

Kashiwahara's parents were both schoolteachers who wanted him to blend into American culture and scolded him when he spoke imperfect English. Yet they also wanted Kashiwahara to learn about traditional Japanese culture, so they sent him to a Japanese-language school on weekends. After the Japanese bombed the U.S. naval base at Pearl Harbor, which marked the beginning of American involvement in World War II, anti-Japanese hysteria—referred to as the "yellow scare"—swept the United States. It was especially severe in Hawaii, where Kashiwahara remembers his parents actually being afraid to speak Japanese, hiding their Japanese-language books, and throwing away their chopsticks out of fear.

Kashiwahara was an average student; he graduated from high school in 1958. After this he decided to go to college on the mainland and enrolled at Washington and Jefferson College in Washington, Pennsylvania. There Kashiwahara was exposed to extreme racism, which had a profound effect on him. As he told *A. Magazine,* "My first two years of college were in Pennsylvania and there was a lot of prejudice then. I couldn't join a fraternity in college because of all-white clauses; it was very traumatic, and I went through a period where I was ashamed of being Asian. I didn't want to speak Japanese or eat Japanese food. It was that bad."

Return to Hawaii

Kashiwahara decided to leave Washington and Jefferson after two years. He returned to Hawaii and enrolled in the premed program at the University of Hawaii. He stayed there for one year and then became interested in broadcasting, ultimately deciding that he did not want to become a doctor. Kashiwahara moved back to the mainland and enrolled in San Francisco State College, where he earned a bachelor's degree in broadcasting in 1963. At that time there was a military draft, and

Ken Kashiwahara

rather than be drafted into the army, he enlisted in the air force and became an information officer. After being stationed in Europe, Kashiwahara volunteered to go to Vietnam.

After serving five years in the military, Kashiwahara returned to civilian life in Hawaii, where he began pursuing a career in television news. He described the reasoning behind his decision to *A. Magazine,* remarking, "I saw the makeup of the population [in Hawaii]: mostly Asian, and I saw the people on television: all white. And I thought, well, for a guy with no experience, this might be a

way to get in." His hunch proved correct, and he was hired by KGMB-TV in Honolulu as a political reporter. "I was terrible at first," he recalled, "nervous and stiff. It took me a full year to get really comfortable." His patience and determination paid off: he became a well-liked reporter, and in 1971 he became a news anchor.

Moving to the network

In 1972 Kashiwahara moved to KABC in Los Angeles, where he served as a reporter and co-anchor of the weekend news broadcasts. Two years later he became a network correspondent with ABC. In this position, Kashiwahara was assigned to cover much more important stories. These included regional stories with national significance—which are frequent in Los Angeles—and important international stories. He covered the American involvement in Indochina, where American-installed governments in South Vietnam and Cambodia were falling prey to guerrilla warfare (in which independent units carried out harassment and sabotage against government troops). Covering these events, Kashiwahara was one of the last American journalists to be airlifted out of Saigon in 1975 as the city fell to the Communist North Vietnamese.

In 1975 Kashiwahara was named chief of the ABC News bureau in Hong Kong. He served at this post for three years and covered many stories, as well as the civil war in Beirut, Lebanon, in 1977. During the 1980s, Kashiwahara covered a wide range of stories for ABC, including Ronald Reagan's presidential campaigns and the spectacular eruption of Mount St. Helens in Oregon. In 1986 Kashiwahara won a national Emmy Award for his story "In the Fire's Path," which was broadcast on ABC's *20-20*. The report detailed the 1985 brush fires that devastated Ojai, California, and surrounding areas. In 1988 he won a second Emmy as a correspondent for the documentary *Burning Question: The Poisoning of America.*

In 1988 and 1989 Kashiwahara accompanied veterans of the Vietnam War on a return trip to Vietnam. The journey resulted in a special report broadcast on the network evening news about three veterans' reunions with children they had fathered while in Vietnam. He also contributed to a one-hour *Nightline* special focusing on eight veterans with post-traumatic stress disorder (a kind of shock suffered by victims of extremely harrowing experiences) who were coming to terms with their wartime experiences. Also in 1989 Kashiwahara covered the aftermath of the Tiananmen Square massacre in Beijing, China, in which hundreds—perhaps as many as one thousand—of unarmed pro-democracy demonstrators were killed by Chinese government troops. Kashiwahara retired from ABC in 1998.

A voice for change

As an Asian American pioneer in the field of broadcast journalism, Kashiwahara is often looked to for wisdom and advice on breaking into this competitive field. He cites determination and the need to stand up to discrimination—for instance, the use of minority reporters only to report stories about, or affecting members of, that minority. "I think the media has to realize that Asian Americans are part of America," he told *A. Magazine.* "We are Americans. Asian Americans ought to be used in stories that have to do with general things in the country, whether it be the economy, or politics, or how Americans feel about the Middle East. What's wrong with asking an Asian American about that? Nothing."

Kashiwahara also believes that in many ways the media are blind to Asian Americans and their struggle for assimilation into the mainstream of American society. In his view, the first black in space, or the first Hispanic, or the first woman, is treated as newsworthy, but when the first Asian went into space, no one noticed. A more blatant example, cited by Kashiwahara, was a *New York Times* article asserting that the U.S. Senate was 100 percent white, when in fact at the time there were two Asian American senators, **Daniel K. Inouye** and Spark Matsunaga.

Kashiwahara is a frequent lecturer on college campuses. He believes that, beginning with his generation, the time has come for Asian Americans to speak out about injustice and racism. "The generation before wanted to remain low-key," he told *A. Magazine,* "and not go out in front. But the next generation and the generation after that are saying, 'It's time to speak out. It is time to assume the responsibility, to take our place in society.'" Kashiwahara was awarded a Lifetime Achievement Award in 1993 from the Asian American Journalists Association. In 2001 he received an achievement award as a Japanese American Visionary from the National Japanese American Historical Society.

Sources:

Chin, Curtis, Lilian Huang, and James Want, "Correspondent Force," *A. Magazine,* vol. 1, no. 1, fall 1992, p. 16.

Huang, Lilian, "A Newsroom of Our Own," *A. Magazine,* vol. 1, no. 1, fall 1992.

Kashiwahara, Ken, telephone interview with Jim Henry, April 20, 1994.

National Japanese American Historical Society, http://www.nikkeiheritage.org (accessed February 28, 2003).

Elaine Kim

Academic, author, activist
Born February 26, 1942, New York City

"[Asian Americans] have moved into cities and towns where few Asian Americans had lived before and are doing things to earn their livelihoods that they could not have imagined in their homelands: Cambodians are making doughnuts, Koreans are making burritos, South Asians are operating motels and taxicabs, Filipinos are driving airport shuttle buses. The lines between Asian and American and Asian American are increasingly blurred."

Elaine H. Kim is a professor of Asian American studies at the University of California at Berkeley. U.C. Berkeley is widely considered the foremost university in the country in the promotion of ethnic studies and the place where much of what we today call multiculturalism—the celebration and acceptance of diverse cultures within one society—first found a national voice. She is a leading national activist and a widely published writer. Kim also produces educational videos and in 1992 made a documentary called *Sa-I-Gu: From Korean Women's Perspective.* This video, which was shot three months after the 1992 Los Angeles riots (sparked by the acquittal of four white police officers accused of savagely beating black motorist Rodney King and videotaped in the process), details the substantial destruction the riots caused in Los Angeles's Koreatown.

Early sense of bigotry

Kim grew up and was educated in Tacoma Park and Silver Spring, Maryland. Her mother and father were both Korean. Her mother immigrated to Hawaii as an infant in 1903 and spent her childhood working on the tenant farms of California and Hawaii. Her father had come to the United States in 1926 as a student.

Both parents were proud of their Korean heritage, and they instilled that pride in their children. In school, however, Kim was subjected to bigotry. In 1994, in a speech she delivered at the University of Maryland, she recalled her harsh experiences: "When I was in the second grade, we read an illustrated book that pictured a globe with a blonde-haired white child standing upright on top of the world, and an upside down Asian child on the bottom, complete with buck teeth, slitted eyes, a long upside-down pigtail, and orange skin. Later on the school bus going home, the girl sitting in front of me turned around, put her arm against mine and said, 'You're *yellow.*'"

Kim also described the physical violence suffered by her brother, reporting, "When I was in elementary and junior high school, gangs of supposedly decent white boys routinely beat my brother up every day after school and hurled epithets... at me when I walked by." She went on to discuss long-standing bad feeling between the Asian

Elaine Kim

American and African American communities, remarking, "It was clear that racism against African Americans was as American as apple pie, and that as an Asian American I was viewed as occupying a space higher than black and lower than white, for which I was supposed to be grateful. Sometimes students would say to me, 'Well, at least you're not black.'"

Return to Korea

Kim graduated from Eastern Senior High School in 1959 and then enrolled in the Uni-

versity of Pennsylvania, where she earned a degree in English and American literature in 1963. From there she went to New York City to study at Columbia University, where she earned a master's degree in English and comparative literature in 1965.

In 1966, Kim left the United States for Korea. "When I was 23 years old," she said in her 1992 keynote speech to the Women's Organization Reaching Koreans, "I went to work in Seoul [South Korea] for a year, armed with an Ivy League education and buoyed by a burning desire to 'become Korean.' I returned feeling neither 'Korean' nor 'American.'" The cultural differences were stunning to the young woman, especially Korean culture's view of women as inferior to men. She stayed in Seoul until 1967, working as a lecturer in English at Ewha University. In 1968, she returned to the States and enrolled in the University of California at Berkeley as a Ph.D. student in English. Again she was confronted with, if not the outright racism of her childhood, a cultural bias that discouraged her interest in studying the literature of non-Western cultures. Frustrated by the English department's closed-mindedness, she transferred to the education department, which she found more open to cultural diversity.

The Third World strikes

In 1969, the Berkeley campus was wracked by strikes started by students of color who felt underrepresented numerically and culturally. The students, whom Kim joined, wanted greater representation on the faculty and student bodies; they also fought for the establishment of ethnic studies programs to emphasize the cultural contributions of non-European societies and to teach the history of non-Europeans in the United States. These strikes were part of a national movement of democratic expression that combined anti-Vietnam war sentiment with civil rights demands from all minorities. Kim was greatly influenced by the strike and the philosophy behind it, and her dissertation, published by Temple University Press in 1982, was a compilation of the work of Asian American writers. Entitled *Asian American Literature: An Introduction to the Writings and Their Social Context,* it was the first scholarly study of Asian American literature and is still considered a major work in the field.

Beginning in the early 1970s, Kim worked to establish Berkeley's Asian American studies program within the newly founded Ethnic Studies Department. She was instrumental in the development of remedial English equivalency programs to help people who speak English as a second language. These courses, which teach critical reading and writing skills, use literature from African American, Native American, Asian American, and Chicano (Mexican American) writers, a practice that became common in the 1990s, but was revolutionary in 1970.

Community activist and author

Kim was granted tenure (a status granted after a trial period to a teacher protecting him or her from dismissal) in 1981, and she began devoting her time to community activities in support of San Francisco-area Korean Americans. The organizations with which she has worked include Asian Women United of California, the Korean Community Center of the East Bay, the Center for Women's Policy Studies, the NOW (National Organization for Women) Legal Defense Fund, the Northern California Korean Coalition, the U.S. Korea Foundation, the Japan Pacific Resource Network, the Association for Asian American Studies, the National Council of the American Studies Association, and Asian Immigrant Women Advocates. From 1998–2000, Kim served on President Bill Clinton's Commission on Women in U.S. History.

Kim has written extensively on issues of concern to Asian Americans. Her first published article, "The Myth of Asian American Success," appeared in 1975 in *Asian American Review.* Her dissertation was published in 1982, and the next year she published *With Silk Wings: Asian American Women at Work.* In 1994 Kim and coauthor L. H. Lang published *Writing Self, Writing Nation.* Other articles by Kim have been published in magazines and newspapers such as the *Philadelphia Inquirer, Newsweek,* the *San Francisco Bay Guardian, A. Magazine,* and *Korean Journal.* She has served as editor of several anthologies, including the highly regarded *Making Waves: Writings by and about Asian American Women* (1989) and *Making More Waves: New Writing by Asian American Women* (1997). Other books include *East to America: Korean American Life Stories* (1996, finalist for the Kirayama Book Prize), *Echoes Upon Echoes: New Korean American Writing* (2002), and *Fresh Talk/Daring Gazes: Issues in American Visual Art* (anticipated for 2003). Kim became active in television productions through her work on *Slaying the Dragon: Asian Women in U.S. Television and Film* (1987–88), *Sa-i-gu: From Korean Women's Perspectives* (1993), *Art to Art* (1994), and *Labor Women* (2002).

The state of Korean America

Kim viewed the riots of April 29 and 30, 1992, in South Central Los Angeles as a pivotal event in the history of Koreans in America. In an article called "Home Is Where the *Han* Is: A Korean American Perspective on the Los Angeles Upheavals," she wrote, "When Koreans in South Central dialed 911 [during the riots] nothing happened. When their stores and homes were being looted and burned to the ground, they were left alone for three horrifying days.... What they had to learn was that, as in South Korea, protection in the U.S. is by and large for the rich and powerful. If there is a choice between Westwood [a wealthy Los Angeles community] and Koreatown, it is clear that Koreatown will have to be sacrificed."

"Today's Asian American communities are maintaining their cultural distinctness," Kim stated in her 1994 address at the University of Maryland, "enabled by modern communication and transportation technology to develop what have been called 'private cultures' and new communities, as Vietnamese refugees settle in Westminster, California, and Korean immigrants gather in Flushing, New York.... [They] have moved into cities and towns where few Asian Americans had lived before and are doing things to earn their livelihoods that they could not have imagined in their homelands: Cambodians are making doughnuts, Koreans are making burritos, South Asians are operating motels and taxicabs, Filipinos are driving airport shuttle buses. The lines between Asian and American and Asian American are increasingly blurred... [suggesting] the permeability of boundaries and borders as well as the possibility of new, hybrid, self-determined identities crafted by Asian Americans themselves."

In 2002, Kim was continuing her work as professor of Asian American Studies and was serving as associate dean of the graduate program at the University of California, Berkeley.

Sources:

Department of Ethnic Studies, University of California, Berkeley, http://ist-socrates.berkeley.edu/~ethnicst/ (accessed March 2003).

Kim, Elaine H., "Asian Americans and Higher Education," address given at University of Maryland Conference on Education Equity, March 2-28, 1994.

Kim, Elaine H., "Creating a Third Space," *San Francisco Bay Guardian,* March 10, 1993.

Kim, Elaine H., "They Armed in Self-Defense," *Newsweek,* May 18, 1992, p. 10.

Kim, Elaine H., "Women's Organization Reaching Koreans: Keynote Speech," November 13, 1992, printed in *KoreAm Journal,* December 1992, p. 32.

Jay C. Kim

Politician, civil engineer
Born March 27, 1939, Seoul, South Korea

"They [Asian Americans] can look at me and say, 'He made it as an immigrant with a strong accent, why can't I?'"

I n a surprise victory, Jay C. Kim was elected to the U.S. House of Representatives in November 1992, becoming the first Korean American to serve in that body. He was elected to represent the newly created 41st District of California, a racially mixed, solidly Republican district outside of Los Angeles. Kim was a political outsider when he was elected, though he had served for two years as mayor of the small town of Diamond Bar, where he made his home. Kim sought election to Congress largely out of the personal conviction that the politicians he encountered were motivated overwhelmingly by self-interest. In an article in *Time,* Kim described what was behind his decision to enter the race: he had just been forced to lay off 20 employees when he read about the pay raises members of Congress had voted for themselves. It struck him that the legislative body was out of step with the problems and concerns of most Americans.

Kim did not initially plan to run for the new district's seat and had even endorsed one of the other candidates in the Republican primary. But when he was approached by people from the party who were dissatisfied with the other two contenders, Kim accepted the challenge. As an immigrant, he faced many obstacles to his election bid—not the least of which was his accent. After more than 30 years in the United States, it was still quite pronounced. Kim especially hopes to be an inspiration to other Asian Americans. "They can look at me," he explained, "and say, 'He made it as an immigrant with a strong accent, why can't I?'"

Born in Korea

Kim was born in 1939 in what is today South Korea. The Korean peninsula had not yet been divided—that occurred after World War II—and was under the control of a brutal Japanese occupation force. By the time Kim left his homeland in 1961, Korea had been liberated from the Japanese, divided by the superpowers of the Soviet Union and the United States, and had suffered through a civil war and military dictatorships. Kim served in the Korean Army in his late teens and early twenties; after his discharge, he immigrated to the United States.

In 1967 Kim earned a bachelor's degree in civil engineering from the University of Southern California. He then continued his education there, earning a master's degree in 1973. After securing his degrees, Kim changed his name from Chang Joon Kim to Jay Kim. He worked as a civil engineer for the next couple of years and then, in 1976, he formed his own engineering and design firm, Jaykim Engineers. His business was based on building roads and water reclamation projects—the type of government-financed work that many congressmen try to funnel to companies in their districts—and benefited from being minority owned. (By law, a certain percentage of all U.S.

government contracts must go to minority-owned businesses.)

Jaykim became very financially rewarding; it also taught Kim a lot about business in general and the way government money is spent. In 1992 Jaykim was one of the many businesses hired to demolish damaged buildings after the Los Angeles riots. This was one of the last projects Kim headed; after his election to Congress in November of that year, he sold the company to avoid the appearance of conflict of interest (a conflict between his private interests and official responsibilities).

Kim's political career

Kim's political career began in 1990 with his election to the city council of Diamond Bar in eastern Los Angeles County. He then served as mayor of Diamond Bar from 1991 to 1993. Kim decided to run for Congress in 1992 in a district that had been created after the reapportionment (division of the state into new districts for purposes of political representation and taxation) following the 1990 census. As a newly created district, there was no incumbent in office, so the election was wide open. There were several Republicans vying for the nomination to run in the general election, and Kim originally supported Charles W. Bader, the mayor of Pomona.

After Kim entered the race his status as a political outsider served as an advantage in an election year marked by anti-Washington and anti-career-politician sentiment. In addition, Kim's entrepreneurial success appealed to the predominantly white-collar, conservative, and affluent voters in the district. Kim surprised both political observers and his

Jay C. Kim

opponents with his victory in the primary election. He then went on to easily defeat his Democratic opponent, Bob Baker, an intelligence analyst and Vietnam veteran whom Kim outspent by a considerable sum.

Kim's political philosophy

Kim is a solid Republican, championing the conservative economic policies that the party traditionally supports. After his election he worked hard to be appointed to the Public Works and Transportation Commit-

139

tee, which oversees government spending on the national infrastructure (the nation's systems of highways, railroads, bridges, and military installations), a close fit with the type of work at which Kim had made his living. He sought this position in order to keep an eye on the way government contracts are awarded, working to eliminate wasteful spending.

Kim does deviate from the Republican party platform in some areas, mostly on social issues. He is against the party's general opposition to abortion, believing that this is a personal decision that should be left out of public policy. He is also opposed to the controversial Republican endorsement of private school vouchers, which would enable Americans to send their children to the school of their choosing. Kim instead favors providing tax credits to families who choose to send their children to private schools.

In the 103rd Congress, Kim was noticeably vocal for a first-year congressman. He took the floor more than the average freshman and spoke out against deficit spending, higher taxes, and government mandates. Kim voted essentially Republican. He opposed the Family and Medical Leave Act, which requires companies to provide guaranteed maternity leave to parents, and he opposed the "Motor Voter" registration bill, which allows people to register to vote when they renew their driver's licenses. Kim also voted in favor of a measure that requires parental notification in the event that a minor seeks an abortion.

Kim and his wife, June, have been married since the 1960s. They have three children.

Sources:

Booth, Cathy, Wendy Cole, and Sylvester Monroe, "California/Jay Kim," *Time,* November 2, 1992, p. 46.

"Jay C. Kim," *Congressional Quarterly,* January 16, 1993, p. 58.

Wendell Kim

Baseball manager, coach
Born March 9, 1950, Honolulu, Hawaii

"I'm proud I never gave up. I'm still doing something I love. I was in the minors for 16 years before getting up here. A lot of people never get up here. I kept working hard to get here. The main thing I've done is survive."

Wendell Kealhapauloe Kim became the first Korean American to work in the major leagues in 1989 when, after over a decade of playing and coaching in the minor leagues, he became the first-base coach for the San Francisco Giants. Since then, he has also coached for the Boston Red Sox and the Montreal Expos. Kim's philosophy is "never be satisfied." He told the *Oakland Tribune*: "When I won a championship in the minor leagues I came back the next year and wanted another one. I've been that way all along. That way you don't make mistakes and screw up. Some guys take it for granted that they've got it made.... I always try to find other things to help us win."

A difficult childhood

Kim was born in Hawaii to a Korean American father and a mother of mixed ancestry. His father, Philip "Wildcat" Kim, was a renowned professional welterweight boxer who, Kim believes, had connections to the crime underworld. He was a brutal man whose anger and abuse dominated the Kim household. He routinely beat his wife and children. Kim sees his father's abusiveness as the result of *his* childhood. He told the *Contra Costa Times* that when his father was a child, "his mother didn't want him. He lived in a crate box behind a market." When Kim was still very young the family left Hawaii and moved to a rough Los Angeles neighborhood between Watts and Compton. Kim was eight years old when his father was killed in a gang-style assassination, probably in connection with a comeback fight he was planning.

The death of Philip Kim brought a certain peace to the Kim home. Wendell began playing Little League baseball and started devoting himself to his studies. He was a tough kid, as was necessary in his neighborhood, but he managed to be one of the top students in his school. He graduated tenth in his class at Banning High School with a 3.4 grade point average. He knew it was not considered "cool" to be seen studying or carrying books, so Kim worked out a unique system for excelling academically without drawing unwanted attention to himself. "I would stay out with the tough guys at my school until midnight on school nights and then stay up for two hours doing my homework," he said in an interview in the *Modesto Bee*.

Wendell Kim

Through most of this time, Kim was essentially on his own. His mother worked full time and told him that she would have to trust in his judgment about what was right and wrong because she didn't have the time or energy to watch after him. He showed considerable strength in maneuvering through his difficult childhood with his priorities intact. The rest of his family was not so fortunate. "My brother went the other way—he's on drugs," he told the *Modesto Bee*. "I've only talked to him once in the last five years. I haven't talked to my sister in fifteen years because of what they did to my mother—hustling her for money for drugs."

Baseball

After high school Kim joined the U.S. Coast Guard to help finance college. He then attended California State Polytechnic University at Pomona, where he played four years of varsity baseball while studying education. While on the Cal State Broncos, Kim set a single-season record for runs scored (93), walks (91), and games played (124), and he was twice named to the All-California Collegiate Athletic Association Team. Still, after college he found that no major league teams were interested in drafting him. He was finally signed as a walk-on by the Giants. He told the *Modesto Bee,* "I was never signed out of college or high school. They didn't want me, I was too short. So I slept in my car two nights in Arizona [at the Giants' spring camp] while waiting for a try-out. I was the only one chosen out of 170 tryouts from all over the country." He was signed in 1973. By 1976 he was playing AA ball in Texas. In 1979 he was playing in Phoenix, where he hit a career high of .313.

Known throughout the Giants organization for his hustle, enthusiasm, and knowledge of the game, Kim was offered a job managing in the Giants' minor league system in 1980. He worked in the minors for the next eight seasons with teams in Clinton (1981–82) and Fresno, California (1983–85), Shreveport, Texas (1986), and Phoenix, Arizona (1987–88). He was named California League Manager of the Year after leading Fresno to the California League title in 1983. He was voted Texas League Manager of the Year in 1986 after leading Shreveport to an 80–56 mark. Kim also led the Phoenix Firebirds to a 77–67 record, coming within one game of the Pacific Coast League play-

offs; he led that team to a 76–67 record in 1988, setting a personal record of five straight seasons above .500.

The majors

In 1989 the Giants brought Kim up to the major leagues, making him first-base coach. Kim quickly earned a reputation as one of the most highly motivated people on the team, described by many as being in nearly perpetual motion. Kim's hard work, zeal, and energy are applied to every task at hand, from coaching to preparing line-up cards, setting up defensive alignments, leading calisthenics, and even pitching at batting practices. Kim was eventually moved to third-base coach.

Kim's fellow players and coaches had high praise for him. Coach Bob Brenly said in the *Vacaville Reporter,* "Every ball club needs a guy like Wendell. He does the job of three or four coaches. And a lot of it is very tedious—charts and tendencies. But Wendell doesn't mind." Giants manager Dusty Baker offered: "Wendell is our everything coach. He does so many different things. Wendell is always up and energetic in everything he does. He's No. 1 in exuberance. He's definitely determined. You don't spend all those years in the minor leagues without being determined."

Kim stayed with the Giants until 1991. Then, from 1997 to 2000, he held a position as third-base coach with the Boston Red Sox. It was with the Red Sox that he gained his reputation as one of the most aggressive third-base coaches in the league. His teammates and fans began to call him "Wave 'Em In Wendell." After Boston, Kim spent a brief time as manager for the Indianapolis Indians, the Milwaukee Brewers' AAA Club. But in 2001, he was called up by Montreal Expos manager Frank Robinson to the position of bench coach. While Kim clearly enjoys his work, he continues to dream of a higher goal: to be the first Asian American to be a manager of a major league team.

Looking back on his career and childhood, Kim once told the *Modesto Bee,* "I'm proud I never gave up. I'm still doing something I love. I was in the minors for 16 years before getting up here. A lot of people never get up here. I kept working hard to get here. The main thing I've done is survive."

Sources:

"History in the Waiting" *ESPN,* http://www.espn.com (accessed March 2003).

Jackson, Ron, "Diminutive Coach Performs Big Job," *Vacaville Reporter,* August 18, 1993.

Montreal Expos, http://www.exposdemontreal.com (accessed March 2003).

Newhouse, Dave, "Kim Escaped from a Rough Childhood," *Contra Costa Times,* July 11, 1992.

Rocha, Elisa, "Mr. Excitement," *Modesto Bee,* August 13, 1993.

Schulman, Henry, "The Life and Times of Wendell Kim—That's Adversity," *Oakland Tribune,* August 23, 1992.

Willa Kim

Costume designer
Born in Los Angeles, California

"I can reflect and help to emphasize what the choreographer is doing in the way of movement. I try to take advantage of the best points of the performer."

With a career in costume design that spans over 30 years, Willa Kim is one of the most decorated artists working in theater. Since her first Broadway show in 1966—Edward Albee's *Malcolm* at the Schubert Theater—Kim has been designing stage costumes to rave reviews. She won Tony awards for Duke Ellington's *Sophisticated Ladies* (1981) and Tommy Tune's *Will Rogers Follies* (1991). She received Tony nominations for Peter Allen's *Legs Diamond* (1988), Andrew Lloyd Webber's *Song and Dance* (1985), Bob Fosse's *Dancin'* (1978), and Joel Grey's *Goodtime Charley* (1975). Among Kim's other laurels are an Emmy for the San Francisco Ballet's production of *The Tempest* (1981); Drama Desk awards for Maria Irene Fornes's *Promenade* (1969), Sam Shepherd's *Operation Sidewinder* (1988), and Jean Genet's *Screens* (1971); and an Obie (an annual award presented for off-Broadway productions by the *Village Voice)* for Robert Lowell's *The Old Glory* (1976).

In addition to her stage work, Kim is credited with originating the sleek look of modern ballet costumes. She was a pioneer in the use of stretch fabrics, which came to replace the thick, wooly nylon that had been the fabric of choice among dancers before Kim. Kim's new designs celebrated the lines of a dancer's body, accentuating the elongated torso. Kim was also the first to experiment with fabric painting, convincing a Brooklyn factory to lend her dyes and to teach her how to color nylons. Her experimental methods quickly became the industry standard.

An artist, not a designer

As a child, Kim, a second-generation Korean American (the second generation of her family to be born in the United States), spent many hours drawing and making paper dolls; she was sure that she would become a painter. "I was trained as an artist, not a designer, and my work reflects that," Kim told *TheaterWeek* in 1991. After receiving a scholarship, she studied fashion illustration at the Chouinard Institute of Art in Los Angeles. She happened onto costume design straight out of art school: "One of my art instructors insisted that I take my portfolio around to art studios and department stores," she explained in *Costume Design: Techniques of Modern Masters.* "I was so delighted when Western Costume asked me to leave it. It was as big as I was and it was so heavy to carry around. The next thing I knew, I was working in the studios."

In the late 1950s, Kim moved from Los Angeles to New York City. Her first New York production was Arnold Weinstein's 1961 Off-Broadway play *Red Eye of Love.* "I had to create 50 costumes with a budget of $250. I used to fall asleep on the floor in the theater and get up and sew at the strangest hours," Kim told the *New York Times* in 1981. In spite of its difficulty, the experience proved to be a great training ground, and Kim found the work exhilarating. She continued designing for the theater, often under similar circumstances, and within five years she was working on Broadway for one of America's premier playwrights as the costume designer for Edward Albee's *Malcolm.*

Then, in 1962, a young choreographer, Greg Tetley, approached Kim to design the costumes for a ballet he was choreographing. Called *Birds of Sorrow,* the production was well received and proved very successful. "[A] lot of choreographers saw that evening of dance and started calling me. Once again, it was something I hadn't thought about doing any more than I had thought about designing," Kim told *Costume Design.* "It seems events kind of occurred and the next thing I knew I was a ballet designer." Since her debut as a designer for dance, Kim has worked regularly with some of the most prestigious ballet companies in the United States, including the Joffrey Ballet, the American Ballet Theater, the San Francisco Ballet, the Alvin Ailey Company, and the Feld Ballets/New York, with whom she has been affiliated for more than 20 years.

The Tonys

After being nominated twice before, Kim won her first Tony Award in 1981 for Duke Ellington's *Sophisticated Ladies.* The production was plagued by problems with directors and choreographers and Kim referred to the show as "a pain in the neck" in the *New York Times* shortly after winning the award. Yet, in spite of the frustrations, she maintained her priorities and justly triumphed with the theater's highest award.

The production that won Kim her second Tony Award was not nearly as frustrating. Working with acclaimed choreographer Tommy Tune, with whom she has collaborated on numerous shows, Kim created the glamorous costumes for *The Will Rogers Follies* from rough sketches supplied by Tune. In spite of a very demanding deadline, Kim told *TheaterWeek,* "It was an easy show to do, compared to a lot of them." The 1991 Broadway spectacular was a far cry from Kim's first New York show with its $250 costume budget; this time she had been given a budget of $1 million, with costumes each costing in the thousands. Because designers were not allowed to make acceptance speeches, when she was awarded her Tony, Kim stood up in the audience and held up a fan inscribed with thanks to Tune and the costume shop of Parson Meares.

The Kim process

When she is designing for the theater, Kim begins by reading the script, researching the period, and then meeting the performers. "It's ideal to wait until the show is cast before beginning the design," she said in a 1989 interview in *TheaterCraft.* In the same way, when she is designing a ballet, Kim insists on seeing the dancers rehearse the finished choreography. "I can reflect and help to emphasize what the choreographer is doing in the way of movement," she explained. "I try to take advantage of the best points of the performer."

Kim says that her favorite part of the designing process is watching things being made in the costume shops. She stays involved from conception to the final stitch, careful to examine the smallest of details.

Kim is also known for lengthy and frequent fittings, because the creation of the design often takes place partly on the body.

While she continues to design for the ballet and has also moved into opera, Kim has often voiced a preference for musical theater. "The challenge is much more exciting," she explained in *TheaterCraft.* "There's more to contend with. Not only the number of people but the complexity of the problem. You have to delineate a character within a time and a period and show a progression of ideas. You also have to flatter the performers."

Kim remains one of the busiest women working in theater, with many projects reflecting her preference for musical theater. She devised costumes for a revival of *Grease,* which opened on Broadway in late spring of 1994. Later challenges included Blake Edwards's stage version of *Victor/Victoria,* starring Julie Andrews, and Tommy Tune's *Busker,* both musicals.

In April 2003, Kim received the Fashion Institute of Technology's Patricia Zipprodt Award for Innovative Costume Design.

Sources:

Duka, John, "She Made 'Ladies' Look Sophisticated," *New York Times,* September 20, 1981, p. D3.

Dunning, Jennifer, "Backstage Partners: Ballet's Kim and Feld," *New York Times,* August 9, 1991.

Howard, Beth, "Designers on Designing: Willa Kim," *TheaterCraft,* March 1989, p. 29.

Kim, Willa, telephone interview with Terry Hong, March 14, 1994.

Pecktal, Lynn, "A Conversation with Willa Kim," *Costume Design: Techniques of Modern Masters,* New York: Backstage Books, 1993.

"Willa Kim Wins 2003 Zipprodt Award," *Entertainment Design,* April 22, 2003.

Wong, Wayman, "Willa-Mania!," *TheaterWeek,* July 8, 1991, pp. 24-27.

Dong Kingman

Artist
Born 1911, Oakland, California
Died May 12, 2000, Manhattan, New York

"For me there is no such thing as Oriental or Occidental. There is only my way of painting with watercolor and I hope whoever sees my paintings will enjoy and understand them as such."

Dong Kingman was one of America's premier twentieth-century artists. A watercolorist, his importance is recognized around the world, and his paintings hang in some of the most prestigious international private collections and museums, including New York City's Museum of Modern Art and Metropolitan Museum of Art, as well the Art Institute of Chicago. He taught painting at Columbia University, Hunter College, and at the Famous Artists School in Westport, Connecticut.

An early ocean voyage

Although Kingman was born in the United States, he left the country at a very early age. His father, a Chinese immigrant from Hong Kong, feared that his older children might somehow be dragged into World War I, then being fought on the European continent. He sold his small dry goods store and returned his family to Hong Kong by ship. It was during this voyage, when Kingman was five, that he first realized he was interested in, and had a capacity for, art. He described the realization in *Dong Kingman's Watercolors,* remembering, "There were many interesting characters aboard, so I began to sketch them day after day to break the monotony.... It was then that I first realized it would be fun to be an artist."

In Hong Kong, Kingman continued to display considerable artistic talent. He was encouraged in this area by his mother, who had painted for years. As a teenager he was sent to Lingnan Branch School, where he studied with Szetsu Wei, a noted Chinese painter. Under his tutelage, Kingman studied both traditional Chinese approaches to art and the works of Western masters. Kingman was especially influenced by the French impressionists, including Paul Gauguin and Pierre-Auguste Renoir. (The impressionists labored to represent objects in the same way that our eye sees them, often in quick bursts of color and blurry forms.) However, he generally prefers Chinese art to that of the West.

In 1929, at the age of 18, Kingman left Hong Kong for the United States where he thought he would be better able to pursue a career as an artist. He arrived in San Francisco, California, and worked at a variety of jobs to support himself and his art. During this period he began to define his artistic sensibilities. While working as a family servant in San Francisco, he spent his spare time painting cityscapes (scenes of the city) in three dimensions—with sunlight and shadow—discarding a key convention of Chinese watercolors, which are traditionally two-dimensional and represent only natural settings. Kingman produced enough work to be included in a show, and critics described his work as a blend of Chinese and Western art, or, to use the terminology of the day, Oriental and Occidental, respectively. Today, Kingman rejects such distinctions. "For me," he has said, "there is no such thing as Orien-

Dong Kingman's *442nd Combat Team at Leghorn*

tal or Occidental. There is only *my* way of painting with watercolor and I hope whoever sees my paintings will enjoy and understand them as such."

In 1936, Kingman was hired as an artist by the federal government through the auspices of the Works Progress Administration (WPA). The WPA was a Depression-era program of President Franklin D. Roosevelt's "New Deal," a series of government-funded programs meant to put the large numbers of unemployed people to work and to channel federal dollars into the stagnant economy. Kingman also mounted his first solo show that year. Held at the San Francisco Art Cen-

ter, it received excellent reviews. Watercolor painting was enjoying wide popularity on the West Coast at this time, and Kingman had the further good fortune to have the patronage of a prominent collector who greatly admired his work and donated several of his paintings to museums.

In 1940, the Metropolitan Museum of Art bought its first Kingman watercolor. This purchase was the first acquisition made by a major American museum of a work by an Asian American artist. In 1941, Kingman's stature was enhanced when he received a two-year Guggenheim fellowship that funded an extended tour of the United States. During

Dong Kingman

ist was drafted into the military, in which he served in Washington, D.C., as an illustrator for the Office of Strategic Services, the forerunner of today's CIA.

In 1945, Kingman was discharged from the military and moved permanently to New York, the city that had so enchanted him. He described his love for cities, which dominate his paintings, in *Dong Kingman's Watercolors:* "I was born, brought up, and have always lived in cities—Oakland, Hong Kong, San Francisco, New York City—and always right in the heart of the asphalt jungle, amid poor people in busy, noisy, congested areas. After many years, I've become familiar with my cities, with their people and animals, and with the ups and downs, ins and outs of their streets, parks, and buildings."

Kingman's work is also marked by the curiously drawn people who inhabit his cities. He explained their origins in *Dong Kingman's Watercolors:* "Many people appear in my paintings, and often they reflect the times in which I was living when I painted them. During the war years, we were bombarded with news of poison gas and H-bombs. This definitely influenced my work, and I painted many figures walking around wearing gas masks and underwater helmets. Later on... I saw hippies, flower children, not-so-honest policemen, and honorable peddlers. There were grass smokers and poppy growers. All these characters, and more, have appeared in my paintings at one time or another."

this tour Kingman produced volumes of paintings and studies of a great variety of American landscapes.

The Kingman cityscape

Kingman's tour of the United States, which produced many fine works, gave the artist a chance to see most of the country. Of all the places he saw, he fell most in love with New York City. In 1942, he had a show at the Midtown Gallery. Again he was awarded wide acclaim in several prominent publications, including *Time, Newsweek,* and *The New Yorker.* That same year, the art-

Teacher and ambassador

Throughout the remainder of the 1940s and early 1950s, Kingman continued showing and selling his paintings. He taught painting at Columbia University and then, in 1948, became a full-time instructor at Hunter College. In 1951, the Midtown Gallery showed a retrospective of his work, marking the tenth anniversary of his first outing with the gallery. Three years later, he toured Asia as part of a U.S. State Department educational exchange program. The tour was very successful and Kingman drew large crowds for the lectures he delivered.

Around 1957, Kingman began teaching annual painting workshops in various countries throughout the world. But one of Kingman's greatest honors as an ambassador didn't come until 1981. The Ministry of Culture of the People's Republic of China invited him to present a one-man exhibit of his works in that country. The exhibit drew over 100,000 visitors.

The Big Screen and the Blank Page

In the 1960s, Kingman made his mark on Hollywood. He received film credits for *Flower Drum Song* (1961) and *55 Days at Peking* (1963), as both films featured his watercolors. Then in 1964 he served as technical advisor for *The World of Suzie Wong*. His artwork also appeared in the films *Circus World* (1964), *King Rat* (1965), *The Sand Pebbles* (1966), and *Lost Horizons* (1973). Around the same time, several books were published featuring his watercolors, including *The Watercolors of Dong Kingman* (1958) and *San Francisco: City on Golden Hills* (1967). Later books included *Paint the Yellow Tiger* (1991), *Portraits of Cities* (1997), and *Dong Kingman: An American Master* (2000). Also in 2000, the Academy of Motion Picture Arts and Sciences presented an exhibition entitled "Dong Kingman: An American Master in Hollywood" to commemorate his earlier work in films.

Reflecting on his long career, Kingman said in *Watercolors,* "Over the years, I've had some difficult times. But whenever I felt discouraged, I would stop and think of how something had always come along which enabled me to continue learning. I would tell myself to have faith and that with time and perseverance I could overcome anything. And I did."

In later years, Kingman made several donations to charitable organizations through the sale of his artworks, including donations to UNICEF, the World Federation of United Nations Association Limited Edition art program, and a number of Hong Kong charities through Hong Kong Rotary International.

Dong Kingman died in his sleep on May 12, 2000. Throughout his career he received several awards, including the Audubon Artist Gold Medal of Honor (1946), the Metropolitan Museum of Art Award (1975), the National Academy of Design 150th Anniversary Gold Medal Award (1975), and the Dolphin Medal from the American Watercolor Society in 1987. The honors continued after his death. In 2001, the American Water Color Society initiated an annual Dong Kingman Award. The same year, the Visual Arts Division of Columbia University School of the Arts instituted a fellowship in his honor. In 2002 the Ministry of Culture of China opened an exhibit entitled "Dong Kingman: Watercolor Master" at the Beijing National Museum, sponsored in part by Century Masters, Inc, a nonprofit organization of cultural and artistic exchange.

Sources:

Dong Kingman: Watercolor Master, http:www.dongkingman.org (accessed March 2003).

Gruskin, Allan D., *The Watercolors of Dong Kingman and How the Artist Works,* New York: The Studio Publications, Inc., 1958.

Kingman, Dong, and Helena Kuo Kingman, *Dong Kingman's Watercolors,* New York: Watson Guptil Publications, 1980.

Maxine Hong Kingston

Author
Born October 27, 1940, Stockton, California

"I began writing when I was nine.... I was in fourth grade and all of a sudden this poem started coming out of me. On and on I went, oblivious to everything, and when it was over I had written 30 verses. It is a bad habit that doesn't go away."

Maxine Hong Kingston is a highly acclaimed writer of both fiction and nonfiction and was one of the first Asian Americans to make it to the top of the literary world in America. Her first book, a memoir published in 1976 called *The Woman Warrior: Memoirs of a Girlhood Among Ghosts,* won the National Book Critic's Circle Award and made her a literary celebrity at the age of 36. Kingston has since written two other critically hailed books. *China Men,* a sequel to *The Woman Warrior,* was published in 1980 and also received the National Book Critic's Circle Award; and in

1989 Kingston published her first novel, *Tripmaster Monkey: His Fake Book.*

Kingston's writing is often cited for its melodiousness and poetry. The *New York Times Book Review* commented, "*The Woman Warrior* is about being Chinese in the way that [the James Joyce novel] *Portrait of the Artist* is about being Irish. It is an investigation of soul, not landscape. Its sources are dream and memory, myth and desire. Its crises are the crises of a heart in exile from roots that bind and terrorize it."

A difficult childhood

Kingston's father, Tom Hong, and her mother, Chew Ling Yan, were both Chinese immigrants. They operated a gambling house in Stockton, California, when Maxine was born in 1940. (She was named after a gambler who always won.) Shortly after her birth, the family opened a laundry where she and her five brothers and sisters joined their parents in working long, arduous hours. Kingston attended public schools, where she was an excellent student. After graduation, with the help of 11 scholarships, she enrolled in the University of California at Berkeley, one of the finest public colleges in the country. She at first intended to study engineering but changed her major to English literature. After her childhood, with its long, hard hours of labor, leaving the engineering program felt irresponsible to the young woman; she had come to believe that everything had to be difficult, and English was easy for her.

Kingston graduated with a bachelor's degree in 1962. In November of that year, she married Earl Kingston, whom she had met in an English course. She earned a

Maxine Hong Kingston

teaching certificate from the state of California and in 1965 taught high school for a year in the city of Hayward. In 1967, the Kingstons moved to Hawaii, where Kingston took various teaching posts. From 1970 to 1977, she taught at the Mid-Pacific Institute, a private boarding school.

The Woman Warrior

Published in 1976, *The Woman Warrior* was an immediate success. In the memoir, Kingston writes of the conflicting cultural messages she received as the daughter of Chinese immigrants growing up in the America of the 1950s. The book also tells the story of the generations of Chinese women that preceded her and the weight she felt as an American trying to emerge from their sometimes stifling presence. The subtitle of the book, *Memoirs of a Girlhood*

Among Ghosts, suggests the book's almost fantastic tone but also refers specifically to the ghosts of Kingston's female relatives and the tragedy of many of their lives—lives lived in the extremely male-dominated society of China. She writes of Chinese folk sayings such as, "When fishing for treasures in the flood, be careful not to pull in girls" and "There's no profit in raising girls. Better to raise geese than girls."

The Woman Warrior received excellent reviews. *Newsweek* called it "thrilling" and "a book of fierce clarity and originality." The *New York Times* termed it "a brilliant memoir." It became a best-seller, was awarded the National Book Critic's Circle Award, and is taught in high schools and colleges all over the country. In the swirl of publicity that followed the book's success, Kingston gave an interview to the *New York Times* about her life and her writing. "I began writing," she said, "when I was nine. The day was very clear to me. I was in fourth grade and all of a sudden this poem started coming out of me. On and on I went, oblivious to everything, and when it was over I had written 30 verses. It is a bad habit that doesn't go away." In *The Woman Warrior*, Kingston's mother can seem domineering and often cruel, but Kingston said, "My mother is the creative one—the one with the visions and the stories to tell. I'm the technician. She's the great inspiration. I never realized it until I finished the book."

China Men and beyond

Kingston's next book, *China Men* (1980), was in many ways a companion to her first. In it she explores the Chinese American experience, this time as it was felt by the men in her family. This book, too, received glowing reviews. The *New York Times* deemed the volume "a triumph of the highest order, of imagination, of language, of moral perception," adding, "It is full of wonderful stories." Again Kingston was awarded the National Book Critic's Circle Award. She discussed her intention in *China Men* in a profile in the *New York Times:* "What I am doing in this book is claiming America. That seems to be a common strain that runs through all the characters. In story after story Chinese American people are claiming America, which goes all the way from one character saying that a Chinese explorer found this place long before [eleventh-century Norwegian explorer] Leif Erikson did to another one buying a house here. Buying the house is a way of saying that America—and not China—is his country."

In 1987, Kingston published a collection of personal essays entitled *Hawaii One Summer.* Then in 1989, she published her fourth book, *Tripmaster Monkey: His Fake Book.* Her first novel, the story is set in San Francisco in the 1960s and tells of Wittman Ah Sing, a manic, playful, highly verbal young man who is one year out of college. After being fired from his job at a toy store, the irreverent Wittman turns his enormous energies to writing a contemporary epic based on an old Chinese novel. The book was a startling departure for Kingston and confused many readers. Still, critics praised it. Reviewers compared the main character to Holden Caulfield of J. D. Salinger's landmark *Catcher in the Rye* and Mark Twain's classic *Huck Finn.* The book won the 1989 PEN West Award.

After the publication of *Tripmaster Monkey,* Kingston gave an interview in which she speculated about the future direction of her work. "I'm beginning to have an idea that Wittman ought to grow up.... American literature is made up of great novels about young men. It has to do with our being a young country.... If I can write a novel in which Wittman grows up to be socially responsible, an effective, good man—forming a community around him, bringing joy to people... then it means I will have made Holden Caulfield grow up; I will have made Huck Finn and Tom Sawyer grow up.... Then I will have helped us all grow up."

Back to school

In 1990, Kingston was invited to join the faculty of the University of California at Berkeley as a senior lecturer in the English department. She couldn't pass up the opportunity to teach at her old alma mater, but she had some new ideas to share with her class. Rather than teaching in an auditorium filled with students that she could never possibly know by name, she insisted on smaller classes. Kingston now makes a point of learning the names of every one of her students and is available for one-on-one meetings with each of her students. In 1997, Kingston was awarded the National Humanities Medal, which was presented by then-President Bill Clinton and First Lady Hillary Clinton.

The Future

Kingston continues to work at the two things she loves the most: teaching and writing. The combination of these two tasks is seen in two of her latest publications. In 2000, she was a contributor to the book *Claiming the Spirit Within: A Sourcebook of*

Women's Poetry and in 2002 she published *To Be the Poet*, a collection based on her 2000 William E. Massey lecture series given at Harvard University. In *The Fifth Book of Peace*, a novel expected to be published in late 2003, Kingston expects to fulfill one of her writing goals by featuring the *Tripmaster* character of Wittman as an adult.

Sources:

Chin, Marilyn, "A MELUS Interview: Maxine Hong Kingston," *MELUS,* vol. 16, winter 1989/90, pp. 57-74.

Kingston, Maxine Hong, *China Men,* New York: Knopf, 1980.

Kingston, Maxine Hong, *Tripmaster Monkey: His Fake Book,* New York: Knopf, 1989.

Kingston, Maxine Hong, *The Woman Warrior,* New York: Knopf, 1976.

Lim, Shirley Geok-Lin, ed., *Approaches to Teaching Kingston's The Woman Warrior,* New York: The Modern Language Association of American, 1991.

Pfaff, Timothy, "Talk with Mrs. Kingston," *New York Times Book Review,* June 15, 1980, p. 1.

"Women Warrior Speaks Peace," http://www.ucberkeley.edu (accessed March 2003).

Harold Hongju Koh

Attorney, professor of law
Born December 8, 1954, Cambridge, Massachusetts

"I learned [from my parents] about the tremendous importance of family, a reverence for tradition, and respect for the elderly, as well as the value of a harmonious society."

From 1998–2001, Harold Hongju Koh served as the Assistant Secretary of State for Democracy, Human Rights and Labor with the U.S. Department of State. Koh earned the nomination for the position through years of dedicated service as an attorney, professor of international law, and a political commentator on foreign policies that protect and promote human rights in the United States and around the world. As of 2003, he was the Gerald C. and Bernice Latrobe Smith Professor of International Law at Yale Law School. He is also the director of Yale's Orville H. Schell Jr. Center for International Human Rights.

Born into an academic family

Koh's parents were both Korean immigrants who had come to the United States to study. His mother arrived in 1948, his father in 1950. They met and married in Cambridge, Massachusetts, home of Harvard University, where Koh's father was studying law. In 1960, the Kohs moved to Washington, D.C., when the elder Koh accepted a position as acting ambassador from South Korea. (He had led the South Korean delegation to the United Nations in previous years.) When his tenure as ambassador ended, the Kohs moved to New Haven, Connecticut, where husband and wife had both been offered teaching positions at Yale. On accepting these, the Kohs became the first Asian American professors in that school's history. Koh's father taught in the law school, and his mother, who held a doctorate in sociology, taught at the undergraduate level.

In an interview with *Asian American Biography,* Koh recalled growing up very much in the mainstream of American society, with very few Asian American friends or classmates. Because of the nature of their profession, his parents immersed themselves in American culture, but they also managed to incorporate some Korean American traditions into the upbringing of their children. "I learned about the tremendous importance of family, a reverence for tradition, and respect for the elderly, as well as the value of a harmonious society," Koh said.

Harold Hongju Koh

A stellar education

After graduating from high school, Koh enrolled in Harvard University, where he won many academic honors, including admission to Phi Beta Kappa. He was also named a Harvard National Scholar, a National Merit Scholar, and a State of Connecticut Scholar. He graduated *summa cum laude* (with highest honors) in 1975 with a bachelor's degree in government. From there, Koh went to Magdalen College at Oxford University in England, where he continued to distinguish himself academically. He was a Marshall Scholar and the president of Magdalen College Middle Common Room. He graduated with first-class honors in 1977 with a master's degree in philosophy, politics, and economics. After returning to the States, he enrolled in Harvard Law School, where he served as developmental editor of the *Harvard Law Review.* He graduated *cum laude* with a J.D. in 1980.

After completing this impressive education, Koh worked as a law clerk to U.S. Supreme Court Justice Harry Blackmun for a year. He then went to work as an associate partner at the law firm of Covington and

Burling. From 1983 to 1985 Koh was an attorney-advisor in the Office of Legal Counsel in the U.S. Department of Justice. During this period he also lectured in the evenings at the George Washington University National Law Center, where he met his wife, Mary-Christy Fisher, who was a law professor there.

Move to Yale

In 1985 Koh joined the faculty of Yale Law School as an associate professor and went on to receive tenure (a status granted to a teacher, after a trial period, protecting him or her from dismissal) five years later. He specialized in international law and human rights, and, as such, Koh became a well-known commentator on cases of international importance. In the 1990s, he was outspoken in his views on the case of John Demjanjuk, the accused Nazi war criminal who was deported to Israel and sentenced to death only to be released on appeal, and on the plight of Haitian refugees and official government policy in dealing with them. On less sensational but no less important issues, Koh is a frequent writer as well. His 1990 book, *The National Security Constitution: Sharing Power after the Iran-Contra Affair,* was very well received; the American Political Science Association named it the most important book of the year contributing to scholarship on the presidency.

Koh has received perhaps the most mainstream media attention of his career as the attorney who argued before the Supreme Court on behalf of Haitians' right to be granted asylum hearings in the United States. In June 1993 the Supreme Court ruled that refugees fleeing a repressive government in Haiti for the United States may be stopped at sea and returned home without asylum hearings. The eight-to-one opinion, with Justice Blackmun the sole dissenter, dealt a blow to the thousands of Haitians taking to the sea in makeshift rafts for a new life in the United States.

For his work on behalf of the Haitians and in other areas of international law, Koh received several awards, including the 1993 Justice in Action Award from the Asian American Legal Defense and Education Fund. In 1992 he was co-recipient of the Human Rights Award from the America Immigration Lawyers' Association Asian Law Caucus. His interest in and opinions on international human rights soon brought him an international audience. In 1993 he was invited to be a visiting professor of the Hague Academy of International Law. Also in 1993, he became the Director of the Orville H. Schell Jr. Center for International Human Rights at Yale University. He held this director's position until 1998, when he accepted the post of Assistant Secretary of State for Democracy, Human Rights and Labor. In this position, his job was to advise the then-secretary of state Madeleine Albright, in all U.S. foreign policy matters concerning worldwide democracy, human rights, labor, the rule of law, and religious freedom. Through this post, he also served on the United Nations (UN) Human Rights Commission, the Organization for Security and Cooperation in Europe, the UN Committee Against Torture, and the UN Conference on New and Restored Democracies (in Benin in 2000). He presented reports and testimony before Congress on several occasions, covering topics such as human rights in Turkey and China and the U.S. policies toward Haiti. Koh left the post in 2001 and returned to teaching at Yale.

Awards and honors

Throughout his career, Koh has published nearly one hundred articles in political magazines and law journals. He has also written several books on human rights and international law. He remains active as one who speaks out for the rights of the minority, as is evident in his 2002 congressional testimony to eliminate all discrimination against women and in his book, *Different but Equal: The International Human Rights of the Intellectually Disabled.* Koh has received dozens of awards and honors including Asian American Lawyer of the Year (1997) from the Asian American Bar Association, the Institute for Korean-American Studies Liberty Award (2000), and the John Quincy Adams Freedom Award (2002) from Amistad America. Koh also holds honorary degrees from eight colleges and has been a fellow in the American Academy of Arts and Sciences since 2000.

Sources:

"Curriculum Vitae," *Yale Law School*, www.law.yale.edu (accessed March 2003).

Koh, Harold Hongju, resume, New Haven, CT, March 1994.

Koh, Harold Hongju, telephone interview with Felicia Paik, April 1, 1994.

Konishiki

Sumo wrestler
Born December 31, 1963, Oahu, Hawaii

Konishiki is amazed by the level of adoration he receives, and in Sports Illustrated *he said, "I'm treated like royalty, I'm a walking god."*

Salevaa Atisanoe, who used the name "Konishiki" professionally, was a champion sumo wrestler from Hawaii. His success in climbing the ranks of the highly traditional world of Japanese sumo wrestling caused quite a stir in Japan, where the sport is considered by many to be closed to foreigners. In 1987, he became the first foreigner to reach the rank of *ozeki* (champion) which is the second-highest rank in the sport.

Growing up in Hawaii

Sale (pronounced like Sally), as the young boy was known, was the eighth of nine children born to his native Samoan parents. They left Samoa in 1959 for the Hawaiian Islands, which had just been made the fiftieth state of the United States. There they hoped to be able to offer their children a better life than was available on Samoa. On the island of Oahu, the Atisanoes lived in a Samoan community with only the most basic of accommodations. Everyone in the family slept in a common room on mats and showered outside. Sale's father, who had been a religious leader on Samoa, established a small church within the community.

Sale was a big child; by the age of 11 he weighed 180 pounds. He went to high school at Honolulu's University Laboratory High, where he played noseguard on the football team and was a champion weight lifter, able to bench press 550 pounds and squat power-lift 600. A few weeks before Konishiki was set to graduate from high school, he was spotted on the beach by a scout sent to Hawaii by a sumo coach named Kuhualua. Kuhualua was a legendary figure in Hawaii in the early 1970s when he became the first non-Japanese sumo wrestler to win a tournament. The scout encouraged Konishiki to meet with Kuhualua, and, even though he knew nothing about sumo—except that it sounded like something he didn't want to do—he agreed to the meeting out of deference to Kuhualua's celebrity status. Kuhualua was able to persuade Konishiki to travel to Japan and give sumo a try. In 1982, weighing 380 pounds, he left for Japan to train at the Takasago stable in Tokyo.

Life as a *sumotori*

Apprentices in the sport of sumo wrestling are called *sumotori,* and in the stables where they train they are subject to a rigid hierarchy in which they must serve those wrestlers above them. Their duties include bathing and feeding superiors, sponging sweat off of them, and running errands, as well as other indignities. In addition, sumotori are subjected to physical abuse reminiscent of the hazing practices common to American fraternities. Writing in *Sports Illustrated,* Franz Lidz described some of the abuses heaped on Konishiki early in his training, reporting, "Stablemasters spat at him, threw salt water into his mouth and whacked him in the knees with bamboo canes. One night an older wrestler stumbled in drunk and knee-dropped the sleeping Konishiki on the head." Although all sumotori are subjected to such things, there is no doubt that Konishiki, as a foreigner, suffered a great deal.

As a competitor, Konishiki became one of the fastest-rising sumos in modern history. He made it into the top of sumo's six divisions after only eight tournaments, setting a record. In 1984 he finished second in one of Japan's most prestigious tournaments, the Emperor's Cup. It was this event that sparked the controversy surrounding Konishiki's nationality. While he is ethnically a Pacific Islander, he is by nationality an American, a Westerner, something that is unforgivable to many of the sport's purists. He has also been criticized by some for relying on his bulk—he weighs 170 pounds more than the average sumo wrestler—rather than employing the grace, strategy, and skill sumos are trained to use. The sport's rules, however, favor extremely heavy competitors. The aim of the contest is to push a competitor to the ground or outside of a 15-foot ring. Matches rarely last more than half a minute, with most lasting a fraction of that.

Controversy continues

As he became more and more famous in Japan during the mid-1980s and beyond, Konishiki generated further controversy. He even began receiving hate mail and death threats. Newspapers demanded that tournaments be canceled if he was going to participate, and one commentator compared Konishiki's arrival in Japan with that of

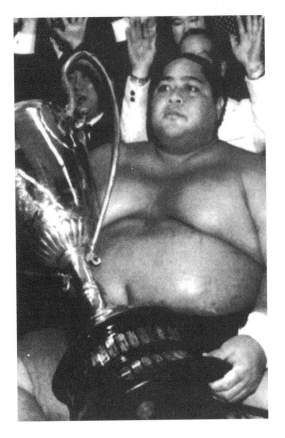

Konishiki

Commodore Matthew Perry's fleet, which had arrived in Japan in the nineteenth century, forcibly opening the country to exploitation by the West. This bad press and rampant hostility hurt Konishiki, and his performance in the ring suffered. He had a couple of bad years, but then he resurfaced as a force to be reckoned with in 1987 when he was elevated to the higher level of *ozeki* (champion), the first foreigner to make it that far. In 1989 Konishiki won his first tournament, the Kyushi.

With his continued success, the governing body of sumo, the Sumo Kyokai, was under pressure by some to elevate Konishiki to *yokozuna* status, while also receiving pressure from detractors not to do so. Konishiki believed he deserved the distinction. He said in *Sports Illustrated*, "*Yokozuna* are like immortals. It's like getting into the Hall of Fame. You stay there for life." One detractor, noted Japanese novelist Noboru Kojima, wrote an essay in a popular magazine in which he said that promoting Konishiki "could lead to renunciation of the identity of Japanese spiritual culture." The title of his essay was "We Do Not Need a Foreign Yokozuna."

Konishikimania

Despite the controversy, Konishiki remained a force in the world of sumo wrestling, and he opened the door to other non-Japanese participants. Although he had critics, in general the people of Japan, the vast majority of whom are sumo fans, loved him. *Sports Illustrated* reported that "old women and young children rub him for good luck like some giant Buddha. Teenage girls swoon at the sight of his huge haunches. Konishiki masks line the shelves of Tokyo toy stores." Konishiki was amazed by the level of adoration he receives, and in the *Sports Illustrated* article he said, "I'm treated like royalty, I'm a walking god."

In 1992 Konishiki married a former fashion model named Sumika who weighs less than a fifth of Konishiki's weight. The wedding was broadcast live on Japanese television, which paid the couple a half million dollars for the rights, and was attended by over a thousand guests, including some of the most influential and important members of Japanese business and political life.

Konishiki continued competing for five more years, but retired in 1997 with a total of 733 career wins. The 6-foot-tall wrestler had a peak weight of over 600 pounds.

Konishiki moved to Japan and became a naturalized Japanese citizen in 1994. But he didn't forget his family and community in Hawaii. In 1996, he helped to establish the Konishiki Kids Foundation, which serves as a cultural exchange program that raises funds for Hawaii youth to visit Japan. Since his retirement, Konishiki has given a number of lectures and appeared on talk shows. He has also pursued a singing career, with his first recording, *Konishiki KMS*, released in 2001.

In 1998, he received the Tokyo Citizen's Cultural Medal of Honor and the UNESCO International Fair Play Award. He has also been inducted into the Hawaii Sports Hall of Fame.

Sources:

"The Fat's in the Fire," *People*, May 11, 1992, p. 47.

Hawaii Sports Hall of Fame, http://www.alohafame.org (accessed March 2003).

Konishiki Kids Foundation, http://konishikikids.org (accessed March 2003).

Lidz, Franz, "Meat Bomb," *Sports Illustrated*, vol. 76, no. 19, May 18, 1992, p. 68.

Tommy Kono

Weightlifter, Olympic medalist
Born June 27, 1930, Sacramento, California

"You have to have a great desire, you've got to be hungry to do well, to improve."

Tame "Tommy" Kono is one of the greatest Olympic athletes in American history. As a weightlifter, Kono won three Olympic medals—two of them gold—in three separate Olympic games and in three weight classes, an unprecedented accomplishment. During his weightlifting career Kono won eight consecutive World Championships and broke seven Olympic records and 26 world records. In 1982 *World Weightlifting,* the official magazine of the International Weightlifting Federation, named Kono the greatest weightlifter in history, and in 1990 he was inducted into the U.S. Olympic Hall of Fame. At that induction ceremony he became—with the great diver **Sammy Lee**—the first of the Asian American inductees. After hearing of his election, Kono told the *Honolulu Star Bulletin,* "I've been nominated often before, but to be picked is something else. I'm just elated."

Early obstacles

Like many Japanese Americans during World War II, the Kono family was detained by the U.S. government in an internment camp. Internment of Japanese Americans was the nation's response to anti-Japanese hysteria after Japan bombed the U.S. naval installation at Pearl Harbor, Hawaii, then a

U.S. territory. The government's professed reason for internment was a fear that Japanese Americans might aid the Japanese in the event of a Japanese invasion of the West Coast. Tommy was 12 years old when his family was forcibly relocated. They were sent to the Tule Lake camp in northern California, where they stayed for the next three and a half years.

Kono was a skinny, asthmatic boy who dreamed of becoming physically fit. "I was so skinny I had to lean forward in the shower," he told the *Star Bulletin,* "so that water wouldn't collect in the hollows by my clavicles." At the age of ten he sent away for information about a correspondence bodybuilding course (one in which instructions are mailed to participants). During his internment, Kono began working out with weights at the suggestion of two young men he met in camp who would change his life forever, Ben Hara and Tad Fujioka. Kono found the training helped him psychologically as well as physically as he endured the shame of being a prisoner of race in his own country.

Kono continued training after his release. He told *Weightlifting USA* that he pursued the sport because he didn't need anything but the weights. "Also, I could continue to lift even after high school." In 1948 he placed second in his first weightlifting competition. "Of course," he said, "there were only two of us in the lightweight class. But I enjoyed it so much, I thought, 'Hey, this is the sport for me!'"

The emergence of a champion

Kono was inducted into the army in 1952 and sent to Camp Stillman in California to prepare for combat in the civil war then being fought between North and South Korea. Kono was originally slated to be shipped off to Korea, but people who knew of his skill as a weightlifter intervened, thinking he was quite possibly an Olympic contender. Kono was transferred to Fort Mason in San Francisco so he could be near Oakland, then the center of American weightlifting. The army funded his training and paid for him to attend the Olympic trials in New York. The Olympics that year were held in Helsinki, Finland, and Kono competed as a lightweight, winning his first gold medal.

Following his Olympic victory, Kono began an unprecedented string of victories in international competition. In 1953 he won the world middleweight championship in Stockholm, Sweden; in 1954 he won the world light-heavyweight championship in Vienna, Austria; and in 1955 he won the world light-heavyweight championship in Munich, West Germany. In 1956 Kono again qualified for the Olympics, held that year in Melbourne, Australia, where he put in a stellar performance: He set two Olympic and two world records, bringing home his second gold medal.

In 1957 Kono's international domination continued when he won the world middleweight championship in Teheran, Iran; in 1958 he repeated his victory at that weight in the championship held in Stockholm; and in 1959 he won his third consecutive middleweight championship in Warsaw, Poland. The following year, Kono went to his third Olympic Games, where he won a silver medal and set an Olympic record.

In all, during his competitive years Kono broke 26 world records in four different weight classes, seven Olympic records, and

Tommy Kono

37 national records. A 1960 article in the *New York Times* described Kono as the world's strongest weight lifter and said that the Russians "admire Kono probably more than any other American athlete." Kono explained this respect from the Russians, traditionally *the* powerhouse in international weightlifting: "That's because the Soviets respect power and I had won over their lifters so many times," he told *Weightlifting USA*. "There were several years (1957 and 1958) when the Russians won every weight class except mine. I was a thorn in their side and maybe because of that, they had respect for me."

Reflections on his career

Kono set an unprecedented string of records and held the title of champion for eight consecutive years. Despite this feat, he says that the greatest satisfaction of such an impressive career comes from having performed as well as he could each time out. "Of course," he told *Weightlifting USA*, "if I performed well and I won, that was even better." He went on to describe the attributes he sees as necessary to become a great lifter: "You have to have a great desire, you've got to be hungry to do well, to improve. No coaching or environment or inducement by financial gains should be the influencing factor. Lifters now should have more incentive because they have all the training camps and things like the Olympic festival. In the past we never had such things. And yet we were able to produce good lifters. And the good lifters kept improving. The bottom line is that in all weightlifting events, you've got to show improvement."

Kono also competed in bodybuilding. He won the Mr. World competition in 1954 and went on to capture three Mr. Universe titles, in 1955, 1957, and 1961. Kono told the *Star Bulletin* that movie star and former bodybuilder Arnold Schwarzenegger, at age 14, saw Kono compete in one such competition.

Following his amateur weightlifting career, Kono worked as a coach. He coached the Mexican national team in the 1968 Olympics held in Mexico City, and then served as coach for the West German team for their home stand at the 1972 Munich games. In 1976 he coached the United States team at the Montreal games, and from 1987 to 1989 he served as coach of the U.S.A. Women's World Team. Kono also served on the board of the United States Weightlifting Federation. In 1990, Kono was inducted into the U.S. Olympics' Hall of Fame. In 1991, he was inducted into the International Weightlifting Federation's Hall of Fame.

Kono lives in Hawaii, where he moved in 1955 when he married Florence Rodrigues, a native of the island of Kauai.

Sources:

Kwon, Bill, "Kono in U.S. Olympic Hall of Fame," *Honolulu Star Bulletin,* July 5, 1990, p. D5.

United States Olympic Committee, http://www.olympic-USA.org (accessed March 2003).

United States Weightlifting Federation, "Tommy T. Kono: Titles and Achievements," press release, 1990.

Fred T. Korematsu

Internment order resister, draftsman
Born 1919, Oakland, California

"I would like to see the government admit that they were wrong and do something about it so this will never happen again to any American citizen of any race, creed, or color."

F red T. Korematsu was one of the few Japanese Americans to defy Executive Order 9066, which called for the internment of all Americans of Japanese descent living on the West Coast during World War II. The order had been issued by President Franklin D. Roosevelt with the rationale that in the event of a Japanese invasion of the West Coast, ethnic Japanese might collaborate with the enemy. Internal government documents dispute this, however, and suggest that the internment was designed to provide a ready pool of hostages to exchange for American prisoners of war should the United States have been in the position of needing them. The order was plainly unconstitutional and a few American citizens refused to obey it. Fred Korematsu was one. He simply refused to turn himself in as 110,000 others did, surrendering everything they owned to the government in the process.

Korematsu managed to avoid capture for only a little over two months, but when he was captured he took the case to court in order to challenge the constitutionality of the policy. The Supreme Court of the United States heard the case and ruled in 1944 that the executive order, while severe in some ways, was justified by the special circumstances of the war. It would be nearly 40 years before Korematsu would get another day in court and be given the opportunity to clear his name.

An American citizen

Korematsu was the third of four sons born to Japanese immigrant parents in Oakland, California. He had been an American citizen all his life by virtue of being born in the United States. His parents ran a flower nursery on 25 acres and spoke Japanese exclusively at home. Korematsu remembers observing traditional Japanese festivals with his family but also spending much of his time on American pastimes such as tennis, basketball, and football.

Korematsu was in his early twenties on December 7, 1941, when the Japanese air force bombed the U.S. naval base at Pearl Harbor, Hawaii. Almost immediately after the surprise attack that killed thousands of American servicemen, a wave of anti-Japanese hysteria swept the country. This mania was particularly fierce on the West Coast, where curfews were imposed and it became illegal for Japanese Americans to travel beyond a 25-mile radius of their residences. Then, on February 19, 1942, President Roosevelt

issued the now-infamous executive order calling for what it termed the "evacuation" of Japanese Americans and resident aliens from the West Coast to "internment camps" located further inland.

Under this scheme, evacuees were first sent to temporary "assembly centers." Korematsu's family was sent to Tanforan, a former horse racing track, where people were lodged in stalls. Korematsu simply refused to go. To avoid capture he changed his name to Clyde Sarah and had his eyelids surgically altered to make himself appear more Caucasian. He worked at several welding jobs and lived in a boarding house while making plans to move east with his fiancee, to where the order did not apply. In an interview with *Asian American Biography,* Korematsu recalled that during that time he "felt just like before, as any American felt at that time, busy doing their own thing, working."

Korematsu's freedom was short-lived, however, and on May 30, 1942, police picked him up as he waited outside a San Leandro, California, pharmacy. He was arrested and taken to the San Francisco County Jail. While there, he was approached by Ernest Besig of the American Civil Liberties Union, who suggested that they go to court to test the legality of the internment. Korematsu agreed to file suit against the government.

Confronting injustice

Korematsu was freed on bail on the charge of ignoring the executive order, and was sent to Tanforan, where he joined his family. They were then all sent to a camp in the Utah desert called Topaz. Meanwhile, Korematsu lost his initial trial on the charges

Fred T. Korematsu

Writing for the majority, Justice Hugo L. Black said, "All legal restrictions which curtail the civil rights of a single racial group are immediately suspect. [But Korematsu] was not excluded from the Military Area because of hostility to him or his race.... He was excluded because we are at war with the Japanese Empire, because the properly constituted military authorities feared an invasion of the West Coast." Writing for the minority, dissenting Justice Frank Murphy noted that the internment order "goes over the very brink of constitutional power and falls into the ugly abyss of racism."

A long wait for justice

After the war Korematsu moved to Detroit to start over. He worked as a draftsman and married his fiancee in 1946, thinking his association with the internment order was over for good. But then, in 1982, four decades after he was arrested, Peter Irons, a historian and lawyer teaching political science at the University of California at San Diego, uncovered new evidence in the case: Irons discovered that the prosecution had possessed documents they did not disclose, showing that military and intelligence authorities in the government had studied whether or not Japanese Americans should be considered security risks. The answer from two separate reports was that they were not—that they were, in fact, remarkably loyal Americans. The final report, by General John DeWitt, commander of the Western Defense Command, had been altered.

Irons contacted Korematsu, along with others who had fought internment, and asked if they would be interested in retrying

of ignoring the order and was sentenced to five years' probation on the felony charge. With attorney Wayne Collins, he then appealed the case to the Ninth Circuit Court of Appeals on the grounds that the order was unconstitutional, so Korematsu could not be guilty of defying it. He lost again. His next step was the Supreme Court, which heard the case in 1944. In December of 1944, shortly after the government closed down the camps and set the prisoners free, the Court handed down its decision.

The final decision was 6 to 3 upholding the constitutionality of the executive order.

the case. Irons also contacted **Dale Minami,** a Japanese American attorney, and asked him to assemble a legal team. In all, some two dozen attorneys from the San Francisco, California; Seattle, Washington; and Portland, Oregon, areas joined forces to retry the cases on a *pro bono* basis, meaning they were doing it for free. On January 19, 1983, they filed suit in federal court in San Francisco arguing that the decision in *Korematsu* v. *United States* should be overturned based on evidence Irons had uncovered showing the government had falsified, suppressed, and withheld evidence from the high court. This new evidence, the attorneys argued, concluded that there was never any "military necessity" to forcibly detain Japanese Americans.

The hearing was held on October 4, 1983, in a San Francisco courtroom packed with Japanese Americans. Korematsu was permitted to make a statement. "I still remember 40 years ago when I was handcuffed and arrested as a criminal here in San Francisco," he told the court. "As long as my record stands in federal court, any American citizen can be held in prison or concentration camps without trial or hearing. I would like to see the government admit that they were wrong and do something about it so this will never happen again to any American citizen of any race, creed, or color." Judge Marilyn Hall Patel overturned the conviction.

Donald K. Takami, a leading member of Korematsu's legal team, stated at the time, "Fred Korematsu represents every Japanese American's desire for the trial they never had, to the extent that the internees felt victimized and unjustly treated. Fred's a regular guy. To me, he's the epitome of the ordinary man who, under extraordinary circum-stances becomes heroic." Korematsu remained in the San Francisco area, where he became a celebrated elder spokesman for the Japanese American community. And *Korematsu* v. *United States* is studied in law schools all over the country as a low point in Supreme Court history as far as adherence to civil liberties is concerned.

In 1998, Korematsu was awarded the Presidential Medal of Freedom, the highest civilian honor in the nation, for his courage in fighting for civil rights.

Sources:

Chin, Steven A., *When Justice Failed: The Fred Korematsu Story,* Austin, TX: Raintree Steck-Vaughn, 1993.

Irons, Peter, *Justice Delayed: The Record of the Japanese American Internment Cases,* Middletown, CT: Wesleyan University Press, 1989.

Irons, Peter, *Justice at War: The Story of the Japanese American Internment Cases,* Oxford: Oxford University Press, 1983.

Korematsu, Fred, interviews with Steven A. Chin, 1991-93.

Margolick, David, "Nisei Carves a Niche in Legal Lore," *New York Times,* November 24, 1984.

Paul Kuroda

Photojournalist
Born February 13, 1954, Fresno, California

"I choose subjects that do not have a voice, that have been trapped in a dark corner of society. I want to bring light to subjects that have been overlooked, that have gone unnoticed, that seem invisible...."

Paul Kuroda is one of the top newspaper photographers in the country. In 1991, as an *Orange County* (California) *Register* photographer, Kuroda was named Newspaper Photographer of the Year by the National Press Photographers Association and the University of Missouri School of Journalism. The competition is one of the most prestigious in the country, and that year 1,750 entrants submitted 35,000 photographs to compete in 35 categories. Kuroda's portfolio consisted mainly of two subjects: illegal Mexican immigrants as they attempted to cross the border into California, and Vietnamese gang members in Orange County, California. Kuroda was lauded for his ability to get close to his subjects, to develop a rapport with them that elevated the images from simple photographs, allowing them to tell a story. In 1992 these remarkable photographs made Kuroda a finalist for a Pulitzer Prize in photojournalism.

Kuroda chooses his subjects carefully. He is especially interested in social issues and told *Asian American Biography (AAB)*, "I choose subjects that do not have a voice, that have been trapped in a dark corner of society. I want to bring light to subjects that have been overlooked, that have gone unnoticed, that seem invisible.... I want to tell stories through my pictures, especially stories that will help rid our world of racism." With his vivid, haunting pictures, Kuroda has earned a reputation as one of the most honest, effective photojournalists working today.

A childhood in poverty

Kuroda was one of three children born to a Japanese mother and a second-generation Japanese American father (one of the second generation of his family to be born in the United States). Kuroda's father had been interned during World War II along with 110,000 other Japanese Americans who were viewed as a security threat and imprisoned for the duration of the war. The family was also stripped of everything it owned, including a successful trucking business. After their release the Kurodas moved to a farm near Fresno, California, where Paul was born and where he lived an impoverished childhood.

Growing up in Fresno was difficult for Kuroda. He told *AAB*, "Fresno is a very small town. It doesn't have the diversity of San Francisco or Los Angeles. It was very difficult to find role models, especially Asian male role models and that led to a lot of problems in my life. I felt like a little boy who never belonged in this world. I spent a great deal of time pondering why I was here." As a shy child he was drawn to the meditative, solitary art of photography and bought himself a camera from the local drug store.

Kuroda's interest in photography continued into college. In 1972, he enrolled in California State University at Fresno, where he studied journalism. Although he spent four years there, he did not graduate. He began his career in journalism as a reporter for the student newspaper. It was difficult financially for him to attend college, and he worked a dizzying variety of jobs to support himself: in the school's library, as a busboy at the local Denny's, selling photo equipment at a mall camera store, clerking at Woolworth's, and delivering Chinese food.

The highlight of Kuroda's academic career came with the production of two 16-millimeter films, which began his career-long dedication to highlighting injustice. One of the films depicted the plight of elderly immigrant Filipino men living in squalor in San Francisco's International Hotel, which at the time was scheduled to be leveled. He hoped his film might prevent the destruction of the men's only home, but the forces of urban renewal were not to be sidetracked. Kuroda's other college-produced film captured the relationship between Japanese farmers organizations and the United Farm Workers. The film displayed the racism of the Japanese toward their predominantly Mexican workers. Unfortunately, Kuroda could not find anyone to air these films, "so," he told *AAB,* "I decided that still photography was it."

The photojournalist emerges

In 1976 Kuroda was hired by the *Clovis Independent and Tribune,* a small-circulation community newspaper. Kuroda learned much about the newspaper business at this paper, but he found the photographic work unchallenging. Two years later he was hired by the *Fresno Bee,* where his skills were better utilized. In 1984 the *Bee* was a finalist for a Pulitzer Prize for its coverage of the

Paul Kuroda

Coalinga, California, earthquake. Leading the coverage were images Kuroda had captured in the immediate aftermath of the quake.

In 1989 Kuroda left the *Bee* to join the *Orange County Register,* a significantly larger paper covering the middle-class suburban communities south of Los Angeles. It was here that Kuroda shot the two series of pictures that solidified his reputation in the world of photojournalism. The first series was on gang violence in Southern California's Little Saigon. Kuroda's photographs told a story of young immigrant men trapped between two worlds: the strict traditions of Vietnam and the permissive American culture plagued by urban violence. Kuroda established a trusting relationship with the young gang members, many of whom were vicious killers. "It helped that I am of Asian descent," he told *Photographer's Forum.* "It would have been very difficult for a photographer of non-Asian descent to do this essay."

The second series he did with the *Register* was on illegal Mexican immigrants. For this series he spent six months with his subjects, again earning their trust—a crucial element of his work. He himself often made border crossings with the illegals in order to get a sense of their predicament. In order to protect the identity of his subjects, Kuroda shot on black and white infrared film. The dark, haunting images reveal no distinguishing features but still manage to convey the desperation and anxiety of the immigrants. Kuroda discussed his philosophy in taking these pictures with *AAB:* "When I take pictures, I try to dissolve any walls within myself that might inhibit me from opening up to the subject. I open up to the point that I become a part of the subject. When I was shooting gang members, I became Vietnamese. When I was shooting the immigrants, I became Mexican. And that's when I become able to take real pictures." Both series helped Kuroda win the Newspaper Photographer of the Year Award in 1991 and to make it to the final round of judging for the Pulitzer Prize.

Shooting for the stars

Kuroda left the *Register* in 1993 feeling that the paper was more interested in profits and circulation than in doing important stories; since his youth, Kuroda has felt that it is important to do work that matters and that makes a difference. He calls it his mission. "It all came back to my mission—to be an agent of change," he told *AAB.* "I'm still reaching for it, still reaching high. I always say, 'Reach for the stars and if you fail, you'll land on the moon; aim for the sidewalk and fail, then you land in the gutter.' People should always have something unreachable, something to always keep you reaching high."

Kuroda went on to become a photo editor for the Associated Press in San Francisco. He is currently responsible for a staff of photographers, covering the area from his hometown of Fresno to northern Nevada.

Sources:

Hofland, Alison, "Paul Kuroda," *Photographer's Forum,* September 1992, pp. 46-52.

Kuroda, Paul, telephone interview with Terry Hong, July 6, 1994.

Michelle Kwan

Figure skater
Born July 7, 1980, Torrance, California

When the United States Figure Skating Association decided to allow Tonya Harding to compete at the 1994 Olympics despite increasing concern over her role in the attack on Nancy Kerrigan, Kwan unwittingly became a minor player in a major international media carnival.

 ichelle Kwan burst into the national spotlight in January of 1994 at the figure skating national championships in Detroit, Michigan, where she placed second behind Tonya Harding. As the second-place finisher, Kwan was guaranteed a spot on the U.S. Olympic team at the 1994 Winter Olympics in Lillehammer, Norway, but due to extenuating circumstances, the U.S. Figure Skating Association decided to put Nancy Kerrigan on the team instead. Kerrigan had been knocked out of contention when she was injured in an assault during the competition. Subsequent investigations led police to believe that Harding, or close associates of hers, may have been involved in the attack as a way of ensuring Harding's victory over her perennial rival. Kwan took the disappointment with a degree of sportsmanship rarely seen in international athletics—certainly not in that year's figure skating. Kwan was quoted in *People* as saying, "It's a bummer for me, but I was kind of hoping Nancy would be able to go. She deserves it." Kwan had become a major force in national figure skating.

Daughter of immigrants

Kwan's father, Danny, immigrated to the United States from Hong Kong in 1971. Her mother, Estella, followed in 1975. Michelle is their third child, born in 1980. Danny Kwan is an administrative supervisor for Pacific Bell and Estella Kwan is the manager of the Golden Pheasant, the family-owned restaurant. Michelle discovered skating after she watched her older brother playing hockey when she was about five years old. She and her older sister Karen soon began taking private lessons. Michelle became something of a prodigy, excelling right away. Her parents tried not to push their gifted

daughter, fearing she might not be able to handle the fame and pressure of competitive skating.

In 1992, while Kwan was preparing for the national junior championships in Orlando, Florida, her father—sensing her high stress level—tried to help her keep the competition in perspective. He told *People,* "I had been telling her about the competition, not to worry." But then he went into her room one night and found her talking in her sleep, saying, "It's nothing, it's nothing," over and over. Michelle placed a disappointing ninth in the competition. Her father decided that he and Michelle needed a change of attitude about the sport. "I went to Michelle and I said, 'You are my daughter.... Skating has cost a lot of time and money and worry to your parents. But when I see you get too stressed out like this, I think it's time to quit.' I told her I just wanted her to have fun, to enjoy skating." She has since been able to do just that.

After the 1992 junior championships, Kwan decided, at the age of 11, that it was time for her to take the test to qualify for senior ranking—a decision she made without consulting her coach, Frank Carroll. She told *People,* "I knew I might get in trouble, but I just had to do it." She passed the test, and since the 1993 competition season, Kwan has been competing in the senior ranks.

The Olympics

When the United States Figure Skating Association decided to allow Tonya Harding to compete at the 1994 Olympics despite increasing concern over her role in the attack on Nancy Kerrigan, Kwan unwittingly became a minor player in a major

Michelle Kwan

ceremonies—all very disappointing for the young girl. Kwan made the best of it, however, and in a statement she released to the press before leaving for Norway, she said, "As the first alternate, I have to keep training and stay focused, in case I'm asked to compete. The only thing that's changed is that now I'll get to go to Norway, and that will be fun." As it turned out, the United States Figure Skating Association allowed Harding to skate at the Olympics, so Kwan spent her first Olympics in the stands.

After the Olympics

When the American media frenzy surrounding the Olympics faded, Kwan was back to her regular training schedule in anticipation of the 1994 World Championships in Chiba, Japan. By the time the championships were held, Harding had been barred from competition after admitting knowledge of the attack on Kerrigan after it happened, and Kerrigan had announced her retirement from amateur competition. This left Kwan the highest-ranked American skater, giving her the additional pressure of needing to place in the top ten just to make sure the American team would qualify for the following year's championships. *Transpacific* magazine described the pressure: "The TV network covering the event went all out to play up the daughter-of-immigrants-with-sacrificing-parents human drama, the it's-a-matter-of-national-honor suspense. The Japanese audience in the stadium must have squirmed at the delicious irony of a tiny 13-year-old Asian girl representing the mighty United States before the world. Many a seasoned veteran would have been crushed by the hopes that millions of Americans were plac-

international media carnival; she would be sent to Norway as an alternate in case the investigation back home implicated Harding in the attack, thus forcing her removal from the team. When the decision to send Kwan was announced, her coach told the *New York Times,* "I don't quite know when we're going or where we're going; all I know is that we're going. We're going there as an alternate unless things change. And then she will be put on the ice."

As an alternate, Kwan was not allowed to live in the Olympic village, train at the Olympic rink, or participate in the opening

ing on her, a Chinese American, to come through in the clutch."

Kwan finished eleventh overall after the compulsories, meaning she would need to deliver a stunning performance in the free-skate. Again the pressure was on the young girl, and again she stood up to it; she executed a brilliant routine, with several triple jumps, and ended up finishing eighth overall, ensuring a place for the Americans in the next competition.

In 1995, she placed second in the U.S. Championships and fourth in the World Championships. Then in 1996, her career took off as she placed first in both the U.S. and World Championships. She also placed first in seven other competitions the same year. In 1997, she placed second in both the U.S. and World contests and first again in both competitions in 1998. More importantly, in 1998 Kwan got her first chance at Olympic competition. Kwan skated a wonderful program and took home a silver medal. Fifteen-year-old Tara Lipinski won the gold that year.

Kwan kept her spirits and her training high and captured first-place titles in U.S championships for 1999, 2000, 2001, and 2002, giving Kwan a total of six U.S. titles and four world championships, which is more than figure skating greats Peggy Fleming or Dorothy Hamill. In 2002, Kwan got her second turn in Olympic competition in Salt Lake City. Unfortunately, it was bronze, not gold, this time around as Sarah Hughes unexpectedly came from fourth place in the short program to the gold winning performance in the long program. Though Kwan was clearly disappointed, she went on to the World Championships to win second place. Though Kwan has remained active in train-ing since then, she has not made clear whether she intends to work toward a third time at the Olympics or if she might opt to turn pro.

Whatever her decision, Kwan has plenty to do off the ice as well. She has served as a national spokesperson for the Children's Miracle Network "Champions Across America" program and has published an autobiography entitled, *Michelle Kwan: Heart of a Champion.* She worked with Electronic Arts to create the first-ever interactive figure skating video game, *Michelle Kwan Figure Skating,* which was released in 1999. Since 1998, Kwan has worked with Walt Disney Studios to produce four television specials and in 2002 she agreed to serve as spokeswoman for the Walt Disney Company for three years.

Kwan's impact on figure skating can be measured not only in the number of medals she has won, but by the even greater number of young people she has inspired in their pursuit of individual goals, especially young Asian Americans. Even as early as the 1994 championships, *Transpacific* had this to say about the inspiring young athlete: "What makes Michelle Kwan's performance so moving is the knowledge that we Asian Americans can count thousands of Michelle Kwans among us, people who shine under difficult circumstances to the credit of all America. We loom large among America's unknown heroes."

Sources:

Kagy, T., "Our Rightful Place," *Transpacific,* June 1994, p. 94

Neill, Michelle, "In the Wings Waits Rising Star Michelle Kwan," *People Weekly,* February 14, 1994, p. 35.

Park, Andrew, "America's Next Ice Princess," *Transpacific,* April 1994, p. 44.

United States Figure Skating Association, http://www.usfasa.org (accessed March 2003).

Fred H. Lau

Law enforcement officer
Born June 26, 1949, San Francisco, California

"Be proud of who you are. And be confident that your past generations were building blocks for your present life, and that your life will be a building block for your children."

As the chief of inspectors for the San Francisco police department, Fred H. Lau is one of the highest-ranking police officers of Asian American descent in the country. As such, Lau is a very visible person in the San Francisco Bay area, a position he fills with distinction. Frequently invited to speak before groups of young people, Lau relishes the opportunity to share his philosophy with others. "It's a matter of self-esteem," he told *Asian American Biography (AAB)* in an interview. "Other ethnic communities have highly visible role models, whereas Asian Americans have been much less visible. I want kids to have someone they can look up to, to say, 'Hey, that's somebody I want to be like.'"

During his more than 20 years on the police force, Lau has received many awards for bravery and outstanding criminal investigations. Among these are the Bronze Medal of Valor, three Meritorious Conduct Awards, two Police Commission Commendations, and numerous Captain's Complimentaries.

Early interest in community service

Lau received his education, from elementary school through college, in his native San Francisco. He attended Garfield Elementary School and graduated from Galileo High School in 1967. During high school, Lau had an experience that he described as significant in shaping his commitment to community service. "It was around 1967. There was a teenage dance in Chinatown's Victory Hall. A big gang fight broke out between two rival groups, and I was struck in the head with a chair and knocked to the ground. A social worker, who eventually became one of my mentors, got me out of there safely. He began to tell me how important it was to stay out of such situations, to get an education. This incident led me in the direction of doing community work."

After high school, Lau became involved with Youth for Service, an agency that worked to enlist African American gang leaders as "street workers" to help convince others to stay away from gangs. Lau was one of the first Asian Americans to volunteer for this service. He continued working with this agency into his junior college years.

Joining the police force

As a community worker, Lau was frequently confronted with the problems of an overcrowded urban environment. These problems often involved confrontations between young people and the police. "There were few recreational facilities," he

Fred H. Lau

told *AAB*. "The streets became the meeting places. The alleys became the playing fields. Large groups of people hanging around led to misunderstandings and confrontations with the police." Lau worked to keep young people out of the criminal justice system, which brought him into contact with officers on the beat. Two such officers, the only two Chinese Americans on the force at the time, encouraged Lau to join the force as well.

Lau's first attempt to join the San Francisco Police Department ended in disappointment when he discovered that he was

three-quarters of an inch below the minimum height requirement of the force—5 feet, 8 inches. Lau felt the height requirement was unfair, however, citing the fact that many Asian Americans are shorter than European Americans. The Asian community joined Lau in challenging the height requirement, and, together, they were able to get it lowered. Lau views this experience as another building block in his own commitment to community.

In the 20 years since joining the force, Lau has advanced through its ranks steadily. In 1980 he was promoted to sergeant/inspector, becoming only the second Chinese American to reach that rank. This was also true of each of his next advancements—to lieutenant (1984), captain (1986), commander (1988), deputy chief (1990), and chief of inspectors (1992). Then in 1996, Lau was appointed as chief of police by the new San Francisco mayor Willie Brown. He held that challenging position until 2002, when he accepted the even greater challenge of a post as Federal Security Director for the Transportation Security Administration at Oakland International Airport. The position was created as part of the Aviation and Transportation Security Act that was signed by President George W. Bush in November 2001, two months after the terrorist attack in New York City in which hijackers crashed two planes into the twin towers of the World Trade Center. Lau's responsibilities include not only implementation and oversight of security measures throughout the airport but also the organization and implementation of a Federal Security Crisis Management Response Plan.

The Lau philosophy

Lau stated his basic philosophy in terms of what he describes as his three families: his law enforcement family, his community family, and, most importantly, his real family. "I have a tremendous responsibility to my three families.... Their expectations are high, but not nearly as high as my own. My families are my foundations. I will never forget them. I will make them proud."

Reflecting on the roots of his own success, Lau points to his greatest role models, his parents, because "of everything they went through, so quietly. They are so caring and loving with us, and with my brother's two sons." Lau lives in San Francisco with his wife, Barbara, who is from Hawaii. His greatest hope is that he will be the sort of role model for his children that his parents were for him. The message he wants to share is: "Be proud of who you are. And be confident that your past generations were building blocks for your present life, and that your life will be a building block for your children."

Sources:

Lau, Fred, "Short Biography of Fred Lau," May 1994.

Lau, Fred, telephone interview with Susan Gall, August 19, 1994.

Oakland International Airport, http://www.flyoakland.com (accessed March 2003).

San Francisco Police Department, "Fred H. Lau, Chief of Inspection," professional resume, August 1994.

Ang Lee

Filmmaker
Born October 23, 1954, Pingtung, Taiwan

ng Lee is an award-winning filmmaker whose vibrant and various films have enjoyed considerable critical and commercial success in the United States, his native Taiwan, and Europe. He was awarded best director by the Golden Globes, the British Academy, and the Director's Guild for his 2000 film *Crouching Tiger Hidden Dragon,* and his 1995 film *Sense and Sensibility* was nominated by the Academy for best picture. Though the genres and subjects of his films vary, they are all deeply entertaining films.

Immigration to America

Ang Lee was born in Taiwan on October 23, 1954. His father was the principal of Lee's high school, so he was expected to do well academically. But when it came time to take the annual college entrance examinations, he failed them. As he told Jeff Yang in the *Village Voice,* "For my generation, that's like death."

Unable to attend college in Taiwan, Lee came to the United States to study. He enrolled in the theatre arts program at the University of Illinois. After graduation he enrolled in the prestigious New York University film school. One of his classmate was Spike Lee, the noted African American and remarkably won both first prize (for *Pushing Hands)* and second prize. The first prize consisted of $500,000 in funding to complete his first feature.

Good Machine Productions, known for producing good quality, low-budget films, found the budget adequate, so they agreed to work with Lee on *Pushing Hands.* The film tells the story of an old *tai chi* master who moves in with his son and his son's white wife. Although the film was made in the United States, it was never released here. In Taiwan it was so successful that Central Motion Picture, Taiwan's largest studio, signed Lee to make another picture. That picture would be *The Wedding Banquet.*

The Wedding Banquet and beyond

The Wedding Banquet tells the story of a gay Chinese American landlord who doesn't want his parents to know that he is gay so he marries a female tenant. The woman goes along with the ruse (trick) to get a green card (the documentation immigrants need to stay in the United States). The film was well received in Asia, the United States, and Europe. Writing in the *New York Times* Stephen Holden said, "It is the unusual film comedy in which humor springs as much from character as from situation." In Taiwan it earned $4 million, which made it the highest-grossing film in that country's history.

In 1994, Lee released *Eat Drink Man Woman,* which tells the story of a widower with daughters who are trying to find him a wife. The film was set in Taipei, and won an Academy Award nomination for best foreign-language film, as well as an Independent Spirit Award. Lee was then hired by a

Ang Lee

film director. While in school, Lee won the best student film award for his thesis, *Fine Line,* a comedy about an Italian man trying to escape the Mafia and a Chinese woman hiding from the U.S. Immigration and Naturalization Service.

After he graduated in 1984 Lee spent the next six years trying to sell a film idea to a Hollywood studio. Although he received encouragement, and studio executives agreed to meet with him, nothing developed. Finally in 1990 he turned to Taiwan. He entered two screenplays in the Taiwan government's annual screenplay competition, prominent Hollywood studio to direct an adaptation of Jane Austen's *Sense and Sensibility*. The film received a Best Picture Oscar nomination, and Lee was voted the Best Director of 1995 by the National Board of Review and the New York Film Critic's Circle. With the success of this film, Lee proved his ability to tackle a variety of genres. His next project was *The Ice Storm* (1997), a film that took place in suburban America during the early 1970s.

Changing genres again, Lee directed *Ride with the Devil* (1999), a Civil War drama starring Tobey Maguire and Jeffrey Wright. His most acclaimed film to date came in 2000 with the most commercially successful foreign-language film ever made, *Crouching Tiger Hidden Dragon.* Lee has described *Crouching Tiger Hidden Dragon* as being *"Sense and Sensibility* with martial arts." The film's kung fu masters battle each other over a legendary sword, but the characters face inner turmoil as well. Lee was awarded an Oscar for best foreign-language film. He also received the best director award from the Director's Guild of America, the Golden Globes, and the British Academy.

In 2003, Lee was working on *The Incredible Hulk,* a film that tells the story of the green giant comic book character of the 1970s. To coincide with its release in summer 2003, the American Museum of the Motion Image in New York planned to show all of Lee's films from May 31 to June 9. The museum's chief film curator, David Schwartz, told *Variety,* "Ang Lee's career is developing in a similar fashion to such great studio system directors as Howard Hawks and John Huston. Like them, Lee has shown his agility in a wide range of genres, moving fluidly between comedies, dramas, epics, and small-scale films."

Lee is married to the former Jane Lin, a microbiologist whom he met while a student at the University of Illinois. They have two children and live outside of New York City. Lee considers spending time with his family to be of utmost importance, and as soon as the hectic pace of the last several years slows down, he plans on doing as much of that as possible.

Sources:

Corliss, Richard, "Ang Lee: Born in Taiwan, Trained in the U.S., Filming Everywhere—Making Movies that Speak a Universal Language," *Time,* July 9, 2001, vol. 158, no. 1, p. 55.

Holden, Stephen. "Inconvenient Marriage of Convenience." *New York Times*, August 4, 1993.

Hornaday, Ann. "A Director's Trip from Salad Days to a 'Banquet'." *New York Times*, August 1, 1993, sec. 2, p. 25.

Rooney, David, "Museum Slots Retros for Lee, Polanski, "*Daily Variety,* March 28, 2003, vol. 278, no. 60, p. 4+.

Yang, Jeff. "Wedding Dues." *Village Voice*, August 24, 1993.

Brandon Lee

Actor
Born February 1, 1965, Oakland, California
Died March 31, 1993, Wilmington,
    North Carolina

"For years I was in my father's shadow, and I resented it. I wanted to be an actor, not do martial arts films. But it finally dawned on me—I am who I am, and I might as well accept it. Once I realized that, doors started to open for me."

Brandon Lee was an up-and-coming actor working on his sixth film—in his first serious role—when he was shot accidentally during the filming of a scene. A gun that was supposed to be filled with blanks had somehow been loaded with a live round. This tragic accident cut short what was by all accounts a budding career in films. When the movie he was working on, *The Crow,* was released a year after his death, Lee received glowing reviews for his performance as a rock musician returned from the dead to avenge his and his girlfriend's murders. Lee was the son of the legendary action-film actor **Bruce Lee,** who also died a mysterious and early death.

A difficult childhood

Lee was born to a Chinese American father and a European American mother in California, where his father was pursuing a film career. When he was a young child, the family moved to Hong Kong, where Lee's father expected to have an easier time making it than in Hollywood, with its rigid racial typecasting. By the age of two, Brandon was taking lessons in the martial art of *jeet kune do* from his father.

When Lee was eight, his father died as a result of brain swelling from an allergic reaction to a painkiller he'd been given. Bruce Lee had achieved cult status by the time of his death, and his films earned enough money for the family to return to the United States. They eventually settled in Rolling Hills, California, a well-to-do community. Being the son of a legendary film star proved difficult for young Brandon. As a student, he was a rebel. He dropped out of high school twice and was expelled for misbehavior just months before graduation from the private Chadwick School in Palos Verdes, California. He finally was able to graduate, however, and went on to study acting, first at Emerson College in Boston and then at various schools and theaters in New York City.

Gives in to action films

Lee was a serious actor, and at age 20 he moved back to Los Angeles to pursue a career in film. He was immediately pigeonholed, however, and was offered little except roles in martial arts movies. He finally gave in and accepted a role in *Kung Fu: The Movie,* a made-for-television vehicle meant to capitalize on the popularity of the 1970s television series. Lee starred with David Carradine in the effort. In 1987 Lee went to Hong Kong and made his first theatrical feature, a Cantonese-language martial arts film called *Legacy of Rage.* In 1989 he made *Laser Mission* and *Showdown in Little Tokyo.*

Brandon Lee

Little Tokyo was an important film for Lee. While it was a typical martial arts movie, it earned him notice. Shortly after that film was released, he was cast in his first starring role in a motion picture titled *Rapid Fire*. Lee was finally at peace with the legacy of his father; while he was not doing exactly the kind of work he wanted to do, he realized that just working was a lot to be grateful for as an actor. A longtime family friend told *Premiere* magazine in 1993, "Brandon said to me, 'You know, for years I was in my father's shadow, and I resented it. I wanted to be an actor, not do martial arts films. But it finally dawned on me—I am who I am, and I might as well accept it. Once I realized that, doors started to open for me.'"

The breakthrough film

Successful actors often have the direction of their careers changed by one film that lifts them from character roles into lead roles and establishes their power as box-office draws. For Lee, this film was to be *The Crow*. Lee had first read the script in 1992 and had lobbied hard for the role of Eric Draven, a comic book hero from a series created by James O'Hara. The producer of *The Crow* originally wanted Christian Slater to star in the film, but when Slater passed on the project, Lee was offered the part.

The film was shot in North Carolina in an effort to save money. Filming began on February 1, 1993. Several weeks into the shoot, Lee appeared on the set to film a scene in which he comes home from the grocery store to find his girlfriend on the verge of being raped by a gang of thugs. One of the thugs was then supposed to pull out a pistol and shoot Lee. Somehow, a live bullet had been loaded into the gun. (Speculation as to how such a thing could have happened centered on bullet fragments that remained in the gun after a close-up shot that displayed the shells being loaded into the revolver.) Lee was rushed to the hospital, and after hours of lifesaving measures, he was pronounced dead at 1:04 P.M. on March 31, 1993. He was 28. His fiancee, Eliza Hutton, had flown in from California and was at his side when he died.

The producers of the film were unsure about whether it should be released. Most of Lee's scenes had already been shot, and those that hadn't could be reworked. With the support of Hutton and Lee's mother, who felt that Lee would have wanted the film completed and released, they finally decided to go ahead with production and finished filming in June. *The Crow* was released in May 1994 and received mixed reviews. Lee's performance, however, was often cited as one of the film's redeeming qualities. *Entertainment Weekly* said, "In *The Crow* Lee displays a sweet, stricken vulnerability. Hidden behind an androgynous rock-star mane, he brings a James Dean quality of wounded adolescent passion to the sort of role most actors ([Charles] Bronson, [Steven] Seagal, etc.) have used merely for displays of robotic rage. Lee's performance is by far the best thing about *The Crow.*"

Although some reviews were unkind, the movie did well at the box office. This was perhaps due to the curiosity surrounding Lee's death, which was widely publicized. Drawn in by Lee's undeniable charisma, viewers could not help but wonder how the young actor's career might have developed.

Sources:

Ascher-Walsh, Rebecca, "How the Crow Flew," *Entertainment Weekly,* May 1, 1994, pp. 18-21.

"Brandon Lee's Last Interview," *Entertainment Weekly,* May 13, 1994, pp. 22-24.

Goodell, Jeffrey, "Chronicle of a Death Foretold," *Premiere,* July 1993, pp. 70-78.

Lipton, Michael, "Lethal Weapon," *People,* April 19, 1993, pp. 80-86.

Lipton, Michael, "Son of Bruce Breaks Loose," *People,* September 7, 1992, pp. 111-13.

Bruce Lee

Actor, martial arts master
Born November 27, 1940, San Francisco, California
Died July 20, 1973, Hong Kong

Long before Bruce Lee became famous for his portrayal of Kato in the 1960s television series The Green Hornet *and for his stardom in a series of Hong Kong-produced martial arts films, he was already gaining fame as the creator of the new martial art* jeet kune do, *which means "the art of intercepting the fist."*

Since Bruce Lee's death in 1973, he has grown into a legend of contemporary American pop culture. His movies have been elevated to cult status, and his name is mentioned in the same breath as those of other Hollywood stars who died young, like Marilyn Monroe and James Dean. Yet Lee was much more than a movie hero; long before he became famous for his portrayal of Kato in the 1960s television series *The Green Hornet* and for his subsequent rise to international stardom in a series of Hong Kong-produced martial arts films, Lee was already gaining fame as the creator of the new martial art *jeet kune do,* which means "the art of intercepting the fist." Lee originated the technique and wrote a book about it called *The Tao of Jeet Kune Do.* His variation incorporated more of the psychological and spiritual aspects of the martial arts than the physical—stripping away everything but the bare essentials.

After playing Kato in *The Green Hornet,* Lee left Hollywood, convinced he would never be able to work there because, as a Chinese American, he would be prohibitively limited in his choice of roles. He went to Hong Kong and began working for an Asian company, making action-adventure films that were hugely successful throughout Asia. While working on his fifth film, *Game of Death,* he died suddenly of brain swelling caused by an allergic reaction brought on by a painkiller. He was 32 years old.

A tradition of performance

Lee's father was a well-known Chinese opera star from Hong Kong who went to perform in the United States in 1940, bringing his wife and three children with him. While he was in the States, his fourth child, Bruce, was born. Lee made his film debut at the age of three months when he appeared as a stand-in for a baby in the American film *Golden Gate Girl.* Shortly thereafter, the Lee family returned to Hong Kong, where Lee's father continued his career in the entertainment industry. Lee spent much of his childhood around film sets. At four years old he had his first walk-on role; at six he had his first speaking part.

As Lee got older, he became involved with street gangs and began getting into trouble. On the streets he was known as Little Dragon. He listed his reasons for becoming involved in this type of life in the biography *Bruce Lee: Fists of Fury:* "Kids [in Hong Kong] have nothing to look forward to. The white [British] kids have all the best jobs and the rest of us had to work for them. That's why most of the kids became punks. Life in Hong Kong is so bad. Kids in slums can never get out." But even as he became more and more immersed in the unsavory side of

Bruce Lee

Hong Kong street life, Lee also cultivated a passion for dancing the cha cha, becoming at one point the cha cha champion of all of Hong Kong. He also developed a passion for physical fitness and began to study the traditional martial art of kung fu. "I always fought with a gang behind me," he said in *Fists of Fury.* "I only took kung fu when I began to feel insecure. I kept wondering what would happen if my gang was not around when I met a rival gang."

Returning to America

Lee studied kung fu at the Wing Chun School, which taught a sophisticated Chinese system of kung fu that was founded by a Shaolin nun some four hundred years ago. Lee excelled at this school and eventually began adding his own techniques to the traditional method, an act of heresy as far as the masters were concerned. Lee was asked to leave, despite his unmistakable gift.

Lee had continued appearing in character roles in films, usually playing a rebel or criminal. He was popular for his good looks and dramatic facial expressions. His pout and scowl became trademarks, helping to set him apart from other young actors. Lee became so well liked that he was offered a film contract before he had finished high school. His parents were concerned that he did not have his priorities straight and opposed his leaving school to accept this offer. When he was arrested for street fighting, they made up their minds that he should stay in school, and to ensure that he would obey them, they sent him to live with friends in the United States until he finished high school.

Lee settled in Seattle, Washington, and graduated from Edison High School. He then enrolled in the University of Washington, where he studied philosophy. He began teaching kung fu to support himself in the early 1960s. In 1964 he married Linda Emery, one of his students. The couple would have a child, Brandon, in 1965 (also see entry on **Brandon Lee**). After the wedding the couple moved to California, where Lee devoted himself to teaching his version of kung fu, which he called *jeet kune do.* Eventually Lee operated three schools of jeet kune do in Seattle; Oakland, California; and Chinatown in Los Angeles, California. He also began to pursue his acting aspirations.

The Green Hornet

In 1966 Lee got his first big break when he was cast as Kato, the sidekick of the cartoonish crime-fighting title character *The Green Hornet.* The show would only last one season and was largely forgettable—except for the persona Lee created as Kato, virtually defining America's perception of the martial artist. Of course, Lee played it in a wildly exaggerated way, with fancy wide stances, flowing hands, catcalls, and high kicks, the exact opposite of the subtle, understated philosophy he actually practiced.

After *The Green Hornet,* Lee made guest appearances on such television shows as *Ironside* and *Here Come the Brides.* He had a small part in the film *Marlowe,* starring James Garner, and was in a few episodes of *Longstreet* with James Franciscus. But Lee was dissatisfied with both the amount and the quality of the work he was being offered—often small, forgettable roles that were stereotypical and demeaning. The final straw came when the starring role in the television series *Kung Fu,* which Lee had helped to develop, went to a white American. This lesson taught Lee about the narrow-mindedness of Hollywood producers, who were unwilling to take any sort of risk, and he decided to leave the country for Hong Kong, where he was sure he would be able to make it as an actor.

The legend is born

In Hong Kong, offers poured in. Lee signed a two-film contract, and in 1971 his first film, *The Big Boss* (retitled *Fists of Fury* in the United States), was released. The movie quickly became the highest-grossing film in Hong Kong. It was unique in that it broke a longstanding tradition in martial arts films—which were generally Japanese—of emphasizing weapons in fight scenes. Lee's film showcased hand-to-hand combat and also introduced more developed plots. Lee explained in the book *Fists of Fury,* "[We] used a minimum of weapons and made it a better film.... People like films that are more than just one long, armed hassle."

Lee's second film, *The Chinese Connection* (titled *Fists of Fury* in Asia, to great confusion), appeared in 1972 and proceeded to break the records set by his previous effort. Lee then opened his own production company, Concord Pictures, giving himself full creative control over future projects. For his next two films, he not only starred, but choreographed, directed, and co-produced as well. The first film from Concord was *Way of the Dragon* (*Return of the Dragon* in the United States). It co-starred a very young Chuck Norris, who would later go on to fame in martial arts pictures. The next was *Enter the Dragon.* Neither movie was released until after Lee's death, which occurred during filming of what would have been his fifth production, *Game of Death.*

Lee's death has spawned a small industry of conspiracy theorists who have suggested all sorts of unprovable reasons for the young man's death. The official version is that he died of cerebral edema, or brain swelling, after an adverse reaction to a painkiller he was taking for a back injury. After his death, *Enter the Dragon,* which was co-produced by major American investors, was released. It has since grossed over $100 million. Lee's final film, *Game of Death,* was released in 1979, but it was a commercial flop, having been haphazardly pasted together with little thought given to content or plot.

Today Lee is a legend. His films are top cult draws and are frequently shown together as mini-film festivals. He undoubtedly helped to create the climate for the commercial acceptability of the action-adventure film, which remains a staple of the big-budget Hollywood film industry.

Sources:

Gross, Edward, *Bruce Lee: Fists of Fury,* Las Vegas, NV: Pioneer Books, 1990.

Sharkey, Betsy, "Fate's Children: Bruce and Brandon," *New York Times,* May 2, 1993, pp. 1, 22.

Sinclair, Abiola, "Bruce Lee: His Life and Times," *New York Amsterdam News,* May 22, 1993, pp. 28, 53.

The Untold Story, Bruce Lee's Life Story as Told by His Mother, Family, and Friends, Hollywood, CA: Unique Publications, 1980.

Uyehara, M., "Bruce Lee: The Man, the Fighter, the Superstar," *The Legendary Bruce Lee,* by the editors of *Black Belt Magazine,* Burbank, CA: Ohara Publications, Inc., 1986.

Gus Lee

Writer
Born August 8, 1946, San Francisco, California

"If you say you're going to write the great American novel, there are too many ways of failing. Whereas, if you say you're going to write about something you know, something where you can see a moral core to the message, and you're truly interested in telling the story, then how can you go wrong?"

Gus Lee began his first book in 1989 as a private memoir. "My daughter asked me to write a family journal and it turned out to be *China Boy,*" he explained in an interview with *Asian American Biography (AAB)*. Not only was the work Lee's first novel, but it was also the first time he had ever attempted fiction writing. The semi-autobiographical *China Boy* introduced audiences to Kai Ting, the American-born son of Chinese immigrant parents who grows up in a predominantly black section of San Francisco, California. The book was widely heralded: the *New York Times Book Review* compared the novel to Amy Tan's *Joy Luck Club* and Gunter Grass's *Tin Drum; Publishers Weekly* referred to it as "the Chinese American experience as [English novelist Charles] Dickens might have described it"; *Washington Post Book World* praised Lee's work as "marvelous"; and *Time* magazine called it "delightful." *China Boy* was a six-month bestseller, a Literary Guild selection, a Random House AudioBook, and one of the *New York Times's* Best 100 for 1991.

In 1994 Lee wrote the second installment in the life and times of young Kai Ting, following him through his training at West Point, where Lee himself was educated. *Honor and Duty* also received glowing praise from the *New York Times Book Review, Publishers Weekly,* the *Chicago Tribune,* the *Los Angeles Times,* and numerous other major publications. It, too, has proven to be a bestseller, and, like *China Boy,* was chosen as a Book of the Month Club selection and a Random House AudioBook.

Born in San Francisco

Gus Lee was the only child born in the United States to parents Tsung-Chi and Da-Tsien (born Tsu) Lee. Lee's four older

Gus Lee

sisters (including one who died in infancy) were all born in China. The once wealthy and aristocratic Lee family had fled China to escape the Japanese invasion and arrived in the United States in 1945 to settle in the poor and mostly African American Panhandle district of San Francisco. "I lived in the Panhandle through junior high school," Lee recalled. "At times it was very tough, but eventually it just became my world. My objective was to become a successful black youth," he added with a laugh. "I never completely mastered it, but it was an honorable objective. Just not one for which I was naturally suited." From the age of nine, Lee worked part time at the local YMCA at various odd jobs.

When Lee was in high school, his family moved to the Sunset district; he graduated from Lincoln High School. He entered the U. S. Military Academy at West Point at the urging of his father, who had been a military officer in China. During Lee's third year, he took an engineering class from H. Norman Schwarzkopf, who would later become famous as the American field commander in the Persian Gulf War. He did well in the class, but not so well in other engineering classes. "The humanities department thought I was a pretty good student, but the engineering department thought I had been dropped on my head. I really was a bad engineering student," he confirmed. "I just didn't do my homework. I read lots of Chinese history, military history, studied the Vietnam War avidly."

With one failed electrical engineering class, West Point discharged Lee, and he was sent to assume his assigned post as a drill sergeant. "It was a painful separation, one that affects me to this day," he said. Although Lee was eligible to be sent to Vietnam, he was not. He returned to California and applied to the University of California at Davis, which initially denied him admission because of his poor record at West Point. It took a letter from then-Major Schwarzkopf on Lee's behalf to ensure the admission. In three quarters, Lee earned his undergraduate degree.

Academic interests

Lee remained at the University of California with the intention of earning a Ph.D. in Chinese history. "I loved the subject, but I didn't have the will to go on that long so I went to law school instead," Lee said. After graduating in 1976 from law school, Lee returned to the army and was sent to Korea, where he served as a criminal defense lawyer. He went back to California in late 1978, when he was assigned to the Presidio in San Francisco. "Then I met my wife, Diane. We had a whirlwind romance and got married after knowing each other for six months. Pretty amazing for a die-hard bachelor like me," Lee recalled.

At his wife's urging, Lee finally left the army in 1979. "But I really hated leaving," he told *AAB*. "I was not comfortable being a Chinese man in the real world. In the army, everyone is green. In the real world, you're the color that's on your face." As a civilian, Lee quickly realized that "the politics of discrimination are always with you, whether you're pro-active or not." He added, "So if it was always going to be there, I decided I might as well do something to make it better."

With that goal in mind, Lee took the position in 1980 of deputy district attorney in Sacramento, California. Three years later, he was a senior deputy district attorney, trial team leader, and police and attorney trainer for Sacramento County. In 1985 Lee was named deputy director for the California District Attorneys Association, where he created and directed skills-based trial advocacy training programs for California's prosecutors, with an emphasis on child sexual assault and domestic violence. (Prosecutors represent the state against the accused in criminal cases.) Four years later, as a senior executive for the State Bar of California, Lee designed and implemented mandatory continuing legal education for California's 130,000 attorneys.

During his legal career, Lee conducted over two hundred criminal trials and received awards for trial advocacy, legal education, community work, and military service, including the University of California at Davis Alumni's 1991 Citation for Excellence, outstanding instructor awards from the California District Attorneys Association and West Point, the army's Meritorious Service Medal with First Oak Leaf Cluster, and the Order of the Silk Purse.

A successful writer

With the success of *China Boy,* his first novel, Lee was suddenly in great demand to give lectures and presentations throughout the United States—demands he fulfilled in addition to those of his legal career. Unable to spend the time he desired with his wife and two children, he finally chose to leave the law field, becoming a full-time novelist in 1993.

No longer professionally tied to California, Lee moved his family to Colorado. "In California, I was under a great deal of stress between my work, my volunteer activities, and my writing. I was gone all the time and was a very inadequate father. The irony was that on the outside, I might have looked like a good father, because I was giving talks all the time about being a good father since I had learned all those lessons of accountability from writing my book. But at that time, I really wasn't doing what I was preaching. So I literally asked the kids if they would be willing to move and leave California in order to get their dad back. I had a genuine fear that they might just say, 'No, thanks, nice of you to ask, but no.' But they said yes, and so we headed for Colorado."

After completing *China Boy,* bringing the work to the public proved virtually effortless, for which Lee credits his agent, Jane Dystel. "I had no problems finding a publisher. It was preposterously easy. But that wasn't my job, it was Jane's. She was the one who made it so easy. Yes, I've been lucky with publishers and editors, but it all starts with your agent," he insisted modestly.

Following the success of *China Boy,* it was Dystel who suggested to Lee that he submit a proposal for a second book. "She told me 'You don't have to write the whole book, just get me a proposal.' So I did and lo and behold, the proposal went to auction and it got sold. So I wrote the book." *Honor and Duty* was published in 1995. This was followed by the 1997 publication of *Tiger's Tale*, a thriller novel that follows the mission of a Chinese American lawyer and army career officer as he goes to Korea in search of a missing buddy. For his next project, Lee took a step away from fiction. In 2003, he published *Chasing Hepburn: A Memoir of Shanghai, Hollywood and a Chinese Family's Fight for Freedom,* a collection of stories through which Lee discovers and shares his own family's history.

Advice for the young writer

Although he cannot explain his gift for writing, Lee offered a few words about taking a project to completion: "I think you need to have a certain amount of relaxed persistence about writing. It's like kung fu or baseball. You can't force it and be successful, but at the same time, you can't not practice and expect to be successful. I paid my dues by having a miserable childhood. So I had angst early on and then had an easy time writing. Although I think it's probably better to have a good childhood and then a lousy time writing.

"The other thing is you really have to have time. If you can't create adequate time for writing, then you'll have to lower your expectations for what you're going to accomplish. Also, I think it's crucial not to focus on what the writing will do for your economics or for your profession. It's very important to focus on what the writing can do for your own learning and your teaching of others. If you say you're going to write the great American novel, there are too many ways of failing. Whereas, if you say you're going to write about something you know, something where you can see a moral core to the message, and you're truly interested in telling the story, then how can you go wrong?"

Sources:

Lee, Gus, telephone interview with Terry Hong, June 6, 1994.

Ming Cho Lee

Set designer, professor
Born October 3, 1930, Shanghai, China

"A career in the arts can be enormously meaningful and have nothing to do with success."

Ming Cho Lee is known as the king of American set design. Having designed the sets for literally hundreds of plays, operas, and dance performances, he is considered the most influential figure in the history of his field. He has also spent many years teaching the craft of set design. In the mid-1990s, after Lee devoted more than 30 years to passing on his skills, it was not an exaggeration to say that more than half of working set designers either were trained by Lee or worked for a time as his assistant.

Born in China

In an interview with *Asian American Biography (AAB),* Lee said that he "came from a very Westernized family [that was] engaged in business." When Lee was six years old, his parents were granted one of the first divorces in China. His father was awarded custody of him because, as Lee explained, "at the time, women usually did not have any rights to the children." During the week, Lee lived with his father, a Yale University-educated international insurance representative; he spent weekends with his mother. "I treasured the time with my mother," Lee told *AAB.* "It was with my mother that I went to theaters, films, operas, and art galleries. It was through my mother

Ming Cho Lee

college would be a better environment for his son. Lee readily agrees, telling *AAB,* "The best thing that could have ever happened to me was to get an American liberal arts education at a small college. It made me look at everything about myself, about education, about society.... My father made a great choice."

At Occidental, Lee was not really comfortable with the English language, so he took as many studio art courses as he could, including watercolor, figure drawing, and basic drawing. "At least I managed to get good grades in art courses," he laughed. "At the time—the late 1940s and early 1950s—abstract expressionism painting controlled the art world, so much so that any kind of representational painting was not considered serious art. Even though I understood abstract painting very well, I had trouble doing it myself." From art, Lee switched to the speech department, which included theater. "Since I had seen quite a lot of theater and opera in Shanghai, I thought it was a good idea that I should at least try theater.... In the theater department, I was very appreciated because I could draw and paint. And that was the beginning."

that I started studying Chinese landscape painting.... If it had not been for my mother, I would not have entered a career in the arts."

Education in America

In 1949, when a Communist uprising led by Mao Zedong took control of China, Lee fled with his family to Hong Kong. Taking his father's advice, Lee traveled to the United States on a student visa and enrolled at Occidental College in California. In spite of a strong Yale connection (Lee's father, stepfather, and maternal uncle were all Yale graduates), Lee's father believed that a smaller

After receiving his degree in 1953, Lee spent one year doing graduate work in theater arts at the University of California at Los Angeles (UCLA). "But I quickly realized that I was just sick of school," he said. He moved to New York at the suggestion of Jo Mielziner, then one of Broadway's most renowned set designers. In 1954, Lee became Mielziner's apprentice, then his assistant. They worked together on and off for six years.

Stage credits

In 1955, Lee designed his first professional show, a revival of the musical comedy *Guys and Dolls* for the Grist Mill Playhouse in Andover, New Jersey. Three years later Lee made his New York debut at the Phoenix Theater as set designer for *The Infernal Machine,* an adaptation of the Greek Oedipus legend by the French dramatist Jean Cocteau. Lee attracted the attention of several important critics for his striking design.

In the late 1950s, Lee began working for set designer Boris Aronson. During this period, Lee's solo career was focused on opera. He designed several productions for the Peabody Institute of Music in Baltimore, the Baltimore Opera Company, and the Opera Company of Boston. In 1961, Lee moved his family to California, where he became designer-in-residence at the San Francisco Opera. He stayed there for one season, returning to New York in 1962. "I came back to do my first Broadway show, which was given to me through Jo [Mielziner]," Lee explained.

He also began a collaboration that would last for 11 years with Joseph Papp, the legendary producer of the New York Shakespeare Festival and longtime artistic director of the Public Theater. Lee assumed the post of principal designer for the Shakespeare Festival's annual summer presentations at the outdoor Delacorte Theater in New York City's Central Park. Because of the festival's budget limitations, Lee created adaptable sets, usually constructed of pipe scaffolding and raw wood planks. This look gave rise to a sculptural style in American set design in the 1960s and 1970s.

In addition to the festival's outdoor productions, Lee designed the sets for many of the company's productions at the Shakespeare Festival's downtown theater, including those for the musical *Hair,* which caused a furor when it opened because of semi-nude scenes. Beyond sets, Lee created an Elizabethan-style (in the style of Shakespeare's era, the 1500s, when Queen Elizabeth I of England reigned), multilevel mobile stage, which, due to its ease of construction, allowed the company to take its open-air productions to parks and playgrounds throughout the five boroughs of New York City.

Lee even redesigned the Delacorte Theater itself, changing its shape from a fan to a horseshoe to bring the audience closer in to the stage, which led to improved sound quality and more fluid staging. Other theater designs credited to Lee include the Florence Sutra Anspacher and Estelle R. Newman theaters in New York's Public Theater complex and the Garage Theater at the Harlem School of the Arts. Lee was also involved in the designs of the Performing Arts Center at the State University of New York at Purchase, the acoustical shell and proscenium (the front of the stage) arch at the Cincinnati Music Hall, and the Patricia Corbett Pavilion at the University of Cincinnati's School of Music.

While designing for the New York Shakespeare Festival, Lee started working as principal designer for the Juilliard Opera Theater, later called the American Opera Center of the Juilliard School of Music. In 1966, Lee began creating sets for the New York City Opera, an affiliation that lasted for seven years. In 1974, he made his Metropolitan Opera debut with his design for

Boris Goudonov and went on to do three more such productions.

In addition to theater and opera, Lee has built a substantial career in designing sets for dance. In 1962, he was chosen by legendary modern ballet choreographer Martha Graham to create the set for *A Look at Lightning.* His affiliation with her company lasted into the mid-1980s. In 1963, Lee began designing for Gerald Arpino of the Joffrey Ballet, eventually creating the sets for eight ballets. Other dance credits include designs for the works of noted choreographers Alvin Ailey, Lew Christenson, and Eliot Feld.

Moving away from Broadway

In spite of Lee's indisputable success in opera and dance, he readily admits to a "terrible Broadway career," having designed sets for many flops. While Lee may not be completely comfortable on Broadway, it was at a Broadway theater, the Brooks Atkinson, that he realized what is perhaps his greatest success—the 1983 staging of *K2,* a drama by Patrick Meyers about two mountain climbers, one of them injured, trapped on an icy ledge near the summit of the world's second-highest mountain, called K2. With its monstrous structure soaring beyond the audience's view, the set won Lee the Tony Award, the Outer Critics Circle Award, the Drama Desk Award, and his third Joseph Maharam Award.

Still, Lee limits his Broadway stagings. When he does agree to a show, he says he must "make sure not to get emotionally involved, to always step back so [he] doesn't find [himself] devastated from the work if something goes wrong." But that kind of objectivity, he maintains, presents other problems. "I don't want to work in that detached way all the time. If you do it all the time, ultimately, it will affect your attitude and your ethics toward the work you're doing. One thing about art is that you must involve your whole heart and soul."

Lee prefers to involve his "whole heart and soul" in regional and experimental theaters such as the Arena Stage in Washington D.C., the Mark Taper Forum in Los Angeles, and the Guthrie Theater in Minneapolis. Away from the demands for profit that drive larger theaters, the smaller venues are more likely to stage new or forward-looking works.

A career in teaching

Beyond his career on the stage, Lee has been teaching for decades. He began at New York University in 1967, then moved to Yale University in 1969. In 1994, his twenty-fifth year at Yale, he chaired the design department at the drama school, commuting three or four days a week between New York and New Haven, Connecticut.

Lee says that he has had very few Asian American students. "It's very frustrating that after more than 25 years of teaching, I've only had one [Asian American] set designer, Wing Lee," he remarked. "I think a career in the arts is not really totally acceptable to Asian families, especially for male offspring. In a way, there seems to be a distrust of the arts. Earning a living at it is very difficult. Asian Americans, especially first-generation Asian Americans, tend to be pragmatic people and it's very hard for them to imagine a life of insecurity for their children. The arts and theater somehow don't always have tangible results. A career in the arts can be enormously meaningful and have nothing to do with success."

Remembering his own decision to enter set design, Lee recalled, "It was a crisis in my family." But after countless awards and fellowships, and at least two honorary doctorates, the only crisis Lee might have to address now is where he will find the time to finish his many projects.

Some of Lee's latest awards include the Obie Award for Sustained Achievement (1995), American Immigration Law Foundation's Washington Immigrant Achievement Award (1998), and the Helen Hayes Award for Outstanding Set Design on the production of *Don Carlos* (2000).

Sources:

Huang, Yu-mei, "The Twists, Turns, Trials and Triumphs of a Theatrical Life," *Free China Review,* January 1984, pp. 63-75.

Lee, Ming Cho, "Designing Opera," *Contemporary Stage Design U.S.A.,* edited by Elizabeth B. Burdick, Peggy Hansen, and Brenda Zanger, Middletown, CT: Wesleyan University Press, 1975.

Lee, Ming Cho, introduction to *American Set Design 2,* edited by Ron Smith, New York: Theater Communications Group, 1991.

Lee, Ming Cho, telephone interviews with Terry Hong, February 6, 1994 and March 6, 1994.

MacKay, Patricia, "Designers on Designing: Ming Cho Lee," *Theater Craft,* February 1984, pp. 15-21.

Rose Hum Lee

Sociologist
Born August 20, 1904, Butte, Montana
Died 1964

"I was a woman, I was in a man's field, and I was Chinese. That meant three strikes against me. The fact that I was able to overcome these barriers is a tremendous encouragement to others, particularly women who belong to minority groups."

R ose Hum Lee was a well-known expert on Chinese American life who achieved success against considerable odds. She is best known for her study *The Chinese in the United States of America,* which examines how Chinese Americans adjusted to life in the United States. When she was appointed chair of the sociology department at Roosevelt University in Chicago, Illinois, in 1956, Lee became the first woman of Chinese ancestry to reach such an important position at an American university.

Early influences

Rose Hum's father, Hum Wah-Lung, immigrated to the United States from China and worked as a ranch hand, miner, and laundry worker in Montana. In 1900 he married Lin Fong, a mail-order bride from China. Mail-order brides were women who corresponded with men through letters and agreed to travel from their homeland to marry them. Lin Fong was a major influence on both Rose and her six brothers and sisters. Even though she was illiterate, Lin

Fong recognized the importance of education, independence, and a love of learning. She helped her children resist the traditional Chinese notion that children should become main sources of income for the family.

A decade in China

Many details of Rose Hum Lee's life are not known, but it is clear that she graduated from Butte High School, in Butte, Montana, in 1921. She was working as a secretary when she met and fell in love with Ku Young Lee, a Chinese student from Philadelphia, Pennsylvania. Despite her mother's objections, they married and left the United States to live in China in the late 1920s. During her decade in China, Lee worked at a variety of jobs, using what she had learned in high school business classes. She worked for the Kwangtung Raw Silk Testing Bureau from 1931 to 1936; the National City Bank of New York in Canton and Kwangtung from 1936 to 1938; the Sun Life Assurance Company in Canton from 1936 to 1938; and the Kwangtung Municipal Telephone Exchange from 1937 to 1938. Each of these jobs helped her to better understand Chinese business practices and everyday life.

When the Sino-Japanese War broke out in 1937 (the term *Sino* denotes China), Lee assisted the Chinese government by working in the Canton Red Cross Women's War Relief Association, the Overseas Relief Unit, and the Kwangtung Emergency Committee for the Relief of Refugees. When the Japanese invaded Canton, beginning an 18-month siege, Lee served as a radio operator and translator. She also worked in hospitals and helped care for war orphans. She adopted one of the orphans and brought her back to the

Rose Hum Lee

United States in 1938. It is unclear whether Lee's husband returned with her to America or remained in China.

Fulfilling a dream

After she returned to the United States, Lee went back to school hoping to become a writer and teacher. She received a bachelor's degree in social work from the Carnegie Institute of Technology in 1942, a master's from the University of Chicago in 1943, and, four years later, a Ph.D. Her studies and her daughter, Elaine, kept her very busy. Nonetheless, Lee found time to write two children's plays. One, *Little Lee Bo-Bo: Detective for Chinatown*, was produced in 1945 at Chicago's Goodman Theatre. Also in 1945, Lee made a move that would affect the rest of her career: she joined the sociology department at Roosevelt University, then a newly established college in Chicago. Roosevelt encouraged diversity among its students and faculty, though there was significant ethnic and racial tension in the United States in the first years after World War II.

Lee's graduate paper charted the growth and decline of Chinese American communities in the Rocky Mountain region. In 1949 she expanded her research to include new Chinese immigrant families in San Francisco. *The Chinese in the United States of America* was the controversial result of this research. Some in the Chinese community criticized Lee for saying that many Chinese people were too closed-minded to become full members of American society. This resistance to her work did not stop Lee's research, however. During the 1950s and 1960s, she studied a wide variety of racial and urban problems. Another major work, *The City: Urbanism and Urbanization in Major World Regions*, was published in 1955.

Meanwhile, Lee's career at Roosevelt University progressed. Eleven years after joining the faculty, she became department chairperson. Three years later, in 1959, she was promoted to full professor. She took a leave of absence from Roosevelt in 1961 to teach at Phoenix College, where she stayed through 1963. There, she continued to teach her belief that racial hatred and separatism must be overcome in order to achieve true democratic equality.

Sources:

"College's First Lady: Dr. Lee Blazes Trail at Roosevelt," *Chicago Sun-Times*, April 10, 1950.
Roosevelt University, biographical material, Chicago, 1994.

Sammy Lee

Olympic diver, physician
Born August 1, 1920, Fresno, California

"I believe that success in life is like the steps of a ladder, with each step being necessary in order to get to the top of one's ambition. Too many of us ask to be boosted up three and four steps at a time, totally ignoring the time spent by our victorious competitors."

S ammy Lee, one of the greatest divers of all time and the recipient of gold medals in two Olympic games, is recognized as one of the world's foremost authorities on the sport of diving. At the 1948 games in London, England, Lee became the first American of Korean ancestry to win a gold medal. At the next Olympic Games, in Helsinki, Finland, in 1952, Lee became the first male American diver to win gold medals at consecutive Olympics. Since then, Lee has remained active in amateur diving, including a stint as coach of the American team and as coach for **Greg Louganis,** another Olympic diver of wide renown. Lee is also a retired physician and surgeon who specialized in treating diseases of the ear.

Standing up to racism

Lee was born to Korean immigrant parents who taught their son that America was a land of freedom and choice for all, regardless of race. This did not alter the fact, however, that racism flourished in the United States. When Lee was in junior high school

Sammy Lee, second from left, with fellow Olympic diving champion, Victoria Manolo Draves

he attended a party given by a classmate. When the hostess's parents realized that Lee, the student body president, was not white, he was asked to leave. Returning home in tears, Lee asked his father why he was not born white. "My father wisely told me how lucky I was to be an American and that if I did not act and perform by showing the fine qualities of my Korean heritage, I would never become a good American," Lee recalled in an interview with *Asian American Biography*.

Lee added that his parents would "use acts of discrimination to their advantage. They told me that prejudiced people were like the pupil of an eye. The more light you try to shine in [it], the more it contracts. Born in America, you have all the rights and privileges. It's in the law. And if you allow these pickpockets, these bigots, to pick from your pocket full of dreams, then you won't have any dreams. Life without dreams is like a bird without wings. You can't fly."

Enchanted by the Olympics

The 1932 Olympics were held in Los Angeles, where the Lee family had by that time settled. Lee told *Swimming World* about this first exposure to international athletics. He was driving by the Los Angeles Coliseum and he noticed its top was ringed with flags from around the world. He asked his father what was happening inside and his father explained that Los Angeles was hosting the Olympic Games, which was a competition by athletes from around the world, in which the best of the best were crowned as champions of the world. "I just got chills up and down my spine. I looked at him and said, 'Poppa, I'm going to be an Olympic champion one day. I don't know what in, but I'll find it.'"

Later that year, Lee found his sport while playing with friends at the local pool; he realized he had a natural affinity for diving. Lee began practicing diving under the tutelage of Hart Crum, a local athlete. However, the pool where Lee practiced was only open to non-whites on Monday, a day referred to as "International Day." By declaration of the health department, the pool was then drained, cleaned, and disinfected by Tuesday morning for use by whites. Despite this racial barrier, Lee continued to train and eventually attracted the attention of Jim Ryan, the ex-Olympic diving coach.

Academics and sports

Lee was valedictorian of his high school class and student body president. He then entered Occidental College with plans to pursue a medical degree. By then Lee was a nationally recognized diver. Like many student athletes, he had trouble balancing his training with academics. By his junior year, Lee's grades had fallen so low that his academic advisor almost declined to recommend him for medical school. Lee told *Swimming World,* "The adviser tried to encourage me to take over my parents' store and forget about medicine." When the United States became involved in World

War II Lee thought he should join the service, but his father talked him into going to medical school.

In 1942, Lee enrolled at Southern California Medical School. That year he also won the national diving championship on the 3-meter springboard and 10-meter tower. In spite of the death of his father, Lee finished his medical training in time to travel to London in 1948 as a member of the U.S. Olympic Diving Team. There he became the first Korean American to win a gold medal when he placed first in the 10-meter platform competition. He went on to win a bronze medal in the 3-meter springboard. He was also the first non-white to win a gold medal in diving. "To be technical about it," Lee told *Swimming World,* "Victoria Draves, who was half-Filipino and half-English, was the first when she won the springboard two days before I won the tower. But as a 100 percent Asian, I was the first, at age 28."

His second Olympiad

Four years later America was fighting an undeclared war in Korea. Lee had entered the U.S. Army's specialized training program in 1942 to help finance medical school. After graduation he had received his post as a lieutenant in the Army Medical Corps and was serving his residency as the 1952 Olympics neared. When the coach of the diving team asked Lee to join the team, Lee asked his commanding officer, "Is it morally right that I should ask to compete in the Olympics again when my country is at war in my ancestral land of Korea?" His commander told him that there were plenty of doctors in the army, but that there was only one Sammy Lee, the diver, and that without his participation, the United States would undoubtedly not win the gold medal.

Lee trained at the Los Angeles Swim Stadium in the evenings while working days at an army hospital. At the Olympic trials, he came in first on the tower, and then, on August 1, 1952, his thirty-second birthday, Lee won his second gold medal.

After the Olympics

In 1953, Lee was presented with the James E. Sullivan Award, the most prestigious award given to America's outstanding amateur athletes. The U.S Department of State sent him on a goodwill tour to ten Southeast Asian countries; he toured the world speaking about the freedom and opportunities available in America.

Lee went on to serve several presidents in diplomatic posts as a representative or goodwill ambassador. He was Dwight D. Eisenhower's personal representative at the 1956 Olympics in Melbourne, Australia; he was a member of the President's Council on Physical Fitness and Sports between 1970 and 1975 under Richard Nixon and Gerald Ford; and he served as Nixon's personal representative to the 1972 Olympics in Munich, West Germany, and Ronald Reagan's representative to the 1988 Olympics in Seoul, South Korea.

In addition, Lee has coached both U.S. professional and amateur diving teams. In 1979, he was the first foreign coach invited to China to evaluate its diving program. He has also coached individual divers, including Bob Webster, who won a gold medal at the 1960 Olympics and the legendary Greg Louganis, whom Lee described as "another son." In 1984, Lee was an Olympic torch runner and flag bearer when the Olympics returned to the Los Angeles Coliseum 50 years after he first saw that stadium ringed with the world's flags.

In describing his philosophy, Lee explained, "I believe that success in life is like the steps of a ladder, with each step being necessary in order to get to the top of one's ambition. Too many of us ask to be boosted up three and four steps at a time, totally ignoring the time spent by our victorious competitors. That's what I used to do. I used to pray every night that someday I would be an Olympic champion. But I remember my dad saying that when I lost a diving contest, 'Never use an excuse of your racial background. Just work harder. If you're not proud of the color of your skin and your ancestral heritage, you'll never be accepted as an American.'"

Sources:

Lee, Sammy, interview with Terry Hong, June 1988.

Lee, Sammy, phone interview with Terry Hong, May 14, 1994.

Professional Diving Coaches Association, http://www.uspdca.org (accessed March 2003).

Wampler, Molly Frick, *Not Without Honor: The Story of Sammy Lee,* Santa Barbara, California: The Fithian Press, 1987.

Tsung-Dao Lee

Theoretical physicist
Born November 25, 1926, Shanghai, China

"Through your consistent and unprejudiced thinking, you have been able to break a most puzzling deadlock in the field of elementary particle physics, where now experimental and theoretical work is pouring forth as a result of your brilliant achievement."—Royal Swedish Academy of Sciences

Tsung-Dao Lee won the Nobel Prize in physics in 1957 in recognition of experimental work he had done that helped disprove a long-held scientific belief in a concept called the conservation of parity. This physical law involved the interaction of colliding subatomic particles (units of matter smaller than atoms) and was first formulated in the 1920s at the birth of modern physics. Lee shared the prize with Chen Ning Yang, and their discovery owes much to the experimental work of Chien Shung Wu of Columbia University. All three are Chinese immigrants to America.

Born in China

Lee was born to Tsing-King Lee, a businessman, and Ming-Chang Chang. His parents emphasized the importance of education. Lee was an excellent student, especially in math and physics, which he enjoyed tremendously. He grew up during an especially tumultuous time in China's history; there was much civil unrest as the old system of imperial dynastic rule crumbled, leaving a series of warlords fighting various civil wars throughout the immense country. Then, in 1935, Japan invaded and occupied large parts of China. Lee was able to continue his schooling, however, and in 1943 he graduated from high school and enrolled in college at the National Chekiang University in Kweichow. The war finally caught up to Lee when his entire university was forced to flee south and consolidate itself with several other war-displaced universities in a quiet part of the country. In 1946, one year after the defeat of the Japanese in World War II, Lee earned a bachelor's degree in physics.

After earning his degree, Lee went to the United States on a government scholarship to study physics at the University of Chicago, then one of the top international centers in the field. Lee studied under Enrico Fermi, one of the world's most prominent nuclear physicists, and earned his Ph.D. in 1950. He wrote his dissertation on white dwarfs—collapsed, super-dense stars with about the same mass as the sun but with a much higher density. After graduating, Lee had expected to return to his home country, but in 1949 the government that awarded him his scholarship to study in the United States fell to the communist insurgency led by Mao Zedong, who established an anti-Western dictatorship. Lee was forced to remain in the United States; he took a job as a research associate in Lake Geneva, Wisconsin, at the Yerkes Astronomical Observatory.

In 1951 he left that job to work as a research associate at the University of California at Berkeley. Later that year, he transferred once again, this time to take a position at the Institute for Advanced Study at Princeton University in New Jersey. There, by a stroke of good luck, he was reunited with a fellow student from his undergraduate days in China, Chin Ning Yang. Lee and Yang became good friends at Princeton and often got together to discuss current problems in the rapidly expanding field of particle physics, in which discoveries were being made at an incredible pace.

In 1953 Lee moved to Columbia University in New York City, where he first served as an assistant professor, and then, in 1956, at the age of 29, as a full professor. He was the youngest person ever to become a full professor at the prestigious Ivy League school. In 1963 he became the Enrico Fermi Professor of Physics.

The Nobel work

Even after moving to New York, Lee continued to meet with his friend and colleague Yang, and they continued to puzzle over the nature of some of the more curious subatomic particles that were being discovered at the time. Physicists had for years been bombarding subatomic particles in high-speed accelerators in order to observe their structures as they split apart at impact. In the course of these experiments, two new particles were discovered called K-mesons. On further experimentation, it was observed that these K-mesons behaved in a way that defied a long-held tenet called the law of conservation of parity. Physicists had noticed that one of these two K-mesons, which appeared identical in all other ways, would decay into two pi-mesons, while the other would decay into three. Established physical law, as elaborated in the law of conservation of parity, does not allow for such difference in behavior; the natural world is expected to behave in entirely predictable, symmetrical ways.

Lee and Yang discussed possible reasons for this discrepancy, and they began experimenting. The question they sought to resolve was whether the two types of K-mesons were in fact the same particle (which would mean the disproving of conservation of parity), or if they were different in a way science was not yet able to observe. The decisive experiment took place during 1956 and 1957; it involved observing the subatomic decay of radioactive cobalt in a controlled environment. The pattern of decay they observed proved that the law of conservation was invalid, a conclusion that surprised the young scientists—they had assumed all along that they would find that the K-mesons were two different types of particles. Their discovery was quickly confirmed by others working on similar experiments. In bringing about the fall of the law of conservation of parity, Lee and Yang greatly furthered the science of particle physics and removed a major obstacle toward achieving Albert Einstein's theoretical goal of discovering a single unified theory governing the major forces of the universe.

The prize

In 1957 the Royal Swedish Academy of Sciences awarded Lee and Yang the Nobel Prize in physics. During the presentation of the awards, the two were lauded with these words: "Through your consistent and unprejudiced thinking, you have been able to break a most puzzling deadlock in the field of elementary particle physics, where now experimental and theoretical work is pouring forth as a result of your brilliant achievement."

Lee has received other honors for his work as well. In 1957 he was awarded the Albert Einstein Commemorative Award of Yeshiva University, and in 1958 Princeton University awarded him an honorary degree. Lee is also a longtime member of the National Academy of Sciences and is a fellow of the American Physical Society.

Lee became a U.S. citizen in 1963, but continued to be concerned for the political and educational climates in his native country. Unfortunately, travel to and from China by U.S. citizens was restricted for many years while China was under Communist control. It wasn't until 1974 that Lee was able to revisit China and begin working on ways to strengthen the scientific community in that country. He started by creating the China-U.S. Physics Examination and Application program in 1980, which offered opportunities for Chinese students to study in America. But Lee also worked with officials in China to set up fellowships that would encourage and support the students in research and practice once their studies were completed and they returned to their own country.

Today, Lee still holds a post at Colombia University, but he travels to China several times a year to work with administrators at such locations as the Center for Advanced Science and Technology in Beijing, The Beijing Institute of Modern Physics, and the Zhejiang Modern Physics Center.

Since 1998, Lee has served as the director for the RIKEN Research Center at Brookhaven National Laboratories. This center is a collaboration between the Tokyo Institute for Physical and Chemical Research (which has the Japanese acronym of RIKEN) and the U.S. lab. The centerpiece of the program is the Relativistic Heavy Ion Collider, a particle accelerator, which Lee and others hope to use in research concerning vacuums or empty space.

Sources:

"An East and West Perspective" *Columbia University,* http://www.columbia.edu (accessed March 2003).

Travers, Bridget, ed., *World of Scientific Discovery,* Detroit, MI: Gale, 1994.

Wasson, Tyler, ed., *Nobel Prize Winners,* Princeton, NJ: Visual Education Corporation, 1987.

Yuan T. Lee

Chemist, Nobel Prize winner
Born November 29, 1936, Hsinchu, Taiwan

"It's very satisfying to promote science and education and see good results. Setting a good example for young people, being a role model, is very important for me."

In 1986 Yuan Tseh Lee shared the Nobel Prize for chemistry with his colleague, Dudley R. Herschbach. The award recognized their groundbreaking research into the nature of chemical reactions. At Harvard University, Lee successfully designed a mass-spectrometer, a technologically advanced detector used in analyzing chemical reactions. His invention, combined with earlier work done by Herschbach, allowed scientists to study how molecules behave when they collide at high speed. Lee is also noted for his work in physics and physical chemistry and has

Yuan T. Lee

received several other awards for his accomplishments.

Education an early priority

Lee was born in Taiwan on November 29, 1936. His mother was an elementary school teacher and his father was an artist and art teacher. Lee was an outstanding student. When he graduated from high school in 1955, he was allowed to enter Taiwan University without taking the required entrance exam.

In college Lee discovered that he loved science—chemistry in particular. His devotion to science was strengthened when he read the biography of Marie Curie, winner of the Nobel Prize in chemistry in 1911. As part of his studies, he conducted research on the separation of the elements strontium and barium in the presence of an electric field.

After he graduated from Taiwan University in 1959, Lee entered graduate school at Tsignua University. He earned a master's degree in chemistry in 1961 and then came to the United States to attend the University of California at Berkeley. In 1965 he received his Ph.D. from Berkeley and spent a year and a half in postgraduate study before moving on to Harvard University.

Study of molecules begins

In 1967 Lee joined Herschbach's research team at Harvard. Earlier in his career, at Berkeley in the late 1950s, Herschbach had proposed a new way to study chemical reactions. It involved beams that consist of molecules moving at very high speeds. Herschbach thought if two beams were crossed, some of the molecules would collide and form new molecules.

In 1963 Herschbach returned to Harvard to continue his research. He performed several successful experiments involving alkali (soluble salt) atoms. At the time, advanced chemical detectors could determine where molecules settled during experiments, what new molecules were created, and whether energy had been created or absorbed. But only experiments involving alkali atoms could be analyzed in this way.

When he joined Herschbach's lab, Lee started to design a better detector, one that would enable scientists to study a wider range of molecules. His detector was the best available in the late 1960s. It was a mass-spectrometer that used magnetic and electric fields to move particles along different paths to separate and identify them. The technical challenges were great, but within ten months the detector was producing important results.

Lee left Harvard in 1968 to become an assistant professor of chemistry at the University of Chicago, but he continued his research into chemical reactions. He left the University of Chicago in 1974 to become a professor of chemistry and principal investigator at the Lawrence Livermore Laboratory at the University of California at Berkeley. While at Berkeley, Lee and his laboratory staff became well known for their work in physics and physical chemistry.

Nobel Prize

In 1986 Lee and Herschbach shared the Nobel Prize in chemistry with John Polanyi, a University of Toronto chemist. Polanyi had studied the same problem as Lee and Herschbach but had taken a different approach. He had focused on the faint infrared light emitted when molecules react to form new substances.

That same year, Lee earned the Peter Debye Award in physical chemistry (1986), bestowed by the American Chemical Society, and the National Medal of Science from the National Science Foundation (1986).

Winning the Nobel Prize opened many opportunities for teaching, lecturing, and research at various universities and scientific organizations around the world. But what Lee wanted most was to contribute to the sci-entific community of his native country. In 1994, he accepted a position as president of Academia Sinica, the most prominent academic and research center in that country. Since the organization is affiliated with the government, Lee reports directly to the president of Taiwan and serves as a national science advisor. He is also chairman of the Taiwan Council of Educational Reform, an organization that advocates the democratization and autonomy of universities in the country, which have historically been controlled by government entities.

Lee continues to travel around the world giving lectures In 1998, he was honored by his alma mater as recipient of the Clark Kerr Award for Distinguished Leadership in Education. At the awards ceremony, he told his audience that he hoped to "take a leadership role in the transformation of Taiwanese society…and to show that good science can be done in a developing country." And on his work in education he said, "It's very satisfying to promote science and education and see good results. Setting a good example for young people, being a role model, is very important for me."

Sources:

"Chemistry: Nobel Prize for 'Detailed Understanding of How Chemical Reactions Take Place,'" *Scientific American,* December 1986, p. 86.

Gwynne, Peter, "Nobel Prizes Focus on Science of the Ultra Small," *Research and Development,* December 1986, p. 37.

Peterson, Ivars, "Chemistry: Probing Reaction Dynamics," *Science News,* October 25, 1986, p. 262.

Zoglin, Richard, Joe Levine, Michael D. Lemonick, Paul Gray, and Barbara Rudolph, "Nobel Prize Winners," *Time,* October 27, 1986.

Maya Lin

Architect, sculptor
Born October 5, 1959, Athens, Ohio

"I would identify myself as Chinese American. If I had to choose one thing over the other, I would choose American. I was not born in China, I was not raised there, and the China my parents knew no longer exists.... I don't have an allegiance to any country but this one, it is my home."

As her senior thesis project at Yale University, where Maya Lin was studying architecture, she submitted a design to a national competition then underway for a Vietnam Veterans Memorial to be built in Washington, D.C. The Vietnam War had been bitterly opposed in the United States, and in many ways the country had not yet healed the rifts that had been opened by the war. The memorial was intended to be a first step in initiating a national dialogue about the costs of the war and the domestic reaction to it; the monument would surely become a heavily visited site.

In entering the competition, Lin was competing with some of the best-known and most highly regarded architects and sculptors in the country. Remarkably, Lin's design was chosen from among 1,420 entries as the winner of the competition. Her idea consisted of a black granite wall inscribed with the names of the nearly 58,000 American servicemen and women who died fighting the Vietnam War. (Vietnamese deaths numbered over two million.) The monument has indeed become one of the most visited sights in Washington and has earned a reputation as a place of great emotion and healing, as the sponsors of its construction had hoped it would. In fact, as the nation commemorated the twentieth anniversary of its withdrawal from armed conflict in Southeast Asia, Lin's monument was the focal point of a great deal of attention, including a 1994 documentary called *Maya Lin: A Strong Vision*, which won the Academy Award for best feature documentary.

Since the construction of the memorial, Lin has gone on to establish herself as one of the premier sculptor/architects in the nation. Other prominent works by her include the Civil Rights Memorial in Montgomery, Alabama; the new lower Manhattan home for the Museum of African Art; and *The Women's Table* at Yale University in New Haven, Connecticut.

Born into an academic family

Lin was born into an academic and artistic family in the rural college town of Athens, Ohio. Her father, Henry Huan Lin, came from a distinguished family of anti-Communist intellectuals and politicians in Beijing, China, and was a well-known ceramist (someone who makes ceramic art pieces) and the former dean of fine arts at Ohio State University. Her mother, Julia Chang Lin, is a professor of literature at Ohio University. Maya was a reclusive child and spent much of her free time engaged in solitary pastimes such as reading and hiking. She also experimented with different arts including silversmithing and bronze casting. She was greatly encouraged in these endeavors by her parents. Lin was an excellent student and was co-valedictorian of her high school graduating class. After graduation, she was accepted at Yale University, where she chose to study architecture.

It was there that she created her now-famous design for the Vietnam Veterans Memorial. Her concept reflected her artistic bias toward simplicity; it called for two highly polished walls of black granite, set in a "V" and inscribed with the names of the dead or missing veterans of the war. In a statement Lin composed to accompany the design, she described the effect the monument would have in terms of motion—that visitors to the site would experience the losses of the war as they "move into and out of it."

Not everyone was happy with the selection of Lin's design; some veterans and their families felt its simplicity and starkness recalled the domestic controversy over the war rather than the heroism of those who fought it. Protesters petitioned for another design—a more traditional, bronze sculpture of three servicemen with an American flag by sculptor Frederick Hart—to take its place. Eventually a compromise was reached: Hart's sculpture would be built as well and would stand 120 feet away from Lin's wall, near the entrance to the memorial.

Moving beyond the memorial

Lin graduated *cum laude* (with honors) from Yale in 1981. In 1982 she coordinated construction of the memorial, which was completed and dedicated that year. But the publicity surrounding her design—much of which was directed at her as well as the monument—had taken its toll on Lin, and she left graduate school at Harvard in 1983 to work at a Boston architectural firm, where she would draw less attention. In the fall of that year she resumed her studies, this

time in Yale's graduate architecture program. In 1985 she graduated with a master's of architecture degree. The next year, Yale awarded her an honorary doctorate of fine arts, and in 1987 Lin moved to New York City, where she set up a studio practice, working simultaneously in sculpture and architecture.

In 1988 the opportunity to work on another large outdoor memorial presented itself when the Southern Poverty Law Center in Montgomery, Alabama, asked Lin to design a memorial to those who had given their lives in the struggle for civil rights. The design she offered was inspired in part by a phrase from the biblical Book of Amos used by civil rights leader Martin Luther King, Jr., publicly on two occasions: "We will not be satisfied until justice rolls down like waters and righteousness like a mighty stream." That phrase is engraved in the Montgomery monument, along with important dates in the history of civil rights and the names of 40 men, women, and children who lost their lives in service to the movement. The Civil Rights Memorial is comprised of a polished black granite wall and conical table over which a thin pool of water flows.

In recent years Lin has created three other pieces of public artwork. In 1991 the Charlotte Coliseum in Charlotte, North Carolina, installed *TOPO,* an environmental landscape sculpture. In 1993 *The Women's Table* was installed at Yale University. The sculpture and water table, dedicated to women—past and present—at Yale, consists of a granite table with a series of numbers spiraling out from its center representing the number of women students at Yale for each year of its existence. With the vast majority of the num-

Maya Lin

bers being zeros, Lin graphically represented women's historical exclusion from Yale.

Also in 1993, as an artist in residence at the Wexner Center for the Arts in Columbus, Ohio, Lin was awarded the first permanent sculpture commission by that newly created, well- respected arts facility. The landscape installation, *Groundswell,* is made of 43 tons of recycled tempered glass and is found in multiple locations throughout the center, highlighting, for instance, a corner near the floor or the sill of a window. Lin continues to devote time to public art. This was followed by Eclipsed Time (1994), a 16-by-30-foot glass and steel clock gracing the ceiling of the Long Island Railroad/Pennsylvania Station terminal in Manhattan. In 1995, she created what she considers to be one of her favorite spaces, Wave Field. Located on campus at the University of Michigan in Ann Arbor, Wave Field is a series of undulating mounds of earth designed to look like rolling waves of water.

Straddling two worlds

Lin has not confined herself to large public commissions and installations, however. She produces highly regarded studio sculpture in such media as beeswax, lead, steel, and broken glass. These have been shown in group shows in New York, Los Angeles, and San Francisco and were exhibited at the Wexner Center for the Arts in 1993 as part of Lin's first one-woman show entitled "Public/Private." Her second major show was in 1997-98, entitled "Topologies." She has worked as a traditional architect as well, having recently designed two houses: one in Williamstown, Massachusetts, and one overlooking the Pacific Ocean in Santa Monica, California. The Williamstown house is a one-story home constructed around a courtyard, reminiscent of traditional Japanese design. In 2002, she designed the Winter Garden as a renovation of the lobby of the American Express Client Services Center in Minneapolis. One of the exterior glass walls is designed with a water running down the side. The waterfall is allowed to freeze in the winter, creating an entirely different effect in lighting and view.

Indeed, much of Lin's work is regarded as Asian in sensibility rather than Western (oriented toward European and North American culture), and Lin readily agrees that her preferences lie with Eastern design. Of the difference between Asian and Western artistic traditions, she wrote in *Art in America*, "Much of the Western architectural training has left me cold. But when I walk into a Japanese garden, I respond immediately. I find its simplicity lets me think and come to my own conclusions." In 2000, Lin published her first book, *Boundaries*, in which she reviews some of her own work.

Lin has been very successful at working in both sculpture and architecture, something her professors at Yale told her she would not be able to do—the conventional

wisdom being that you have to choose one or the other. The *New York Times* interviewed Lin about her success in these two fields. "It's been exceedingly difficult," she admitted, "and at times downright discouraging. There's an incredible suspicion that if you're interested in two different disciplines, then you treat them lightly. I love architecture and I love sculpture, but I could never choose. Sculpture to me is like poetry, and architecture is like prose."

Though Lin has tried to stay away from monument building, she did submit sketches (when asked) for a possible World Trade Center memorial to honor those who were killed in the September 11, 2001, terrorist attack on that site. She is also working on an idea of her own which she calls the Extinction Project: a memorial for extinct plant and animal species that would serve to encourage and promote environmental protection. Most of her current projects involve public spaces and special designs for private homes and apartments. Lin lives in New York City with her husband, Daniel Wolf, an art dealer, and their two daughters.

Of her ethnicity, Lin wrote in *Art in America*, "If you ask, I would identify myself as Chinese American. If I had to choose one thing over the other, I would choose American. I was not born in China, I was not raised there, and the China my parents knew no longer exists.... I don't have an allegiance to any country but this one, it is my home."

Sources:

Gandee, Charles, "Life after Vietnam," *Vogue*, February 1993.

Lin, Maya, "Maya Lin," *Art in America*, September 1991.

Tauber, Peter, "Monument Maker," *New York Times,* February 24, 1991, p. 48.

Zinsser, William, "I realized her tears were becoming part of the memorial," *Smithsonian,* September 1991, pp. 33-35, 42.

Jahja Ling

Conductor, pianist
Born 1951, Jakarta, Indonesia

"Classical music has to be passed on to the next generation, and that's why working with young people gives me tremendous joy."

Jahja Ling is considered one of the most talented young conductors of classical music in the world. He has earned a reputation for insightful and highly expressive interpretations of music as both conductor and pianist and has amassed an impressive list of guest conducting engagements with some of the most renowned orchestras in the world. As of summer 1995, he held two posts: resident conductor of the Cleveland Orchestra and music director of the Florida Orchestra.

Jahja Ling was born into a family of ethnic Chinese in Indonesia, where there is a large Chinese community. His father, who was educated in the Netherlands, enjoyed many aspects of Western culture, especially classical music. His grandmother was a violinist and provided the Ling household with the piano that young Ling first began to play when he was nine years old. Even at that age, Ling was able to reproduce pieces on the piano from simply hearing them. At six,

he began formal piano instruction and by age 12 had taught himself Tchaikovsky's *Piano Concerto No. 1*. When he was 17, he won the first of two Jakarta Piano competitions, and when he graduated from the Jakarta Music School, his sights were set on becoming a soloist. Ling traveled to the United States as the recipient of a Rockefeller grant to study at the Juilliard School of Music in New York under the tutelage of famed teacher Mieczyslaw Munz.

Early conducting experience

While in New York, Ling got his first taste of conducting as the director of his church choir. He became interested enough to sign up for a conducting course at Juilliard, where another teacher, John Nelson, recognized his talent and encouraged him to pursue conducting seriously.

After graduating from Juilliard in 1975 with a master's degree in music, Ling was accepted into the highly competitive conducting program at the Yale University School of Music. Ling's career as a conductor began while he was a student of Yale's Otto-Werner Mueller. He earned a doctor of musical arts degree from Yale in 1985.

While training as a conductor at Yale, Ling also sought to maintain his position as a pianist. He entered several piano competitions, winning the bronze medal at the 1977 Artur Rubinstein International Piano Master Competition in Israel and a certificate of honor at the 1978 Tchaikovsky International Piano Competition in Moscow. In 1979, Ling was accepted as a scholarship student into the noted conducting program at the Berkshire Music Festival at Tangle-

Jahja Ling

Bernstein, Colin Davis, **Seiji Ozawa**, Andre Previn, and Gunther Schuller. This opportunity also provided Ling with the recognition that would quickly propel him into the professional ranks.

Continued success

In 1981, Ling joined the conducting staff of the San Francisco Symphony as part of the Exxon/Arts Endowment program, serving as assistant conductor and then associate conductor until 1984. During his tenure there, Ling founded the San Francisco Symphony Youth Orchestra and in a short time created a top-quality ensemble.

In 1984, Christoph von Dohnanyi, music director of the Cleveland Orchestra, offered Ling a job as associate conductor. Ling's performance led to his appointment the following season as the Cleveland Orchestra's resident conductor, becoming only the fourth person to hold the title. "This orchestra needs people with very strong integrity and that integrity he's got," said Dohnanyi about Ling. "He's modest, and maybe in some ways, too modest, but he's a terrific musician and a wonderful colleague."

Throughout his career, Ling has demonstrated his commitment to developing the talent of young musicians. He told *AAB*, "Classical music has to be passed on to the next generation, and that's why working with young people gives me tremendous joy." In 1986, Ling founded the Cleveland Orchestra Youth Orchestra, quickly becoming a very popular leader among the young people with whom he worked. In 1993, due to his increasingly busy schedule, he stepped down as music director of the ensemble.

wood in rural Massachusetts. As Ling recalled in an interview with *Asian American Biography (AAB)*, "1979 was a critical year. I came to Tanglewood as an unknown and was given a lot of encouragement. [Legendary conductor Leonard] Bernstein even told me that I would be a big conductor one day." Not wanting to disappoint the man he would later regard as his mentor, Ling proved his worth and the following summer was awarded a Leonard Bernstein Conducting Fellowship to the festival. In this capacity, he studied with some of the world's most accomplished conductors:

In 1988, Ling won two distinctive honors. He was one of three conductors to receive the Seaver/National Endowment for the Arts Conductor's Award, a career development grant made to American conductors judged to be of extraordinary promise. That year Ling was also appointed music director of the Florida Orchestra, which serves the Tampa Bay area. Since becoming music director in Florida, he has been credited with bringing a degree of confidence and a high level of expectation to an organization that was losing ground. The doubling of subscriptions (memberships to the orchestra through which season tickets are distributed) since his arrival as music director has been attributed to his dynamic leadership and commitment to the community.

Recordings and successes

One of Ling's most notable appearances with the Florida Orchestra was at Super Bowl XXV in January 1991. Ling led the orchestra in the performance of "The Star Spangled Banner" with pop singer Whitney Houston before a worldwide audience of 750 million. Subsequently, the recording of the performance on Arista Records earned a gold record with sales of more than 860,000 copies. Ling's other recordings include an album of classical trumpet works with Rolf Smedvig and the Scottish Chamber Orchestra, which earned a Grammy nomination in 1990, and the Dupre Organ Symphony and Rheinberger Organ Concerto with soloist Michael Murray and the Royal Philharmonic Orchestra.

Ling has earned critical acclaim as a guest conductor of many of the world's leading orchestras. Along with what are known as the "Big Five" orchestras (those in Boston, Chicago, Cleveland, New York, and Philadelphia), he has led the ensembles of Cincinnati, Detroit, Florida, Minnesota, Montreal, and San Francisco, among others. In 1988, he made his European debut with the Leipzig Gewandhaus Orchestra as the first conductor of Chinese descent to lead the German ensemble. Other engagements abroad have seen him take the podium of the Hong Kong Philharmonic, Netherlands Radio Philharmonic, Royal Philharmonic, National Symphony Orchestra of Taipei, and Tokyo's Yomiuri Nippon Symphony.

One of the highlights of Ling's career was his New York Philharmonic debut in 1993. Substituting for the ailing Kurt Masur, Ling conducted the world premiere of Ellen Taafe Zwillich's *Symphony No. 3*. He recalled the significance of the event, explaining, "Because of the world premiere, there were 13 critics in the audience. Having so many critics there was added pressure, but receiving good reviews from all of them was very satisfying."

In addition to his conducting duties, Ling continues to perform at the keyboard. He has appeared as soloist and conductor/soloist with the Cleveland, Florida, and St. Paul Chamber orchestras. He sees these performances as an opportunity to enhance his ability to communicate as a conductor, explaining, "When you play with the orchestra as part of the team, it makes a feeling of being a colleague. It makes the music flow better and they know what you mean musically."

In the summer of 1994, Ling conducted the Los Angeles Philharmonic in a performance of Tchaikovsky's *Symphony No. 2*. *Los Angeles Times* contributor Martin Bernheimer began his review thus: "His name is Jahja Ling. Remember it." He continued, "Ling capitalized on expressive restraint, crisp articulation, dynamic variety, and rhythmic propulsion. It was lovely."

Classical music ambassador

Since 1990, Ling has directed free concerts of the Cleveland Orchestra in several of the city's downtown locations for Fourth of July celebrations, drawing as many as 100,000 listeners. "It gives me great joy when I can see so many people at concerts they wouldn't normally come to," he told *AAB*. "There's a danger that classical music is thought only to belong to the elite, and we need to change that. When you can touch people with music, you have made an important connection." In 1999, Ling was given a greater opportunity to reach more listeners as he took over the duties of Blossom Festival director. The Blossom Festival is the summer season of the Cleveland Orchestra with concerts of classical and pop music performed at the outdoor amphitheater of Blossom Music Center in Cuyahoga Falls, Ohio.

To keep his life's goals in perspective, Ling adheres to this philosophy: "Stay focused.... Never think you are higher or lower than where you are.... Aim for the target." Ultimately, he would like to take the reins of a major orchestra while continuing with his guest conducting engagements. Paramount to his plan is finding a post that will not only provide him with quality conducting opportunities but will also allow him to spend time with his wife, Jane, and sons Gabriel and Daniel.

Sources:

Bernheimer, Martin, "Ling: Surprise Debut with Philharmonic," *Los Angeles Times,* August 4, 1994, p. F1.

Cleveland Orchestra, http://www.clevelandorch.com (accessed November, 2002).

Fleming, John, "From Red, White and Blue to Gold," *St. Petersburg Times,* November 22, 1991.

Ling, Jahja, interview with Marilyn Eppich, July 8, 1994.

Rosenberg, Donald, "Jahja Ling: A Consummate Wielder of Orchestra Baton," *Cleveland Plain Dealer,* April 3, 1994.

"They Loved Ling in L.A.," *Cleveland Plain Dealer,* August 6, 1994, p. B4.

Thomas, Michael, "A Man of Many Movements," *City Reports,* October 15, 1992.

Lisa Ling

Television host
Born August 30, 1973, Sacramento, California

"I've learned that the values that my family lived by have become a part of me. And their struggles as immigrants taught me to appreciate what it means to be American, without forgetting what it means to be Chinese."

L isa Ling has emerged as one of her generation's top and most experienced reporters. She entered broadcast journalism at the age of sixteen and has been rising steadily ever since. In 2003, she left after three years with ABC's daytime talk show *The View* to become the host of *National Geographic's Explorer.* While on *The View,* Ling served to voice opinions for the younger, twenty-something generation.

Ling grew up in a traditional Chinese American family in Sacramento, California. Her father, whose parents had immigrated from China, was an aircraft inspector for the U.S. Air Force, and her mother immigrated to the United States from Taiwan in 1968 to study at Sacramento State University. Though her family wanted Ling to pursue a career in law or medicine, Ling knew what she wanted and went after it. In an interview with *Gold Sea Asian American Profiles,* Ling recalled her parents' reaction to her pursuit of a career in television. "They just didn't think that a career in television would be the most wise decision. But then, I'm probably one of the most obnoxious and boisterous people that they have ever met, so they just said, 'You know what? You can probably pull it off.'"

One of only a few Asian Americans

Ling attended high school in Sacramento near her father's air force base. She was one of only a few Asian Americans students at her high school. She says that when she was younger, she was embarrassed by her Asian heritage because it made her different. She reports being the brunt of several wise-cracks, which she said hurt her deeply. In her senior year of high school, she began reading and learning about her Asian heritage. She read many books by Chinese and Chinese American authors, and discovered a deep interest in Chinese history.

Ling began her career remarkably early. At the age of sixteen, she was chosen to be a host of *Scratch,* a nationally syndicated entertainment-based teen show. Ling earned the role after her teacher suggested she audi-

Lisa Ling

tion at her local mall. She got the job, and began traveling the country to cover events for the show. Though the experience was rewarding and fun for Ling, she had to miss a lot of school and spent a lot of her time traveling. Just as her time at *Scratch* was ending, and Ling was ready to head to Boston to attend Boston University, producers at Channel One saw her work and offered her a job.

Ling jumped at the opportunity. The new show, based in Los Angeles, was aimed at high school students. Ling shifted her college plans—from Boston University to the University of Southern California, which she could attend while working full-time for

Channel One. Ling committed herself to excel in both her schoolwork and her new career. She threw herself into the two endeavors, leaving little time for anything else. Her dedication paid off. Before her twenty-fifth birthday, she became Channel One's senior war correspondent.

In that position, Ling covered a wide variety of stories, including the 1992 referendum elections in Russia, held after the breakup of the Soviet Union. She also covered the dramatic unrest in Afghanistan, both pre- and post-Taliban. She traveled to North Africa to cover the ongoing civil war in Algeria. Her position has taken her to dangerous places for stories such as the one she did on drug trafficking in Colombia. On the other hand, her afternoon tea with the Dalai Lama, the Buddhist spiritual leader of Tibet, was both exotic and tranquil.

While on assignment for Channel One, Ling often worked side by side with older network correspondents. This exposure gave her confidence and experience beyond her years, and would help her later in her career. While working for the show that reached eight million teenagers, Ling tried to make her reporting accessible and familiar, "I absolutely have a classroom in mind…filled with the students from my old high school. I think, what would my friends in high school think of this?" It was this friendly attitude that earned her a certain celebrity among viewers of the show.

While she was still working for Channel One, some viewers formed a fan club, and one classroom even sent her a check for $22 after a story was broadcast showing the damage done to Ling's home in a California earthquake. These experiences awed her,

"Being recognized is great, but it's very weird. I'll never get used to that."

The View

But Ling would gain even more celebrity, and become one of the most recognizable Asian Americans on television, when she was named as a co-host to ABC's daytime show, *The View,* in 1999. Journalist Barbara Walters created and produced *The View* to be a forum for women of different ages and backgrounds. Ling was chosen to represent the younger demographic. On *The View,* Ling bantered with the other cohosts about subjects ranging from health and beauty to hot political issues of the day.

While at *The View,* Ling also pursued other projects. In October 2000, she began to contribute research and stories to *USA Today's Weekend* edition. In addition, she worked on several documentaries for the Public Broadcasting Service (PBS); she produced eight documentaries for the PBS network. Ling was also selected to host the 2001 television special *"Teen People's* 20 Teens Who Will Change the World."

Ling knows her status as a celebrity can help her influence young people. In September 2001, she hosted a forum for teens entitled "The Day It All Changed," referring to the terrorist attacks on the World Trade Center in New York and The Pentagon in Washington, D.C. Using her footage from Afghanistan to help teens understand global aspects of politics and society, she hoped to encourage young people to recognize the responsibility they have to the world.

Ling's achievements and style were being noticed by mainstream publications. She was named one of *Cosmopolitan* magazine's

"Fun, Fearless Females," and one of *Rolling Stone* magazine's "Hot Reporters." During her time at *The View,* Ling further bolstered her professional resume by serving as a correspondent for weekend ABC news. One thing that Ling loves about her job is that she is constantly learning something new. Ling told *Gold Sea Asian American Profiles,* "I can't believe that I'm actually getting paid for getting fed knowledge. I'm learning so much every day, and I'm actually getting paid for it. I couldn't ask for a better job."

While at *The View,* Ling participated in a genealogy project on her family that was broadcast on the show. The reporter who grew up ashamed of her heritage had come a long way. Ling discovered that her family had once been scholars and high-ranking government officials in China. Ling has made guest appearances on *Hollywood Squares, The Tonight Show with Jay Leno,* NBC's television show *Ed, Spin City, The Late Show with Craig Kilborn,* and *Dangerous Minds.* A testament to her position as a recognized celebrity was her selection to appear in television commercials for Old Navy khakis.

After *The View*

Ling announced that she would leave *The View* after December 5, 2002, to begin a new adventure as the host of *National Geographic's Explorer.* After the September 11, 2001, attacks on New York, she felt a growing interest in returning to reporting. She says that the time was right for the move. "If I don't do it now, I may never want to do it," she said. "Two years from now, I may be thinking about settling down and may not

want to travel." In 2003, viewers of *National Geographic's Explorer* could look forward to Ling's energy and journalistic background as she tackles her new job. Her insatiable curiosity and the show's theme—to cover the world and all that's in it—seem a perfect fit.

Sources

"Ling remembers visits to Afghanistan in Penn State Speech," *U-Wire,* http://www.uwire.com/content/topae103101001.html (accessed March 20, 2003).

"Lisa Ling named next host of National Geographic Explorer," *MSNBC News,* http://www.msnbc.com/news (accessed March 20, 2003).

"Lisa Ling," *The View,* http://www.abc.abcnews.go.com/theview/hosts/ling.html (accessed March 20, 2003).

"The Perky One," *Gold Sea Asian American Profiles,* http://goldsea.com/Personalities/Linglisa/linglisa.html (accessed March 20, 2003).

Lucy Alexis Liu

Actress
Born December 2, 1968, Queens, New York

"I think that if I weren't an actress, if I decided that I wanted to go into hotel management, I would do that as ferociously as possible, too, just because I love to live my life passionately."

cting on television and in hit movies, Lucy Liu determinedly works against old stereotypes of passivity for Asian American women. She has stamped her own imprint on roles originally written for non-Asians or for men, and now happily appears as the lead instead of being side-

Lucy Alexis Liu

A city girl

Lucy Liu's parents, immigrants from China, raised Lucy and her brother and sister in the working-class urban setting of Jackson Heights, Queens, New York. Her biochemist mother and engineer/business-man father "worked ferociously" according to Liu, and the children were "latchkey kids" who watched television in their apartment after school. It was a conservative, frugal upbringing, bilingual in Mandarin Chinese and English, with an emphasis on education and a strong work ethic.

Liu adored watching the comedy spy show, *Get Smart.* She also liked to pretend to be the super-heroine Wonder Woman, with a pair of "magic" silver bracelets on her wrists. She had no early ambitions to be an actress, but as she told an interviewer for the *Yesterdayland* Web site, she "wanted to be something or somebody different when I was younger. It was kind of a cultural thing." She summed up her feelings about growing up Asian American: "You go through a period when you don't like being Asian; you want to be 'American.'"

Graduating in 1986 from Stuyvesant High School, one of New York's best and most competitive public schools, Liu attended New York University for her fresh-man year, but then transferred to the University of Michigan. There, having regained an interest in her Chinese roots, she majored in Asian languages and culture, but she also explored fine arts and performing arts. When she won the role of Alice in the avant-garde Andre Gregory stage version of *Alice in Wonderland* during her senior year in college, she discovered a passion. From that

lined as exotic ethnic "color." Liu has spo-ken out against ingrained prejudice in the movie business: "I think that ultimately being Asian in this business is something you have to consider because sometimes people aren't as open... People are afraid and they don't think the public is smart enough to understand that this is America and that there are all kinds of people out there. The studios keep putting out the Won-der Bread and what they think is safe."

point forward, she focused her attention on acting as a profession.

Starting from scratch

With no connections in show business, Liu joined the thousands of other aspiring actors in starting "from scratch." Soon after college, she moved to Los Angeles to strive for a break in television or films. Supporting herself by waitressing and teaching aerobics, she got her first television role (playing a waitress) on *Beverly Hills 90210* in 1990. During the early 1990s she also acted in a Hong Kong movie, *Ban Wo Zong Heng.* Liu was also a cast member in well-regarded California theater companies such as the Pan Asian Repertory Theater and East West Players. She eventually gained small parts in episodes of several popular television series, including *The X Files* and *ER* (three episodes), among others. Her roles were typically, as she put it, "the immigrant who had been washed ashore...in accents and very dramatic." In 1996, she had a supporting role as a college student on *Pearl,* a short-lived situation comedy. Small parts in movies also came along, including a brief appearance in *Jerry Maguire,* starring Tom Cruise and Renée Zellweger, in 1996.

Her big break came in 1997, when Liu won the role of Ling Woo, one of the lawyers in the cast of the popular television series, *Ally McBeal.* Liu had auditioned for—and lost—another role, but the show's producer-writer David E. Kelley then wrote a part for expressly for her. During the show's final seasons, Liu was a member of the regular cast of *Ally McBeal,* and she was nominated for an Emmy Award. The character of Ling Woo was controversial among viewers. She was described as "assertive" at best and, more often, "cold and calculating," "icy," and "a woman who lives to sue her enemies." Liu herself said of Ling Woo, "she doesn't have time to mince words and protect other people's feelings....I like how aggressive she is. I like that she doesn't apologize for anything that she does." Some critics felt that this portrayal, while defying perceptions of Asian American women's docility, perpetuated another outdated image: the ruthless "Dragon Lady" type.

Action hero

The exposure she earned with her role on *Ally McBeal* led to prominent roles in movies like 1999's Mel Gibson thriller, *Payback.* In 2000 Liu played Princess Pei Pei in Jackie Chan's comedy, *Shanghai Noon.* She was disappointed that she got to perform only one kick while filming with the martial arts star. Liu was the last of three to be cast in the "angel" crimefighter roles for the movie, *Charlie's Angels,* a tongue-in-cheek update of the 1970s television series. Liu played Alex Munday, whom she described as "smart and very strong," making good use of her long-time martial arts study in many fight scenes. *Charlie's Angels* earned more than $300 million in worldwide distribution, and made Liu a household name. As an action movie featuring a trio of tough yet beautiful women, it was especially popular with young girls. Asian American girls regarded Liu as a "Wonder Woman" of their own.

Liu continued her focus on action films with a starring role opposite Antonio Bandaras in 2002's *Ballistic: Ecks vs. Server.* Her role, Agent Sever, was originally written for a man. Agent Sever was a trained assassin obsessed with revenge. Liu's fighting abilities were showcased in *Ballistic,* which required three-and-a-half months of intensive martial arts training. Liu turned in a memorable cameo appearance as the murderess, "Go-to-Hell Kitty," in 2002's Academy Award-winning musical, *Chicago.*

In 2003, Liu appeared in the big-budget sequel, *Charlie's Angels: Full Throttle.* Liu has said that she wouldn't mind making *Charlie's Angels 5,* if the demand for sequels continues. She was part of the ensemble cast of *Hotel,* an independent film set in Italy. Also released in 2003 was director Quentin Tarantino's long-awaited *Kill Bill,* which Liu described as "an homage to all the martial arts movies." Liu learned Japanese for her role as an underworld boss, and enjoyed the on-location shooting in Beijing, China.

As Liu takes her career in a new direction, she became executive producer (and star) of an update of the old Charlie Chan detective series. In addition to her duties as producer, Liu will play the sleuthing granddaughter of Charlie Chan (always portrayed by non-Asians in the past). Hong Kong movie legend, John Woo, has agreed to be the movie's producer.

Comedy is always of interest to Liu, and she has done voice-overs for animated television shows including *Futurama* and *King of the Hill,* and was the first Asian American woman to host *Saturday Night Live.* Liu has agreed to participate as producer of an action comedy in a project with Danny DeVito's Jersey Films.

As Liu's career continues to develop, it will be interesting to see if she stays with action roles, or branches out into more everyday characters. While promoting *Ballistic,* Liu noted, "One of the things that you have to look out for is becoming trapped in a place where people want to see you all the time doing one thing." She has mentioned that she would like to return to theater work and to make smaller independent films, in addition to the action blockbusters.

On her own time

For many years (predating her movie combat roles), Liu studied Kali-Escrima-Silat, a form of martial arts that traces its origins to the Philippines and Indonesia. It places an emphasis on stick fighting. She also pursues an array of outdoor activities, including skiing and rock climbing.

Liu has an abiding interest in the visual arts, especially photography. In 1993 her work was exhibited at New York's Cast Iron Gallery. Titled "Unraveling," the show included photographs she had taken in Hong Kong and collages of photographs from Pro-Choice demonstrations in Washington, D.C. After the New York show, she was awarded a grant to travel in China to study and make artworks. She later exhibited mixed-media photo collage work based on her China experiences in a Venice, California, art gallery.

As a native New Yorker, Liu visited the site of the September 11, 2001, World Trade Center attacks during the rescue efforts and participated in fundraising for the victims. Liu has also been a fundraiser for the Susan G. Komen Breast Cancer Foundation. She is motivated by a personal experience she had when she was in her early twenties. After having a noncancerous lump surgically removed from her breast, she realized the importance of breast cancer awareness. She expresses the belief that "I think you should take anything that happens to you and turn it into something positive."

Sources:

"Biography for Lucy Liu," *IMDb.com 2001,* http://us.imdb.com/Bio?Liu,%20Lucy (accessed April 4, 2003).

Chang, Yahlin, "Taking No Prisoners," *Newsweek,* September 30, 1998.

"Interview: Lucy Liu," *Yesterdayland.com 2000,* http://www.yesterdayland.com/features/interviews/liu_1.php (accessed April 4, 2003).

Krulik, Nancy E. and Nola Thaker, *Angels: The Inside Scoop on the Stars of Charlie's Angels,* New York: Aladdin Library, 2000.

Moran, Julie, "Lucy Liu Breast Cancer Scare," *ET Online,* August 29, 2001. http://www.etonline.com/celebrity/a6154.htm (accessed April 4, 2003).

Riefe, Jordan: "Lucy Liu Goes Ballistic," Static Multimedia, *Destroy-all-monsters.com 2002.* http://www.destroy-all-monsters.com/liuinterview.shtml (accessed April 4, 2003).

"'Unraveling' in Soho," *Asian New Yorker,* September 1993.

Gary Locke

Gary Locke

Politician
Born January 21, 1950, Seattle, Washington

"Democrats have a positive, specific plan to turn our nation around."

Gary Locke has achieved a number of firsts. He was the first Asian American governor of a U.S. state when he was elected in Washington in 1996; and he was the first Chinese American to head a county government (King County, Seattle) in North America. In a state where the Asian American population is just 6 percent, Locke reaches beyond his own ethnic group, to serve all people.

Seattle childhood

Gary Locke was born January 21, 1950, in one of Seattle's poorest neighborhoods, the second of five children. His mother. Julie, was a Chinese immigrant mother and his father, James, a World War II army combat officer. James Locke owned a restaurant,

Pike Place Market, and later a grocery. Locke grew up speaking Chinese at home, learning English only after starting kindergarten.

A straight-A student and a Boy Scout, Locke was accepted at Yale University in the late 1960s, where he wanted to study political science. Though able to keep up academically, he often felt a little out of place socially. Many of the other students came from wealthier families. Locke was homesick, and he found himself missing Seattle. Nevertheless, he was determined to finish what he started; he graduated from Yale in 1972, and went on to earn a law degree from Boston University in 1975.

After earning his law degree, Locke returned to Seattle and took a job as a King County deputy prosecutor, which eventually led him into politics. He started out campaigning door-to-door for politicians, and he discovered he liked the work of grassroots campaigning. He was hooked on politics, and ran successfully for the state house of representatives in 1982. One of his main campaign promises was to work for reform in Seattle schools to improve education for poor and minority students.

His colleagues recall that in his first years in the state legislature, Locke played the role of angry agitator, and often made enemies. Over time, he became known more as a consensus builder who would fight for his bills aggressively and eventually pull all sides together to broker an agreement.

He rose in the state legislature to chair the powerful house appropriations committee, where he acquired a reputation for brilliance in budget-writing.

Many saw him as a rising star, predicting he would become Washington State governor some day—and their predictions came true in 1996. His reputation and sphere of influence continued to grow. By 2003, he had become known nationally as a Democratic Party leader.

Before embarking on his mission to help shape his state, he set out to help shape his "hometown" of the greater Seattle area.

Locke's leadership skills passed a crucial test in late May 1994, when he was put in the position of bringing environmentalist and pro-growth forces together on the Seattle area's regional growth-management plan. Locke found a way to get developers and environmentalists to agree to a compromise. The compromise, announced moments before elected officials from King County, Seattle, and the area's suburban areas were to start voting on twenty-year growth policies, stunned—and pleased—many.

Locke made his run for King County executive at a time when the county was gaining new clout. His taking office coincided with the merger of King County with agencies of the Seattle metropolitan area.

The day Locke was sworn into office, county government grew from 7,000 to 11,000 people. The county council was expanded to give suburban representatives the majority for the first time. Locke's job as regional leader was second in power to the governor.

Locke threw himself into office, becoming the region's leading decisionmaker. Yet, his critics chastised him at first for making decisions too slowly. Locke defended his pace, saying that his advisers suggested that he take things slowly, hire the right people, and get them working together. "Reshaping government takes time," he told *Asian American Biography.*

Becoming governor

Locke decided to run for governor in the 1996 election. As the Democratic candidate, he won 59 percent of the vote. At that time, Washington was home to large and important corporations, including Microsoft and Boeing. During his first term, he faced the beginning of the nationwide economic downturn. Voters reelected him to a second term in 2000, but then his path became even bumpier. Early in his second term, Boeing announced plans to leave Washington, moving to a state with lower taxes, landing a serious blow to the Washington state economy.

Although he was chosen by the Democratic Party to give their response to President George W. Bush's 2003 "State of the Union" address, many criticized his speech, saying it did not explain the Democrats' vision for the future. Locke, like many governors, was struggling with the challenges of balancing a state budget with rising unemployment and other economic woes.

In 2003 the United States engaged in war with Iraq. Secretary of Homeland Security Tom Ridge urged the governors of all fifty states to activate their National Guard troops in case they were targeted by terrorists. Locke, who said the federal government has not provided enough funding for the states to implement new security measures to combat terrorism, did not follow the suggestion.

The politics of inclusion

Locke frequently talks about a Nordstrom-style government, referring to the department store chain famous for its excep-tional customer service. Locke's way of adapting the Nordstrom philosophy to government is to treat people with respect and to make government more accessible to ordinary people. He is proud of his Asian American heritage, and visited China during his second term as governor. However, he is careful not to place too much emphasis on ethnicity, since Asian Americans represent just over 5 percent of the Washington's population.

Locke's first brief marriage ended in divorce. In 1992, a blind date with a television journalist, Mona Lee, resulted in his second marriage after a long courtship. The couple has two children.

Sources:

Donahue, Bill, Don Campbell, and Tina Kelley, "American Tale: Washington Governor Gary Locke Explores His Roots in Jilong, China," *People Weekly,* November 24, 1997, vol. 48, no. 21, p. 169.

Gupta, Himanee, "Locke Faces Big Tests with Growth-Plan Vote—County Executive Learning Nuances of Job," *Seattle Times,* May 23, 1994.

Gupta, Himanee, "Opposing Sides Praise County's Agreement on Grand Ridge," *Seattle Times,* May 19, 1994.

Hickey, Jennifer G., "Could the Buck Stop Here?" *Insight on the News,* February 18, 2003, vol. 19, no. 5, p. 14.

Kno, Fidelius, "Man of the Year: Gary Locke's Star Rises in the Northwest," *Asian Weekly,* December 4, 1993.

Lim, Gerard, "Gary Locke's for Honest, No-Frills Legislation in King County, Washington," *Asian Week,* March 1994.

Moody, Fred, "The Man Who Mistook His Life for the Legislature," *Seattle Weekly,* February 27, 1991.

Murphy, Kim, "Washington State Battle Inspires Asian Americans," *Los Angeles Times,* November 1, 1996, vol. 115, p. A30.

Schaefer, David. "Two Very Private Candidates—If You Find Locke off Duty, He's Likely to Have a Wrench in Hand," *Seattle Times,* October 31, 1993.

John Lone

Actor
Born 1952, Hong Kong

"Ideally, acting, even directing, is about revelation and sharing. I've been lucky to have the opportunity, the good fortune, to have a life and career which lets me experience that so often."

John Lone

J ohn Lone is an actor who made his mark in Off-Broadway productions in New York, primarily in the plays of **David Henry Hwang,** before moving on to motion pictures. He first came to national prominence in the film *Year of the Dragon* in 1986. The next year he played the title role in Bernardo Bertolucci's Academy Award-winning film *The Last Emperor.* Since then, he has appeared in several other major films, including the 1993 adaptation of Hwang's Broadway hit *M. Butterfly.*

Born into poverty

Lone's actual date of birth is not known. He was born in Hong Kong sometime in 1952. At about the age of ten, the orphaned Lone was taken by his guardian from his impoverished home to join the Beijing Opera, which had fled the Chinese mainland during the Communist revolution of the 1940s. The company took in and trained even poor children who showed promise. Lone remained in the company's isolated, almost monastery-like setting for several years, studying classical Chinese theater, which includes elements of poetry, dance, mime, singing, acrobatics, and martial arts.

In his mid-teens, Lone grew curious about the outside world and with his guardian contrived a story about an ill grandmother so that he could escape the rigid, isolated, and archaic world of the Beijing Opera. Their plan proved a success, and Lone spent months living in Hong Kong. During this time he was exposed to American and European films, and he found he enjoyed them more than he did the Chinese films he had known before.

Eventually Lone began acting again. His acting and athletic abilities, as well as his extremely good looks, did not go unnoticed for long. He was offered a ten-year film contract to star in martial arts films for a major Hong Kong studio and was also asked to join the Maurice Bejart dance company of Brussels. He declined both offers, however, having decided to pursue an acting career in the United States.

Life in America

Lone first settled in Los Angeles and attended Santa Ana Junior College, where he earned an associate of arts degree and became fluent in English. He then began studying acting and looking for work as an actor. Although life in the small town of Santa Ana had been protected and relatively free from racism, Hollywood proved to be much less tolerant and offered the young actor very few opportunities. As he struggled to find work, Lone was told again and again that he did not look Chinese enough for Asian roles and that he was too foreign for leading-man roles.

In the early 1980s, however, Lone landed the lead role in David Henry Hwang's play *FOB*—an abbreviation for "fresh off the boat," slang for new immigrants—which was being staged at the Joseph Papp/New York Public Theater. *FOB* won wide critical acclaim, winning an Obie Award for both Hwang and Lone. (The Obies are theater awards for Off-Broadway productions awarded by the *Village Voice*.) The relationship between Lone and Hwang was strengthened by the success they shared in this production. The *New York Times* referred to Lone as "the key ingredient in Mr. Hwang's plays." Lone quickly gained a reputation as Hwang's finest interpreter, the actor best suited to Hwang's style and characters, and he acted in several of his plays to continued critical acclaim. Among the Hwang plays in which Lone appeared in the early 1980s were *The Dance and the Railroad, The Sound of a Voice,* and *The House of Beauties.*

A career in film

In 1984 Lone made his first feature film, playing the title role in *Iceman,* the story of a prehistoric man found frozen in the Arctic ice. Lone won the role after the director saw him in *The Dance and the Railroad* at the Public Theater. In spite of working 17-hour days in heavy makeup and enduring five months of Arctic winter, Lone found the work exhilarating. He was thrilled to play the part, telling *New York Newsday,* "This has been the most challenging, most exciting role. I know that sounds corny, but I really mean it. My first film role, and it is perfect." The director, Fred Schepisi, was thrilled too. "John is a brilliant, exploratory actor," said Schepisi. "He has enormous technical resources, and he's a perfectionist. He works until he intensely understands the details. Only then is he free to produce the unexpected."

Following *Iceman,* Lone portrayed the leader of the Chinese Mafia in *Year of the Dragon,* a film that sparked angry protests from the Asian American community for its stereotypical and generally negative portrayal of Chinese Americans and the life of Chinatown. Lone did not let the protests affect his performance or his feelings about the film, which he supported.

In 1987 Lone spent six months in China filming the title role in Bernardo Bertolucci's epic motion picture *The Last Emperor*, which won the Oscar for best picture. Almost immediately following his return, he appeared in *The Moderns* as a strange businessman/art collector living in the now-legendary American expatriate (having left their native country) community of 1920s Paris. He then portrayed a Hong Kong businessman in a political thriller, *Shadow of China*, and an underworld crime lord in a gangster film, *Shanghai 1920*. Both of these films were produced by Asian companies and directed by Asians, with dialogue in English and an international cast. These undertakings were inspired by the success, commercially and critically, of *The Last Emperor*, which took in over $100 million around the world.

In 1993 Lone returned to the work of David Henry Hwang, starring in the film adaptation of Hwang's Broadway hit *M. Butterfly*. For the title role of the captivating opera star—a man posing as a woman—who carries on a long affair with a male French diplomat who does not suspect his lover's true identity, Lone drew heavily on his training with the Beijing Opera, which traditionally casts boys and men in female roles. In 1994 Lone appeared in *The Shadow* opposite Alec Baldwin. The next year, Universal Pictures released *The Hunted*, starring Lone and Christopher Lambert. His next film was *Rush Hour II* (2001).

Lone has chosen to portray a variety of characters that would be the envy of many ethnic actors. In a 1994 press release Lone said, "Ideally, acting, even directing, is about revelation and sharing. I've been lucky to have the opportunity, the good for-

tune, to have a life and career which lets me experience that so often."

Sources:

Block-Korenbrot Public Relations, "John Lone," press release, 1994.

Broeske, Pat, "Shanghai Surprise," *Los Angeles Times Calendar*, December 2, 1990, p. 26.

Hilton, Pat, "The Sudden Success of John Lone," *Drama-logue*, October 10, 1985, pp. 14-15.

"John Lone," *New York Times*, July 31, 1981, p. C2.

Watson, Steven, "The Primitive Innocence of a Lone Iceman," *New York Newsday*, April 22, 1984.

Bette Bao Lord

Writer, activist
Born November 3, 1938, Shanghai, China

"Becoming a novelist was not a girlhood dream but a middle-aged happenstance. Perhaps if I had known what I now know about the agony of the blank page, the imperative of endless revision, the rigors of technique, I would never have begun a first novel."

Bette Bao Lord is a bestselling author of novels and works of nonfiction. Her books, including *Eighth Moon: The True Story of a Young Girl's Life in Communist China; Spring Moon; Legacies, A Chinese Mosaic;* and the children's book *In the Year of the Boar and Jackie Robinson,* have all been highly praised and translated into several languages. Lord is also a political activist who serves on many boards and is currently chair of Freedom House, an organization established in 1941 by First Lady Eleanor Roosevelt to promote democracy and keep watch over the preservation and violations of political and civil rights in countries around the world. She is a frequent lecturer on foreign affairs, specifically on events in her native country of China.

A family torn apart

Lord was born during a tumultuous period in Chinese history. The country was fighting against a brutal Japanese invasion—one of the many conflicts of World War II—and her father, Sandys Bao, had been commissioned into the army as a colonel. Sandys was an electrical engineer who had been educated in England, and his expertise was needed in the war effort to help build a crucial power station in China's interior. He was in grave danger for much of the war, but he managed to survive.

When the Japanese were defeated in 1945, Sandys Bao was sent to the United States by the Nationalist government of China to buy heavy equipment to help rebuild the devastated country. It was intended that he go to America alone. Eventually, however, he was able to persuade the authorities to allow his wife, Dora, and two of his three daughters to join him. The youngest girl, Sansan, was left behind with relatives because Sandys and Dora thought the long ocean voyage would be too difficult for the infant. They planned to have her come later, or, when Sandys finished his work, to return to her soon.

But China's troubles were not over yet. Shortly after the family left, civil war broke out between the Nationalist government that

Betty Bao Lord

had assumed power after the withdrawal of the Japanese and the rural, Communist insurgency led by Mao Zedong. The war was long and bloody, and in 1949, the Communists emerged victorious. Because Sandys was a former colonel in the Nationalist army he would have been considered a traitor in the new China, so he could not return. Worse yet, under the oppressive leadership of Chairman Mao, China became isolationist, cutting off its ties with the rest of the world, especially the West (primarily Europe and North America). The Baos knew it would be extremely difficult, if not impossible, to get young Sansan out of the country.

Starting over

The family settled in Brooklyn, New York, where Bette went to grammar school. She wrote about the experience years later: "I docked in Brooklyn on a sleepy Sunday and was enrolled in P.S. 8 in Brooklyn Heights on a sneezy Monday. Dopey and Bashful was I because I didn't speak a word of English.... On that first day at school, the principal asked, 'How old are you?' My mother translated. Though eight, I stuck up ten fingers ... the two extra fingers were because Chinese are considered a year old when born, two upon the new year.... I was the shortest fifth grader in all of the five boroughs [of New York City]. No one gave it a thought. Weren't Chinese known to be small?"

Young Bette Bao adapted well, however, and became a good student. Soon, the family moved from Brooklyn to Teaneck, New Jersey, a suburb of New York City. There Bao was very popular and continued to excel academically. She was elected secretary of the student council and was a member of the debating team. After graduating, she enrolled in Tufts University in suburban Boston, Massachusetts.

Bao wrote, "By college, visions of Nobel Prizes danced in my head. And so I signed up to study how to make a better living through chemistry." She had difficulty with chemistry, however, and "the head of the department ... made me an offer I couldn't refuse: 'Major in chemistry and flunk, or transfer out and pass.'" Bao transferred out of the chemistry program and instead majored in history and political science. She earned her bachelor's degree in 1959. From there she went on to earn a master's degree at Tufts's Fletcher School of Law and Diplomacy in 1960.

The writer emerges

In 1962, Bao was working in Washington, D.C., as the director of the Fulbright Exchange program after having worked in Hawaii for two years. In the U.S. capital she was reunited with Winston Lord, a man she'd met in college. They were married that year. Also in 1962, Bao Lord's mother concocted a plan in which she pretended to be terminally ill in an effort to get the Chinese authorities to allow her youngest daughter to visit her in Hong Kong. It worked, and Sansan was allowed to visit her mother, after which they both fled to the United States.

The next year, Lord was encouraged by her friends to write the story of her sister's life. The idea was intriguing and she quit her job to devote herself to the project fulltime. She interviewed Sansan extensively, and in 1964 Harper published *Eighth Moon: The True Story of a Young Girl's Life in Communist China*. The book did remarkably well both critically and commercially. It was issued as a *Reader's Digest* condensed book and continues to be taught in high schools. Bao Lord also gave birth to a daughter that year, Elizabeth Pillsbury Lord.

Travels with her husband

Winston Lord, meanwhile, was continuing to climb the ranks of the Washington diplomatic corps. In 1965, he was sent to Geneva, Switzerland. In 1968, with the election of Richard Nixon to the presidency, Lord, a Republican, was given a post as a top aide to Henry Kissinger, Nixon's secretary of state. Five years later, Winston Lord traveled to China on a diplomatic mission and was allowed to bring his wife. It was the first time Bette Bao Lord had returned to the country of her birth. Photographs taken during this trip were published in the *Washington Post,* and she signed a contract with Harper & Row to write an account of her return to China.

In 1976, the Republicans were voted out of office and the Lords decided to leave Washington. They moved to Colorado, where Lord began work on her book detailing her return to her homeland. Originally intended as a nonfiction account of her travels, the book eventually became a novel. She wrote about the experience later, saying, "Becoming a novelist was not a girlhood dream but a middle-aged happenstance. Perhaps if I had known what I now know about the agony of the blank page, the imperative of endless revision, the rigors of technique, I would never have begun a first novel." All the agony was worth it, however. Entitled *Spring Moon* (1981), the book was a resounding success. It was nominated for a National Book Award, was on the *New York Times* bestseller list for 30 weeks, and earned an award from the Literary Guild. In 1984, Bao Lord published her first children's book; intended for fifth and sixth graders, *In the Year of the Boar and Jackie Robinson* is a fictionalized account of her first year in America.

Ambassador's wife

In 1985, Winston Lord was appointed American ambassador to China, and Bao Lord returned with him to her native country. While stationed in Beijing, she immersed herself in the local arts commu-

nity; in 1988, she coproduced the play *The Caine Mutiny* at the People's Art Theater. The production was directed by American film star Charlton Heston, and the premiere was attended by Herman Wouk, the play's author.

Although Bao Lord had no official title in the diplomatic corps, she was an invaluable assistant to her husband during this period, which was an especially difficult one for the rulers of China. By the end of their stay in Beijing, the city was in the midst of a student-led pro-democracy movement. Lord's ambassadorship ended in April of 1989, but Bao Lord stayed behind to help interpret events for CBS News. She had left, however, by the weekend of June 3rd, when government troops shocked the world by gunning down as many as one thousand unarmed students who had been occupying downtown Beijing's Tiananmen Square.

In 1990, Bao Lord published her second work of nonfiction, *Legacies, A Chinese Mosaic,* which relates the story of her return to China as the wife of the American ambassador. The book became a *New York Times* bestseller and a Book of the Month Club selection. It has been translated into ten languages, and was named one of the top ten books of nonfiction for 1990 by *Time* magazine. In 1996, she published *The Middle Heart,* a novel set in China over a twenty-year time period in China, ending in 1989.

Spokesperson for freedom

In the spring of 1993, Bao Lord was named chair of Freedom House, a New York-based organization that, among other things, issues yearly reports on the state of freedom in the world. As such, she is a frequent contributor to newspapers and magazines of national importance. She wrote a column for *USA Today* in 1993 about the growing racial and ethnic conflicts around the world, and, more disturbingly in her eyes, here in America. "More and more," she wrote, "we define ourselves by race, ethnicity, creed, and class. More and more, we build brick walls of suspicion and shun opening doors. More and more, good will is in short supply.... The United States has a leading role and a large stake in nurturing democratic values and institutions," she asserts. "But we must practice at home what we trumpet abroad."

Sources:

Fox, Mary Virginia, *Bette Bao Lord: Novelist and Chinese Voice for Change,* People of Distinction series, Chicago: Children's Press, 1993.

Lord, Bette Bao, "Practice of Liberty Begins at Home." *USA Today,* December 20, 1993, p. 13A.

Lord, Bette Bao, telephone interview with Jim Henry, April 18, 1994.

Lord, Bette Bao, "Walking in Lucky Shoes." *Newsweek,* July 6, 1992, p. 10.

Greg Louganis

Olympic diver, dancer, actor
Born in 1960

"After I hit my head [during a dive at the 1988 Olympics], I suddenly became an underdog. So that made each dive more important. I also knew, but no one else knew at the time, that these were going to be my last competitive dives."

In the words of Preston Levi, director of research at the International Swimming Hall of Fame, Greg Louganis is "the diver of the century." His list of firsts, honors, and records is long and impressive; during his career he won 47 national diving titles, six Pan-American gold medals, five world championships, four Olympic gold medals, and one silver medal. He earned his first Olympic medal in 1976 when he won a silver in the springboard diving event. He went on to dominate the sport of international diving as few athletes have dominated any sport. At the 1984 Olympics in Los Angeles, he performed a 3-somersault tuck—a dive so difficult it had killed a man a year earlier—with near perfect marks. His final score in the diving competition that year was 710.91, giving him the gold medal with a score 67.41 points higher than that of the silver medalist. In so doing, he became the first diver ever, man or woman, to score above 700 points. He also became the first man in 56 years to win the springboard and platform titles at the same Olympics. In 1988 at the Olympic Games in Seoul, South Korea, he repeated this feat, winning two gold medals again. This made him the first man ever to take home two gold medals from two successive Olympics.

In March 1995 Louganis's autobiography, *Breaking the Surface,* stunned the nation with its disclosure that the great athlete had AIDS. The book and Louganis's subsequent interviews reveal that the road to success has often been a difficult one for Louganis, both as a gifted child and as a world-class competitor in sports.

Raised by adoptive parents

Louganis's biological parents were teenagers of Samoan and Northern European descent who gave him up for adoption soon after he was born. After nine months in a foster home, he was adopted by Peter and Francis Louganis and raised in El Cajon, a suburb of San Diego, California. His adoptive father was a bookkeeper for a fishing company and later became a tuna-boat controller for the American Tuna Boats Association. In his autobiography, Louganis describes his father, who died in 1991, as an abusive alcoholic.

At the age of 18 months, Louganis was already taking dance lessons, where he learned the practice of visualization. This discipline would prove crucial to his later diving technique. To help students memorize new dance combinations, the teacher would dim the lights, turn up the volume of the music, and ask the children to visualize the routine from beginning to end. "I didn't leave the room until I could do the routine flawlessly in my head," Louganis recalled in an interview with *Asian American Biography (AAB).*

Beginning at the age of three, Louganis performed in dance recitals and local talent

Greg Louganis

competitions. His athleticism and poise gave him a self-confidence onstage that he did not possess at other times. In school he was treated cruelly by the predominantly white students, some of whom called him "nigger" because of his dark skin. To complicate matters, Louganis suffered from a serious stutter, dyslexia (although this went undiagnosed until he was in college), and asthma. These compounded the name-calling and undermined his sense of self-confidence. At the age of 12, suffering serious depression and using drugs, Louganis attempted suicide.

Throughout his childhood Louganis compensated for the ridicule he endured in school by concentrating his energies on dancing and gymnastics, which he had taken up on the advice of a doctor who believed that vigorous exercise might help his asthma. When the young boy began practicing his acrobatics off the diving board into the family pool, his mother decided to enroll him in a diving class.

His first championship

In 1971 Louganis scored a perfect ten in the diving competition at the Amateur Athletic Union (AAU) Junior Olympics. Among the spectators at that event was Dr. **Sammy Lee**, a gold medalist in diving at the 1948 and 1952 Olympics. Lee thought Louganis was the greatest diving talent he had ever seen. In 1975 Louganis's father hired Lee as a coach to help his son prepare for the 1976 Olympics in Montreal. Louganis, who was still only 16, finished sixth in the springboard, but won the silver medal in the platform. The 18 months following the Olympics were dismal for the young diver. "When I came back from Montreal," he told *AAB,* "a lot of my friends at high school wouldn't talk to me because they thought I had changed. It was very hard on me at the time."

In 1978 Louganis hired a new coach, Ron O'Brien. That year, he won four national diving titles, a world championship, and a scholarship to the University of Miami in Florida. In freshman English class, he was given the word "dyslexia" as a vocabulary subject. When he looked it up in the dictionary, he learned it was a fairly common condition that distorts a person's ability to read and is often misdiagnosed as a learning disability. He was elated. "For the first time, I knew I *wasn't* retarded," he told *AAB.*

After two years of study at Miami, Louganis transferred to the University of California at Irvine, where he would be closer to O'Brien, who was coaching at the world-famous Mission Viejo Club near San Diego. In 1980 Louganis graduated with a degree in theater and dance. The 1980 Olympics were held that year in Moscow, in what was then the Soviet Union. Despite the doctrine that the games are to be free from political concerns, the U.S. team, by order of President Jimmy Carter, boycotted the games in protest of the Soviets' 1979 invasion of Afghanistan. Louganis was heavily favored to win both diving events, and had the United States not boycotted the games, he could well have won two medals at three consecutive games.

Olympic gold

At the 1984 Olympics, Louganis went into the first event, the springboard, under great pressure; as the reigning world champion in both the springboard and the platform, he felt the judges expected more from him than from his competitors. Nevertheless, he was able to pull off a stunning performance and rack up the incredible score of 710.91, winning gold medals in both events. The next year, Louganis received the Sullivan Award, presented to the nation's outstanding amateur athlete. On a more personal note, Louganis was finally breaking out of his intense shyness and beginning to speak publicly about the difficulties of his childhood. By sharing these experiences he overcame their power and was able to help other young people meet similar challenges.

Louganis was 28 years old when the next Olympic Games were held in Seoul, Korea, in 1988, and the diver was secretly carrying a great burden. His sexual partner—a man called Tom in the autobiography—with whom he had been in a turbulent relationship for six years, was diagnosed with AIDS. Louganis was tested and found that he was HIV positive. He began getting treatment and agonized over whether or not to tell the Olympic committee, ultimately deciding not to tell.

By this time, Louganis had accumulated 47 national diving titles, six Pan-American gold medals, five world championships, and the two Olympic gold medals. It was widely expected that he would continue in his championship form. During a preliminary round of diving, Louganis hit his head on the board during a dive, digging a three-inch gash across his forehead. Louganis writes in his book that, while he was being stitched up by the gloveless Olympic physician James Puffer, "so many things were going through my mind. Did I get any blood in the pool? ... Could I have infected Ron [his coach]? Then I worried about Dr. Puffer, who wasn't wearing any gloves."

The burden of being the defending champion also weighed on him. "If I came back without two medals," he told *AAB,* "I would have been considered a failure.... After I hit my head, I suddenly became an underdog. So that made each dive more important. I also knew, but no one else knew at the time, that these were going to be my last competitive dives."

In spite of the obstacles, Louganis won the gold medal in both events. He was awarded the Olympic Spirit Award at the closing ceremonies, acknowledging him as the most inspiring athlete among the 9,600 assembled in Seoul. He had finished the most impressive career in competitive diving's history and left behind a legacy of accomplishment few have matched in any sport.

A career in acting

After retiring from competitive diving, Louganis pursued a career in acting. He has danced with the show *Dance Kaleidoscope,* starred in *Cinderella* with the Los Angeles Civic Light Opera, performed in *The Boyfriend* at the Sacramento Music Circus, sung and danced with the Cincinnati Pops Orchestra, and appeared in the Off-Broadway production of *Jeffrey,* a comedy about a dancer in the chorus of the musical *Cats* who succumbs to AIDS. Another noteworthy performance was a 1995 one-man show, *The Only Thing Worse You Could Have Told Me...,* which is a comedy about a gay man and his family. Louganis has also appeared in numerous movies and television shows. Moreover, he is a regular commentator for high-profile diving competitions and has appeared in commercials.

In 1994, Greg announced that he was gay during a videotaped presentation at the Gay Games IV. A year later, during an interview with Barbara Walters, he revealed that he had developed AIDS. Soon after, in 1995, he published an autobiography titled *Breaking the Surface*, which became a bestseller and in 1996 the book was made into a Showtime television movie.

Once Louganis told the story of his illness, he received some criticism but also much support from the sports world. According to a *Newsweek* article, the chair of the Seoul Olympic organizing committee said it wasn't "morally right" for Louganis to have competed in the final round after cutting his head, but experts say there was no real threat of infecting other swimmers. Even Puffer, the doctor who stitched up Louganis's head (and has since tested negative for the HIV virus) agrees that the chance of infection to himself was minimal.

The fact that Louganis maintained his silence reveals that the sports world is not particularly kind to gay participants. *Newsweek* reported that Louganis had trouble finding people to room with him at the Olympics because fellow competitors suspected he was gay. Other gay swimmers confirmed that there is a great deal of gay-bashing in the sport. To come out as a homosexual during the Olympics would have, undoubtedly, caused an uproar in the media and the sports world. Publishing his autobiography has put an end to this painful silence for Louganis. "For me," he wrote, "this book means no more secrets." Louganis remains active in his southern California community by talking with youth groups about drug and alcohol dependency and rehabilitation and promoting organizations working on treatments for and education about dyslexia. He has also turned his attention toward his interest in pets by co-authoring the book, *For the Life of Your Dog: A Complete Guide to Having a Dog in Your Life from Adoption and Birth Through Sickness and Health.*

Sources:

Anderson, Dave, "The State of the Art," *New York Times,* August 8, 1984.

Hirshey, Gerri, "Art of a Diver," *Rolling Stone,* September 22, 1988, pp. 87-91.

Leerhsen, Charles, "True to the Olympic Ideal," *Newsweek,* October 10, 1988, pp. 63-64.

Louganis, Greg, http:www.louganis.com (accessed November 2002).

Louganis, Greg, with Eric Marcus, *Breaking the Surface,* New York: Random House, 1995.

Louganis, Greg, telephone interview with Terry Hong, February 10, 1994.

Neff, Craig, "It's a Bird, It's a Plane, It's Supergreg!," *Sports Illustrated,* August 20, 1984, pp. 80-83.

Reibstein, Larry, "Public Glory, Secret Agony," *Newsweek,* March 6, 1995, pp. 48-51.

Skow, John, "A Soaring, Majestic Slowness," *Time,* August 20, 1984, pp. 62-63.

FIELD OF ENDEAVOR INDEX

Volume number appears in **bold**.

ACADEMIA
Kim, Elaine   **1**
Koh, Harold Hongju   **1**
Lee, Rose Hum   **1**
Mukherjee, Bharati   **2**
Natividad, Irene   **2**
Park, Linda Sue   **2**
Takaki, Ronald   **2**
Tien, Chang-Lin   **2**

AEROSPACE
Chawla, Kalpana   **1**
Chiao, Leroy   **1**
Onizuka, Ellison   **2**
Wang, Taylor   **2**

ARCHITECTURE
Lin, Maya   **1**
Noguchi, Isamu   **2**
Obata, Gyo   **2**
Pei, I. M.   **2**
Yamasaki, Minoru   **2**

ART
Aruego, Jose   **1**
Kingman, Dong   **1**
Lin, Maya   **1**
Noguchi, Isamu   **2**
Ono, Yoko   **2**
Say, Allen   **2**

BUSINESS AND INDUSTRY
Aoki, Rocky   **1**
Bajaj, Kavelle R.   **1**
Campbell, Phyllis   **1**
Isaki, Paul   **1**
Matano, Tom   **2**
Mehta, Sonny   **2**
Ming, Jenny   **2**
Mow, William   **2**
Natori, Josie   **2**
Quereshey, Safi U.   **2**
Siv, Sichan   **2**
Wang, An   **2**
Yan, Martin   **2**
Yang, Jerry   **2**
Young, Shirley   **2**
Zee, Teddy   **2**

COMEDY
Barry, Lynda   **1**
Cho, Margaret   **1**
Morita, Pat   **2**

COMPUTER INDUSTRY
Bajaj, Kavelle R.   **1**
Qureshey, Safi U.   **2**
Wang, An   **2**
Yang, Jerry   **2**

DANCE
Barredo, Maniya   **1**

FASHION
Kim, Willa   **1**
Ming, Jenny   **2**
Mow, Willam   **2**
Natori, Josie   **2**
Sui, Anna   **2**
Wang, Vera   **2**

FILM
Carrere,Tia   **1**
Chen, Joan   **1**
Chiang, Doug   **1**
Gotanda, Philip Kan   **1**
Hwang, David Henry   **1**
Kahanamoku, Duke   **1**
Lee, Ang   **1**
Lee, Brandon   **1**
Lee, Bruce   **1**
Liu, Lucy   **1**
Lone, John   **1**
Mako   **2**
McCarthy, Nobu   **2**
Morita, Pat   **2**
Nair, Mira   **2**
Ngor, Haing S.   **2**
Ono, Yoko   **2**
Quo, Beulah   **2**
Reeves, Keanu   **2**
Salonga, Lea   **2**
Shyamalan, M. Night   **2**
Takei, George   **2**
Tomita, Tamlyn   **2**
Wang, Wayne   **2**
Wong, Anna May   **2**
Wong, B. D.   **2**
Zee, Teddy   **2**

INDEX